Zoom in, Zoom out
Crossing Borders in Contemporary European Cinema

Edited by

Sandra Barriales-Bouche and Marjorie Attignol Salvodon

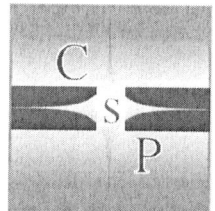

CAMBRIDGE SCHOLARS PUBLISHING

Zoom in, Zoom out: Crossing Borders in Contemporary European Cinema, edited by Sandra Barriales-Bouche and Marjorie Attignol Salvodon

This book first published 2007 by

Cambridge Scholars Publishing

15 Angerton Gardens, Newcastle, NE5 2JA, UK

British Library Cataloguing in Publication Data
A catalogue record for this book is available from the British Library

Copyright © 2007 by Sandra Barriales-Bouche and Marjorie Attignol Salvodon and contributors

All rights for this book reserved. No part of this book may be reproduced, stored in a retrieval system, or transmitted, in any form or by any means, electronic, mechanical, photocopying, recording or otherwise, without the prior permission of the copyright owner.
ISBN 1-84718-135-X; ISBN 13: 9781847181350

WE DEDICATE THIS BOOK TO ALL THE PEOPLE WHO CROSS BORDERS EVERY DAY, AND WHO ARE CONSTANTLY NEGOTIATING THE SHIFTING BORDERS OF IDENTITY

TABLE OF CONTENTS

List of Tables ix
Acknowledgements x

Introduction 1

Part I: Imagining An(Other) Europe:
Unsettled Borders And Re-Negotiated Identities 15

Chapter One
Imagining European Subjects as Chaotic Borders:
Cédric Klapisch's *Pot Luck* and *The Russian Dolls*
Mireille Rosello 16

Chapter Two
Borders and Bridges in the Films of Fatih Akin
Janis Little Solomon..34

Chapter Three
Permeable Borders in *Notre Musique*
Jehanne-Marie Gavarini 53

Part II: Mapping New Borders:
Genre, Co-Productions, And Technology 69

Chapter Four
Borders in/of the Balkan Road Movie
Nevena Daković 70

Chapter Five
Spanish Co-Productions: Commercial Need or Common Culture?
An Analysis of International Co-Productions in Spain from 2000 to 2004
Alejandro Pardo 89

Chapter Six
Database Cinema and the Museification of National Histories
Olivier Asselin 128

**Part III: European Film And Its Other Borders:
Cross-Cultural, National, And Transnational Perspectives** 155

Chapter Seven
Immigration in the Post-Industrial Age
Claudio Mazzola 156

Chapter Eight
Changing Direction: Recent Irish Cinema Revisits its Borders
Ruth Barton 170

Chapter Nine
Gnome is Where the Heart is: The New Europe
in German-Language-Cinema
John E. Davidson 186

Contributors 208

Index 211

LIST OF TABLES

Chart 1: Co-Production Treaties Signed by Spain

Chart 2: Projects with Spanish Participation Funded by EURIMAGES and IBERMEDIA

Chart 3: Evolution of Film Production in Spain (1995-2004)

Graph 1: Percentage of International Co-Productions in Spain (1995-2004)

Chart 4: Evolution of Co-Productions in Western Europe (2000-2004)

Chart 5: Typology of International Co-Productions in Spain

Chart 6: Co-Producing Countries with Spain (2000-2004)

Chart 7: New Typology of Spanish Co-Productions (2000-2004)

Graph 2: New Typology of Spanish Co-Productions (2000-2004): Percentage by Categories

Chart 8: Top 25 Spanish International Co-Productions at the Domestic Box Office (2000-2004)

Chart 9: Top 25 Spanish International Co-Productions on the European Market (2000-2004)

ACKNOWLEDGEMENTS

SANDRA BARRIALES-BOUCHE I am very grateful to the following people for their unconditional support during the preparation of the manuscript: my colleague Marjorie Attignol Salvodon, whose great professionalism, energy, and patience made the job much easier; Ángel G. Loureiro, for helping me discover the passionate world of Spanish Cinema during my first semester as a graduate student at the University of Massachusetts at Amherst; my students at Suffolk University, because teaching and advising them has been the most rewarding learning experience of my life; Johanna, for her friendship; my parents and Alberto, for everything; and finally, Luis, for having invited me to cross borders ten years ago.

MARJORIE ATTIGNOL SALVODON I warmly thank the people who facilitated the process of turning an abstract idea into a concrete book: Sandra Barriales-Bouche for being a fantastic co-editor with endless enthusiasm, diligence, and a sense of humor; the students in my French Cinema class at Suffolk University, especially Mara Cates and Kristin Seabolt, for their keen appreciation of films; Jehanne-Marie Gavarini for film-watching companionship in Boston; and Samba Gadjigo for teaching me about African cinema at Mount Holyoke College.

We both thank Amanda Millar and Andy Nercessian at Cambridge Scholars Press for planting the seeds of this project; our wonderful colleagues in the Department of Humanities and Modern Languages at Suffolk University; Johanna Collins for her careful and precise editing when we needed it the most; and the nine contributors to this collection whose insightful work brings this book to life.

INTRODUCTION

SANDRA BARRIALES-BOUCHE AND MARJORIE ATTIGNOL SALVODON, SUFFOLK UNIVERSITY

According to Patricia M. Goff (2000), it is preferable to focus on "the ways in which borders are made meaningful in Europe," than on "whether borders continue to be meaningful" (534). This means that the cultural, historical, and political factors that have influenced the proliferation, shape, and nature of borders in contemporary Europe are central. Borders have marked historical periods, geographical spaces, and ideological positions. They are "double-edged" in that they remain instrumental in both opening up Europe to new possibilities (European Union) and revealing Europe's centuries-old conflicts and divisions (inter-European wars).[1] How does one think about this apparent dichotomy of European borders as both hopeful and ominous? In studying the varied discourses that have influenced the making of borders in Europe in this essay, we discuss the porosity of borders across space and time through the historical events, ideas, and political realities that constitute Europe. We focus on key foundational myths related to the democratic ideal, religious identities, and transitional epochs in Europe, exploring how significant twentieth century events, such as World War I and World War II, the wars in Yugoslavia, the fall of the Berlin Wall, and the recent history of extra-European immigration, have turned Europe's seemingly "stable" borders into "porous" ones. Though European borders are often imagined as "stable," many scholars have recently shown this idea to be a myth—an idea that we are going to discuss in the next section of this chapter.

---

[1] By inter-European wars, we refer to the major wars that have taken place in Europe in the twentieth century, that is to say, World War I (1914-1918), World War II (1939-1945), and the wars of Yugoslavia (1991-1999).

Europe's Porous Borders: Myth and Realities

Mirrors reflect and refract images. In Josep Fontana's book on Europe and the myths subtending European history, *The Distorted Past: A Reinterpretation of Europe*, he uses the metaphor of the mirror to offer new interpretations of ideas that have influenced how we think about European history (Fontana 1995). Fontana's first chapter, "The Barbarian Mirror," calls into question the egalitarian ideals of the Greek *polis*, which effectively counter the values that succeeding generations have attributed to Greek democracy: "The overworked image of a Greek *polis* inhabited by free citizens who collectively participated in government is a mirage" (5). Indeed, according to Fontana, the legacy of European history merits a critical engagement. It is not a matter of replacing one set of myths with another set of myths, rather it is a matter of embracing a new vision of European history. He writes, for instance:

> It serves no purpose to demythologize the Greek miracle in order to replace it by other myths: Indo-European, Egyptian, Phoenician or Minoan. What we must do is replace the notion of a single creative people—as well as the Carthaginians, Etruscans, Celts, etc.—which made possible the evolution based on the whole mass of their contributions, of a culture which embraced many shared elements (8).

This view shifts the traditional perspectives that have come to define European history.[2] Fontana uses the concept of the "barbarian" in this analysis of a Europe constructed from varied origins and contributions of many different peoples to undo the dichotomy separating "us" and "them," or Europe and the rest of the world.[3] Fontana compels us to examine the implications of imagining European history not as a series of fixed and stable events understood by unchanging notions. He suggests that European history is engendered from contributions from a multitude of places, interests, and peoples. The much-touted Greek origin

---

[2] *The Distorted Past* is part of a series, entitled "The Making of Europe," that defines Europe in a context of exchange and interaction. The Series Editor, Jacques Le Goff, writes: "Europe is bordered by the Atlantic, Asia, and Africa, its history and geography inextricably entwined, and its past comprehensible only within the context of the world at large. The territory retains the name given it by the Ancient Greeks, and the roots of its heritage may be traced far into prehistory. It is on this foundation – rich and creative, united yet diverse – that Europe's future will be built" (Fontana 1995, vi).

[3] Fontana reminds us of the meaning of the word "barbarian," writing that "the word "barbarian" originally designated the individual who was incapable of expressing himself fluently in Greek: the word was simply an onomatopoeic formation to echo the articulatory difficulties of a person who cannot speak well and stammers (a common element in the xenophobic myths of all races)" (4).

of democracy, then, is one element, among many, in contemporary configurations of democracy in Europe.[4]

Furthermore, Fontana's chapter on religion and religious identity in Europe, "The Christian Mirror," also disavows any notion of an uncomplicated European religious heritage. Reminding us that "the first enemy against whom the crusade was preached was Islam" (Fontana 1995, 54), he invokes the notion of "frontiers" in the evolution of Christendom:

> When there is talk of the great awakening of the year 1000, it is forgotten that the period was also one of social and religious conflict thus leading to the fixing of new frontiers: external frontiers which would separate Europe from the Muslims and from eastern Christianity, but also other internal frontiers, which would mark off a part of society itself.

In highlighting the diverse origins of the group of believers in Europe, Fontana questions the traditional conceptualization of Christendom. If Islam was the first enemy designated by the Crusades, Jews were the "internal enemy" (Fontana 1995, 72) whom the Church targeted to blame for any "collective misfortune." The religious inheritance of Europe, then, is one of great complexity and rife with conflict; the borders created around different religious groups sustain the separation between peoples and their religious identities.

Borders of identity in Europe—whether they are political, religious, or geographical— are reinforced during pivotal moments, such as the Crusades, the Renaissance, the Reformation, and the Enlightenment. These times of transition have heralded innovative ideas, new practices, and alternative systems of thought. They have occasioned both liberating and repressive changes. Many scholars, for instance, have debated the "underside" of the European Enlightenment in regards to slavery, women's roles, and the limits of progressive thinking in eighteenth-century Europe.[5] In this light, Jacques Derrida's call for a "new Enlightenment" is significant: "A Europe that can show another politics is possible, that can imagine a political and ethical

---

[4] Jacques Derrida (1996) accentuates the arbitrariness of identity: "Je n'ai qu'une langue, ce n'est pas la mienne" ('I have one language and it's not mine') seems confusing but, in fact, it is an eloquent response to a complex historical reality for Algerian Jews living in Algeria, a country the French colonized from 1830 until 1962. As an Algerian Jew, Derrida may be considered a person dispossessed of French identity twice: he acquired French citizenship by decree, because the Crémieux doctrine granted citizenship to all Jews living in Algeria in 1870, forty years after France colonized Algeria, while later experiencing the withdrawal of his French citizenship by law, under the Vichy government in France during World War II. The idea of "origin" is complicated by historical circumstances for individuals like Derrida, and for continents like Europe.

[5] See Emmanuel Chukwudi Eze (1997) and Louis Sala-Molins (1987).

reflection that is heir to the Enlightenment tradition, but that can also be the portent of a new Enlightenment, able to challenge binary distinctions and high moral pronouncements" (Derrida 2004, 3). A critical engagement with the foundational myths of Europe requires an acknowledgement that "a construction and re-creation of myth is part of the making of a collective consciousness" (García 1993, 5). Indeed, the borders of identity in European history have revealed the conventional nature of borders and the different European historical contexts that have witnessed their creation. Any work must consider the totality of European history, which is powerfully summarized in Peter Bugge's concise statement that "Heritage must be all-inclusive: the Acropolis as well as Auschwitz and everything in between" (Bugge 2003, 73). As we have seen, the existence of European borders depends on ubiquitous Others: for the Renaissance thinkers, the Other represents the Middle Ages (popularly referred to as "the Dark Ages"); for the Crusaders, the Other is the non-Christian, non-believer; for the adherents to Western democracy, the Other represents those who deviate from the values embodied in the Western European democratic model. Historically speaking, the relationship to the Other is fraught with prejudice, myths, and ignorance; in discussing the meanings of borders in Europe today, we accept that Europe is still in the process of becoming, as it engages with its complex history.

In *Postwar: A History of Europe since 1945*, Tony Judt's sweeping history of Europe after the end of World War II, he examines the experiences, events, and ideas that have molded Europe historically (Judt 2005, 753). European borders, as the contrasts between the map in the frontispiece of his book and the one in the back reveal, have been in constant flux over the past six decades. Inter-European wars, decolonization, extra-European immigration, and the collapse of the Iron Curtain are all events that have shaped the social, political, ideological, and cultural borders of contemporary Europe. Judt's assertion that Europe's geography is not "absolute" but rather "relative" reflects the reconfiguration of European borders in the twentieth century. The relativity of borders is echoed in Annsi Paasi's article, in which he states that "[...] boundaries do not embody any eternal truths of places. Rather they are socially constructed and power relations are decisive for their constitution" (Paasi 2001, 23). War and immigration are two prime examples of complex sociological phenomena that have further complicated the nature of borders in Europe. And in the twentieth century, Paasi reminds us, "more than 60% of Europe's present boundaries have been drawn during the 20th century" (22). Though distinct in origin and nature, the wars of ethnic cleansing in Yugoslavia, the rising immigration from Europe's former colonies to European capitals and the ensuing xenophobia, as well as religious and cultural intolerance in Europe, have all raised challenging questions about the meaning of borders in European history. Can the social, cultural, religious, and geographical divisions within Europe be transcended? Will the reconfiguration of borders by immigration inspire a more fluid understanding of European history, especially as it relates to immigration from the proverbial "jewels" of Europe's colonial crown? Will the European Union's mission to create pan-European unity succeed over time, thereby transforming the very nature of borders?

To restate Patricia M. Goff's expression, the ways in which borders are made meaningful in Europe are crucial for understanding how Europe, European identity, and the nature of borders have been reconfigured in the twentieth century. Europe is now facing itself in the mirror; Europe is now addressing the limitations of its foundational myths of democracy, religious identity, and ideals because the wars in Yugoslavia, extra-European immigration, and the fall of the Berlin Wall have all reconfirmed the instability of borders in Europe. Etienne Balibar evokes the idea that the "[...] Balkan War manifests the impasse and impossibility of European unification" (Balibar 2002, 73), and sounds the bells of Euro-pessimism. Yet the German writer, Peter Schneider (2005), when describing the socio-cultural borders and the ensuing conflicts for those people negotiating Turkish-German identity, calls for Muslim integration in German society. This idea expresses absolute confidence in Germany and the likelihood that it will easily survive the divisive borders of cultural identity, race, and religious difference that mark its current socio-political landscape. As European borders continue to shift, the distance between Balibar's Euro-pessimism and Schneider's Euro-confidence may be bridged with the emergence of new conceptualizations of identity. The meanings created by the multi-layered and transversal dimension of European borders show the significance of borders at different historical moments, during large-scale conflicts such as war, and in the midst of transitional periods, when the signals for a new era can no longer be ignored. By addressing its foundational myths, Europe may begin to see the "Other" reflected in itself, its own mirror, and begin to shift the traditional ways of imagining European history and European identity as a stable, fixed and permanent entity.

The Question of Borders in European Film

Throughout the centuries —most drastically during the twentieth century— Europe has witnessed the shifting and provisional nature of its borders. The instability of geographical borders in the continent has run parallel to the crisis of European identity. European identity, like the geographical borders of Europe, is in the process of being redefined. The boundaries of European subjectivity are less clear than they seemed in the past. As Wendy Everett (2005) explains,

Contemporary Europe and its multiple identities are perhaps best envisioned as a form of fractal geometry, pattered by chaos, with national and regional differences endlessly breaking down into ever more complex sub-divisions that reflect differences such as gender, sexuality and ethnicity (5).

Realizing that a monolithic sense of European identity has been a historical mirage only increases the uncertainty that Europeans experience during recent troubling contexts such as the tension between nationalist dispersion and unification or globalization. If the borders that demarcate Europe have become porous, that porosity also calls into question the very same concepts of border and identity, which now demand a more complex approach than the one structured in binary terms of in/out or us/them. There has been a change in the European mentality that can be easily identifiable as a new conceptualization of Europe as a fluctuating signifier.

We inquire into the transcendence of this new vision of Europe in European cinema or, in other words, we ask whether the porosity of European borders has had an impact on European film and how deep this impact has been. Judging from the most recent studies on European cinema, it is evident that all the confusion, instability and uncertainty conveyed by the term "Europe" is retained in the label "European cinema." The limits and borders of European cinema seem to be as porous as those of Europe. Scholars of European cinema have confessed their insecurity when identifying what films can fit the label "European cinema" or what makes, in the end, a film "European." As Tim Bergfelder (2005) says, European cinema, like Europe itself, is in transition or in a state of "indeterminacy or 'in-between-ness'" (320). European cinema is in the process of questioning not only the borders of Europe but also its own borders.

In the era of globalization, in which the project of "one Europe" seems more achievable than ever, European cinema is, like Europe itself, at an impasse between two opposite forces: homogenization and preservation of diversity. One important question seems to be whether it is possible to integrate the variety of national European cinemas at a supra-national European level and to have cinema reflect the changes proposed at the political level for Europe: taking as a starting point a supposedly common European heritage, to create a supra-national European cinema that becomes, in its unification, a strong global player. As desirable as this project seems, it raises concerns about the role of those European countries that are not members of the EU in such an integration.

If we analyze the emphasis that the European Union has put on supra-national European film initiatives, we would have to conclude that EU politicians see European cinema playing an important role not only in any future integration of the nations included in the Union, but also in the awaited success of European cultural exports in intra-European and global markets. Politicians see great potential for cinema to promote a cultural idea of Europe and to increase European commercial competitiveness internationally. The decision of European authorities to celebrate the centenary of cinema in 1995-1996 as a pan-European commemoration shows not only their pride in the European films of the past, but also their faith in the performative power of cinema for the Europe of the future.

There have been many attempts to create a pan-European film industry recently, and the attitude towards old initiatives, like co-productions, has changed. As Thomas Elsaesser (2005) explains, while in previous decades European authorities disdained co-productions for being "Europuddings," more recent co-productions have earned legitimacy and are now considered a crucial part of European integration (506). The MEDIA programmes and Eurimages are considered the most important initiatives towards a borderless European film industry in a borderless Europe, also capable of crossing the boundaries of international markets. When measuring the success of those programs, some critics are more approving than others, but all agree that MEDIA II is less respectful of linguistic and cultural diversity than MEDIA I, paying more attention to commercial competitiveness than to multiculturalism. Regarding Eurimages, critics acknowledge its commitment to the formation of European identity, but they also criticize its lack of "economic muscle and cultural political agenda" (Wayne 2002, 29) and the vagueness in its definition of Europe's identity "beyond general references to diversity and common cultural heritage" (Jäckel 2003, 76). Contemporary supra-national European film projects face at least two challenges: on the one hand, films need to keep a balanced combination of European commonalities and European social, historical, and cultural heterogeneity; on the other hand, films need to keep their European idiosyncrasy while being competitive enough to succeed in global markets. But some projects have revealed the impasse in which EU film industries find themselves. While some European representatives at the GATT conversations in Uruguay in 1993 opposed the treatment of cinema as any other commercial good and justified their position by defending film as a cultural product, some European authorities do not mind approving the omission of cultural distinctiveness in certain large-scale pan-European film projects if this transformation enables them to compete in global markets. The second and more pragmatic approach makes the European film industry fall into the globalization paradox, since it relies on the use of English and Americanized formulas in order to survive or to obtain the funds that later will support more "authentic" European or national films.[6]

---

[6] See Martine Danan (2002) for an analysis of this paradox in the case of French cinema.

The dilemma of European cinema, like that of Europe itself, is whether or not to reflect national borders. Although some of the measures proposed to invigorate European cinema—education of children's appreciation of European cinema in schools, creation of one TV channel dedicated exclusively to the screening of European films (Jäckel 2003, 146)—emulate the ones used by European countries to maintain their own national cinemas, European cinema needs to decide whether to keep the boundaries of the nation at a supra-national level or cross the stable borders of national cinemas towards a post-national era. Rosalind Galt (2006) sees the ethical dilemma of European cinema in the challenge of "how to become European—as opposed to simply continuing an older model of national cinemas—without degenerating into the filmic correlative of Brussels bureaucracy, the Europudding" (2). European cinema is in an unstable position between the national and the global, as if it were trying to reach the difficult balance that Gerard Delanty (2005) envisions for what he calls "cosmopolitan Europe":

> It is possible to conceive of European identity as a cosmopolitan identity based on a cultural logic of self-transformation rather than as a supranational identity or an official EU identity that is in a relation of tension with national identities. As a cosmopolitan identity, European identity is a form of post-national self-understanding that expresses itself within, as much as beyond, national identities (405).

Stuart Hall (1992) explained that European movies from the late 1980s and early 1990s revealed the collapse of borders in Europe (46). While acknowledging the collapse of borders provoked a shock back then, today's filmmakers seem to have accepted such a collapse just as the way Europe and the world are and will be for a while. Contemporary European cinema shows Europe as a space demarcated within porous borders by exploring the interconnections between geographic, historical, and cultural boundaries as well as the contact zones between local, regional, national, and global borders. European films question the borders of Europe and, in the end, the feasibility of a traditional conceptualization of borders. European cinema shows Europe as a space that needs to be redefined and at the same time as an entity that challenges any easy definition. Rather than reconfirming a stable and fixed sense of European identity and providing answers, European cinema shows the tensions and contradictions that undermine Europe today, and raises questions about the limits of European identity. If we follow critics like Everett (2005), who considers the critical gaze a feature of European cinema (11), then we would have to conclude that the self-awareness and the "in-between-ness" present in contemporary European films make them more European than ever.

Contemporary European cinema invites us to cross the traditional borders of Europe, European identity, and European cinema and this call is also a crucial responsibility for those who create the theoretical and critical discourse on European cinema. If we accept Catherine Fowler's statement (2002) about how European cinema is an invention of the critics (1), it is urgent for critics and scholars to trespass the traditional theoretical borders with which they have demarcated the field of "European Film." It is very important to acknowledge that the apparently pure and stable borders of European cinema have always been a convention used by critics to distinguish European cinema from its Others, specifically Hollywood cinema. The narrative of "European cinema" has been constructed upon binary categories, but the identification of European film with a particular cinematic tradition, such as auteur or art movies is no longer realistic or useful. For instance, Elsaesser (2005) invites us to go beyond a negative vision of Hollywood and construct a more comprehensive history of the connections between Hollywood and European cinema to prove their interdependence in a global world.

Contemporary European cinema demands a more complex framework that can acknowledge the porous nature of its borders. Ian Aitkin (2005) proposes globalization as the new theoretical framework to analyze European film. Elsaesser and Aitkin are not the only critics to suggest that we abandon the framework of national borders and embrace a transnational perspective in our analysis of European cinema. Bergfelder (2005) proposes the creation of "an alternative history of European cinema" that would "avoid narratives and discourses of containment, replacing these with critical travelogues, charting the fluidity of identities, and tracing the brief encounters between films and shifting audience formations" (329). It is also time for European Film Studies to acknowledge in its analysis the period of transition in which European films find themselves. In the context of the transformations that Europe is undertaking, *Zoom in, Zoom out: Crossing Borders in Contemporary European Cinema* attempts to serve as a testimony to the multiple ways in which filmmakers are questioning the many borders of the continent and its cinema. Most other volumes that deal with European film still present a sum of articles on particular national cinemas without attaining a pan-national perspective. In this book "European" does not mean a juxtaposition of individual countries from the same continent, but rather it refers to the post-national perspective in films made in Europe during the 1990s and the beginning of the twenty-first century that question European borders.

Zooming in and out in Contemporary European Cinema

Zoom in, Zoom out: Crossing Borders in Contemporary European Cinema treats the phenomenon of 'crossing borders' in European cinema as a symptom reflecting the ongoing challenges that Europe is urgently confronting. European films have become a vital cultural space where the relationship between borders and identity is being renegotiated. This volume examines the performative dimension of European cinema in the reformulation of European identity: a significant number of films not only attempt to describe the current transformation of Europe, they also aim to guide the process. The films discussed here self-consciously address the question of European identity while overtly crossing geographic, cultural, linguistic and aesthetic borders. While making the crossing of borders in Contemporary European films the common subject of all the articles, we maintain diverse themes and perspectives as subtopics. We have included articles not only about films that deal thematically with border-crossings, but also articles that examine movies that cross borders in relation to genres, techniques, or aesthetic approaches. The articles have different theoretical approaches (Film Theory, Cultural Studies, History, Sociology, Philosophy, and Psychoanalysis) and cover films from a variety of cinematic traditions (French, German, Greek, Irish, Italian, Spanish, and Yugoslavian).

This book is divided in three sections. The first section, *IMAGINING AN(OTHER) EUROPE: UNSETTLED BORDERS AND RE-NEGOTIATED IDENTITIES*, includes three articles on films by three of the most important filmmakers in Europe today: Cédric Klapisch, Fatih Akin, and Jean-Luc Godard. In all of these films, the unsettled nature of borders mirrors many of the urgent cultural, political, and economic challenges that Europe is currently facing. The three directors coincide in offering films that directly acknowledge the fluctuating nature of European borders. Mireille Rosello's article discusses the notion of a "chaotic border" through "the visual construction of a self-ironic allegory that both invents and mocks a disorganized, messy, inarticulate, rudimentary, and yet dynamic and optimistically chaotic European subject" in the two most recent films by Klapisch: *L'Auberge espagnole/Pot Luck* (2002) and *Les Poupées russes/The Russian Dolls* (2005). Rosello analyzes the interconnections between the redrawing of administrative borders (around states, countries, cities or new supranational entities) and the redrawing of the conventionally erected borders of storytelling practices and units of cultural information. According to Rosello, *L'Auberge espagnole* self-consciously addresses the fractal structure of Europe and the European subject by offering a metanarrative that, far from being closed, is still "becoming" and needs "to be continued." Janis Solomon's article analyzes three films by Akin, one that involves crossing ethnic borders within Germany (*Kurz und schmerzlos/Short Sharp Shock* [1998]) and two others that deal with geographic border crossings from Germany to Istanbul (*Im Juli /In July* [2000] and *Gegen die Wand/Head-On* [2004]). Solomon explores the transnational imaginary that is being proposed in Akin's films, in which literal and figurative borders are constantly renegotiated. Solomon's analysis confirms the crucial role, that according to Elsaesser, cinema plays for the "hyphenated" members of the European nations (119). Akin, a Turkish-German director, uses his films to bridge differences between the two cultures to which he belongs. Solomon's article shows how his work locates itself geographically as well as culturally, artistically, and politically in multiple frames of reference that transcend the national. Jehanne-Marie Gavarini's article examines the "borderless" quality of Godard's *Notre Musique* (2005), a film modeled after one European literary masterpiece: Dante's *Divine Comedy*. According to Gavarini, far from reinforcing any canonical vision of Europe, the movie questions European unity and moral standards in the aftermath of Sarajevo's siege and in the context of globalization. The article analyzes all the different borders that *Notre Musique* trespasses: geo-political (reflecting the doubts and questions that Godard has about a utopian vision of Europe), philosophical (refuting binary structures), narrative (taking the audience on a circular ride), artistic (self-consciously playing between reality and fiction), and linguistic (exploring the fragile condition of translation).

The second section, *MAPPING NEW BORDERS: GENRE, CO-PRODUCTIONS, AND TECHNOLOGY*, comprises three chapters on films that explore the interdependence between the transformation of European borders and the reformulation of genre frames, co-productions, and new technologies in contemporary European cinema. After studying the formula, constitutive elements, and borders of the Balkan road movie as genre, Nevena Daković's article explores how the real border-crossings shown in Balkan road movies convey more abstract journeys that expose Balkan identity also as a border-crossing between the past and the present, the Balkans and Europe, the official and mythical history, and among different social groupings. Daković's analysis of two opposite paradigmatic films (Sotiris Goritsas' film *Balkanisateur* [1998] and Milcho Manchevski's *Dust* [2001]) shows that the instabilities of the Balkan road movie and Balkan identity are interdependent. Daković defines the Balkan road movie as a multilayered genre that reflects the floating quality of Balkaness by representing both the Europeanization of the Balkans and the Balkanization of the world. Alejandro Pardo's article focuses on a crucial dimension of today's European Cinema: the reinvigoration of co-productions and their role as promoters of a common European culture and identity. Taking as a case study the proliferation of Spanish co-productions in particular, Pardo examines the economic, cultural, and political motivations underlying European collective film projects. The new typology Pardo proposes to classify Spanish co-productions reflects that, far from making European integration the main goal of the European collective projects, economic motivations prevail over cultural ones most of the time. Pardo's article shows a significant contrast: in the co-productions in which Spain chooses Latin American countries as its partners the cultural interests prevail in opposition to the more financial-oriented co-productions in which Spain chooses other European countries as its allies. Olivier Asselin's article examines the impact of the digital revolution on the discourse of European national cinemas, by analyzing how the database model has become a cultural category that puts an end to narratives' domination in contemporary culture. Asselin's main question is whether the digital revolution has had an impact on the representation of national histories, which have been transmitted in a narrative form, or, in other words, whether the crossing of narrative borders onto digital ones in recent historical films imply an erosion of the traditional limits of national history. Asselin's analysis of a recent historical film (Sokurov's *The Russian Ark* [2002]) and Peter Greenaway's most ambitious project *The Tulse Luper Suitcases: A Personal History of Uranium* [2003], shows that, despite the different digital experimentations the directors undertake in their works, historical continuity and cultural totality persist as artistic goals in a trend that Asselin considers "defensive and perhaps reactionary."

The final section, *EUROPEAN FILM AND ITS OTHER BORDERS: CROSS-CULTURAL, NATIONAL, AND TRANSNATIONAL PERSPECTIVES,* contains three chapters focused on films that defy socio-political borders in subtle yet provocative ways through the image of the traveller and the immigrant. The articles in this section underscore the ways in which the use of the travel motif and of different journeys in European cinema is inextricably linked to the cross-cultural and transnational impulses impacting the limits of Europe and the European nations. After contextualizing Italy's relationship to internal immigration in the context its reunification in the nineteenth century and in its struggle to define a sense of national identity after World War II, Claudio Mazzola's article considers the main differences between the first generation of Italian filmmakers who reacted to the phenomenon of Eastern-European immigration in their films during the early nineties and the second generation of directors who are making films on the same topic during the first years of the new millennium. In order to show the differences between the two generations, Mazzola compares Gianni Amelio's *Lamerica* (1993) and Marco Tullio Giordana's *Quando sei nato non ti puoi più nascondere* (2005). He shows that the second generation of filmmakers is more willing to accept the porosity of borders between "us" and "them" and therefore to question older perceptions of immigration and Italian identity in the context of globalization. Ruth Barton's article examines the motif of the stranger throughout the history of Irish cinema to analyze the ways in which the "outsider" has enabled the "insider" to better understand himself/herself and her/his relationship to Ireland. Barton's article also explores how the motif of the traveller has been transformed in the most recent Irish films to represent Ireland's relationship with mainland Europe or with the countries that now contribute to the new immigrant culture in Ireland. In recent films such as *Yu Ming is My Name* (2003), *Adam and Paul* (2004), and the *The Traveller Girl* (2005), Barton assesses the ways in which the borders of contemporary Irish immigrant identity are being crossed. For John Davidson, the "new Europe" found in German-language cinema reveals the connections between the local and the global. He discusses German identity in relation to language and place in a new era he defines as post-national. Through the juxtaposition of two distinct contexts, identities, and histories—the Southern United States and Germany—Davidson discusses *Schultze Gets the Blues* (2003) at length to situate difference in post-national Europe. By examining the borders of cultural identification and belonging, Davidson accentuates the multiple contradictions at work in German-language film through the interplay of local, national, and transnational identities. As a whole, the essays in *Zoom in, Zoom out: Crossing Borders in Contemporary European Cinema* frame the self-conscious gesture by European filmmakers to define European cinema as a work-in-progress, or at the very least, as a project that, like Europe itself, raises as many questions as it answers.

Works Cited

Aitkin, I. 2005. Current problems in the study of European cinema and the role of questions on cultural identity. In *European Identity in Cinema*. 2nd ed. Edited by W. Everett. 79-86. Bristol, UK: Intellect Books.

Bergfelder, T. 2005. National, transnational or supranational cinema? Rethinking European film studies. *Media, Culture & Society* 27.3: 315-331.

Bugge, P. 2003. A European cultural heritage? Reflections on a concept and a programme. In *Rethinking heritage: Cultures and politics in Europe*. Edited by R. S. Peckham, London: I.B. Tauris.

Danan, M. 2002. From a "prenational" to a "postnational" French cinema. In *The European cinema reader*. Edited by C. Fowler. 232-245. London and New York: Routledge.

Delanty, G. 2005. The idea of a cosmopolitan Europe: On the cultural significance of Europeanization. *International Review of Sociology* 15.3 (November): 405-421.

Derrida, J. 1996. *Le monolinguisme de l'autre, ou la prothèse de l'origine.* Paris: Galilée.
—. 2004. Une Europe de l'espoir. *Le Monde diplomatique* (December): 3.
Elsaesser, T. 2005. *European cinema. Face to face with Hollywood.* Amsterdam: Amsterdam University Press.
Etienne, B. 2002. *Politics and the other scene.* London: Verso.
Everett, W., ed. 2005. *European identity in cinema.* 2nd ed. Bristol, UK: Intellect Books.
Eze, E. C., ed. 1997. *Race and the enlightenment*, Cambridge, MA: Blackwell.
Fontana, J. 1995. *The distorted past: A reinterpretation of Europe.* Translated by C. Smith. London: Basil Blackwell.
Fowler, C. 2002. *The European cinema reader.* London: Routledge.
Galt, R. 2006. *The new European cinema. Redrawing the map.* New York: Columbia University Press.
García, S. 1993. Europe's fragmented |deiítities and the frontiers of citizenship. In *European identity and the search for legitimacy.* Edited by S. García. London: Pinter Publishers.
Goff, P. M. 2000. Invisible borders: Economic liberalization and national identity. *International Studies Quarterly* 44: 533-562.
Hall, S. 1992. European cinema on the verge of a nervous breakdown. In *Screening Europe. Image and identity in contemporary European cinema.* Edited by D. Petrie. London: British Film Institute.
Jäckel, A. 2003. *European film industries.* London: British Film Institute.
Judt, T. 2005. *Postwar: A history of Europe since 1945.* New York: The Penguin Press.
Paasi, A. 2001. Europe as a social process and discourse: Considerations of place, boundaries and identity. *European Urban and Regional Studies* 8(1): 7-28.
Sala-Molins, L. 1987. *Le code noir, ou le calvaire de Canaan.* Paris: PUF.
Schneider, P. 2005. The New Berlin Wall. *New York Times Magazine* 5 (December): 66-71.
Wayne, M. 2002. *The politics of contemporary European cinema. Histories, borders, diasporas.* Bristol, UK: Intellect Books.

PART I:

IMAGINING AN(OTHER) EUROPE: UNSETTLED BORDERS AND RE-NEGOTIATED IDENTITIES

CHAPTER ONE

IMAGINING EUROPEAN SUBJECTS AS CHAOTIC
BORDERS: CÉDRIC KLAPISCH'S *POT LUCK*
AND *THE RUSSIAN DOLLS*

MIREILLE ROSELLO, UNIVERSITY OF AMSTERDAM

In this chapter, I propose to test the notion of a "chaotic border" by focusing on the visual construction of a self-ironic allegory that both invents and mocks a disorganized, messy, inarticulate, rudimentary and yet dynamic and optimistically chaotic European subject, in two films by French director Cédric Klapisch: *L'Auberge espagnole* or *Pot Luck* (2002) and its sequel, *Les Poupées russes* or *The Russian Dolls* (2005).

Klapisch, who studied film in Paris and at NYU in the 1980s, became highly visible in 1996-7, which was a turning point for him as a filmmaker and as a public voice. Two films, *Chacun cherche son chat* (1996) (*When the Cat's Away*) and *Un Air de famille* (1996) (*Family Resemblances*) established him as a sensitive reader of contemporary culture. The first one is a collective portrait of one of the most popular Parisian neighborhoods and *Un Air de famille*, awarded three Césars, is an adaptation of a play by the famous screenwriting team Agnès Jaoui and Jean Pierre Bacri. Both films became spectacular box office hits.

At the same period, the director (who had already put his camera at the service of his political agenda in 1994, when AIDS was the most urgent public health issue)[1] became a visible public figure. Along with 66 French filmmakers who advocated civil disobedience, he signed the well-publicized manifesto when the so-called "loi Debré," a series of anti-immigration measures, was discussed at the National Assembly. The bill was concocted as a response to the "affaire des sans-papiers de Saint-Bernard," one of the very first movements organized by undocumented migrants who refused to continue living invisible and clandestine lives in France. Klapisch is very much a contemporary public intellectual whose deliberately unpretentious but thoughtful interventions are not

---

[1] In 1994, he had already participated in the "3000 scenarios against AIDS" campaign, directing two short films, *La Chambre* and *Poisson rouge*.

so much the equivalent of the 19th century Stendhalian realist mirror but rather a self-conscious and self-referential attempt at participating in the construction of contemporary Europe.

I suggest that his own interventions on behalf of undocumented migrants participate in the construction of what I am here calling a "chaotic border," here within his own work rather than within or around Europe. The supranational border around what is now called "Fortress Europe" has already been described and denounced as the walls of a medieval castle, a sort of reinforced xenophobic super state-line.[2] I argue that the chaotic phenomena that *L'Auberge espagnole* and *Les Poupées russes* focus on are both radically different but also inseparable from the type of issues that Klapisch and other directors confronted in 1996. Seen by more than 3 million spectators in France, the two films address European borders as they exist today and how they may exist tomorrow, with Klapisch exploring what he sees as the future the enlarged community of nations.[3]

---

[2] From that point of view, historically speaking, European 21st century productions can be seen as catching up with many 20th century postcolonial novels and films that were grappling with the issue of diglossia, multilingualism and creolization as early as the 1950s and 60s. Caribbean artists wishing to embrace their Creole culture, African writers worrying about the weight of Europhone languages, Maghrebi authors who experienced the process of "Arabisation" after 1962, and children of immigrants whose parents speak a different tongue from the one they study at school (French or English or German) have already exposed the limits of an ideology that presupposes that everyone's mother tongue is the same as the national tongue. Twenty-first century Europe is facing an even more complicated problem, as one strong gravitational pull goes in the direction of preserving the diversity of language while another force seems to be at work to create a pecking order between languages.

[3] Klapisch explains in an interview that *Les Poupées russes* is part of his most recent reflection on the relationship between Europe and globalization: "Aujourd'hui les questions actuelles sont: la Russie, la Turquie ou la Hongrie vont-elles faire partie de l'Europe ? Et plus largement, pour moi, la question est de savoir si l'on veut être citoyen du monde. Mon opinion est qu'il faut se forcer à ne pas penser les choses d'une façon nationale. L'Europe n'est qu'une première étape. L'apprentissage de base de l'être humain doit être d'apprendre à découvrir les autres" (Today, the relevant questions are: will Russia, Turkey and Hungary be part of Europe? And for me, the larger issue is whether we want to be citizens of the world. My sense is that we should make an effort not to think nationally. Europe is only the first stage. The main educational project of each human being should be to learn how to discover others) (Tourné 2005). He suggests elsewhere that he is also commenting on the Turkish issue which is at the core of any discussion about the future enlargment of "l'Europe des 25": "Avant de choisir la Russie, j'avais pensé à la Turquie: l'idée était la même, parler de l'Europe dans ce qu'elle n'est pas encore..." (Before opting for Russia, I had thought of Turkey: the idea was the same, to talk about what Europe is not yet...) (Ferenczi 2005).

Depending on which reading we privilege, *L'Auberge espagnole* might be summarized in two very different ways. Adapting Gérard Genette's famous account of the whole of Proust's *La Recherche*, we could say that this exuberant and deliberately non-linear narrative tells the story of how "Xavier devient écrivain" (Xavier, the hero, becomes a writer).[4] And from that point of view, it is important to keep in mind that the element of becoming, of experimenting is just as important when we study the narrative techniques that he is using within the story (this is the work of a beginner who hesitates and often rewrites the narrative) as when we look at what his plot and autobiographical trajectory tell us about the emergence of a European subject/map. Like Xavier, like the story, Europe is in becoming, unable to totalize, to properly add up what is lost and what is gained.

At the end of *L'Auberge espagnole*, he looks at photographs of all of his new friends, at old pictures of himself including one of the child who dreamed of being a writer (to write books), he replaces the old Rimbaldian "I is an other" (je est un autre) by a chaotic assemblage where "I" and others, his nationality and that of his housemates, but also aspects of his own personality are either embraced or discarded. The result is not only chaos but what Xavier calls "a vrai bordel" (a right mess). "Je ne suis pas ça, ni ça, ni ça ... je ne suis plus ça ... Je suis lui, et lui, et lui aussi et lui. Je suis elle, je suis Français, Espagnol, Anglais et Danois; je ne suis pas un mais plusieurs" (I am not this, nor that, nor that, I am no longer that... I am he, and he, and he too. I am she, I am French, Spanish, English and Dan... I am not one but many). In the background, the spectator hears echoes of barely audible noises, something that hesitates between a cacophony and a polyphonic ensemble. "Je suis comme l'Europe, Xavier concludes, je suis tout ça, je suis un vrai bordel" (I am like Europe, I am all of this, I am a real mess). Xavier has crossed borders but also become a chaotic border himself. The camera work reflects the chaotic multitude that he has become: layers of past identities are superimposed, each new identity photograph that he shows to the camera lingers a little after he chooses another one, creating a ghostly effect. Photos of the past come alive then become still again. A mosaic of small quadrangles then divides the screen into equal fragments, with the meaning remaining unclear. Voices, his and others, repeat bits of sentences. He is the writer who both secretes and reflects the reality of his new subjectivity, by dint of trials and errors, a messy and unfinished process that the spectators can read as an intuition rather than a proposal. Moreover, this occurs in the 14th and last chapter of the film but characteristically, Xavier's voice acknowledges that that process of creation is the "beginning," what gave birth to the story that we have just enjoyed. Xavier has become a writer.

---

[4] See Genette's *Figures III*. Paris: Seuil, 1972.

But we do not have, naturally, to take Xavier's point of view for granted and a "reading for the plot," as Peter Brooks would say (Brooks 1984), would yield the following result. The film is a collective portrait of a group of students who cross borders as they arrive in Barcelona on the Erasmus exchange program that has linked universities from France, Germany, Denmark, Italy, and England. They have all come to the same city in order to study in Spanish. Due to financial constraints and a lack of administrative superstructure that is very comically and creatively filmed when Xavier explains the application process, they are more or less forced to share a house. This experiment in international cohabitation is the Spanish Inn of the title, a place of friction, messiness, constant mistranslation where each character constantly remains at a level of linguistic and cultural semi-incompetence that makes dialogues both difficult and fruitful.[5] The border between languages becomes as chaotic as the borders between nations and what they represent.

This multidimensional narrative experiment suggests that the chaotic movement pulls in two simultaneous and sometimes antagonistic directions: one the one hand, new European experiences teach Klapisch's main character, Xavier, how to tell stories in a different (more chaotic) way and on the other hand, the way in which he tells the chaotic story of his Europe gives a chaotic aspect both to Europe and to his own European subjectivity. In other words, I am not reading the group of students as Klapisch's allegory of what currently constitutes "Europe" and "Europeans," I am reading the film itself as an attempt to make us consider what would be the elements and the storytelling practices that would be required for us to construct such an allegory, and also what the consequences of such a pedagogical approach would be. Klapisch's story stages, in the realm of visual fiction, some of the theoretical problems that philosophers, social and political scientists have been writing about.

One of the most obvious proposals is this performative description of a chaotic zone of turbulence that replaces the way in which we used to represent national borders. Stories themselves are affected because borders are not simply redrawn, moved from one place to another (for example from around states to around the new supranational entity) but redefined as borders. The way in which individuals imagine crossing a border or living in what Mary-Louise Pratt called a contact zone is also evolving rapidly (Pratt 1992). The two processes go hand in hand even if they have a slightly different impact on the cultural categories that visual narratives such as films invite us to mobilize. The re-

---

[5] The title of both films creates interesting problems of translation: Klapisch, as he explains in an interview, toyed with "Europudding," which was thought to be unappealing by his English-speaking team. Eventually, "Pot Luck" was preferred although the phrase only keeps a portion of the French expression, leaving out the allusion to Spain for example (Brooks 2003).

drawing of European borders is officially described as a dismantling of state limits. The fact that people are free to move about within Europe, i.e. across state lines that used to be strong symbolic and practical divisions around countries, means that our narratives of international movement are transformed.

In *L'Auberge espagnole*, the moment when students cross a state-line is completely de-emphasized. Other recent European films deal with the disappearance of the border by making fun of the extinct ritual. For example, in Wim Wenders's *Lisbon Story*, the hero, Philip Winter is a sound engineer who travels from Frankfurt to Portugal's capital city to meet an American director. When he crosses borders, he talks to the non-existent border guards and jokes about what he is smuggling in the trunk of his car or pretend to be surprised not to have to show his passport.[6]

In *L'Auberge espagnole*, the fact that borders no longer function in this way is simply not worth representing. The crossing of the European state-line between France and Spain, for example, is never even represented. What happens, on the other hand, is that the nature and the quality of what constitutes a border, or what constitutes an important moment of passage has changed radically and from that point of view, Klapisch's chaotic representations of a "bordélique" resemble Etienne Balibar's descriptions of "fractal," "incomplete" (frontière non-entières) or deterritorialized borders. In *We, the People of Europe?*, he argues that

> ...sometimes noisily and sometimes sneakily, borders have changed place. Whereas traditionally, and in conformity with both their juridical definitions and "cartographical" representation as incorporated in national memry, they should be at the edge of the territory, marking the point where it ends, it seems that borders and the institutional practices corresponding to them have been transported into the middle of the political space. They can no longer function as simple edges and external limits of democracy that the mass of citizens can see as a barrier protecting their rights and lives without ever really interfering with them (Balibar 2001, 109).

And as John Crowley points out in his review of Balibar's book, the immediate consequence of this type of restructuring is that the way in which one crosses a border becomes a completely different protocol. Rather than being a sort of no-man's land around the city, a vacuum where contact is rare, "Instead, the type of deterritorialized borders whose emergence Balibar is right to

---

[6] See Ewa Mazierska's analysis who suggests that "Road films provide an excellent opportunity to explore both the variety and differences of national and regional cultures in Europe, as well as the common 'European identity,' of which migration and traveling are often regarded as an important component" (Mazierska 2001).

emphasize are places of intense friction."[7] The film is keen on emphasizing that the deterritorialization of the border is not the same thing as its disappareance. The intense friction manifests itself in different ways, even before Xavier's departure.

For example, when he tries to collect all the documents that are necessary for his application to the Erasmus program, the administrative labyrinth is visualized on the screen by the proliferation of official documents that are superimposed over the moving images. The absurdity of static bureaucracy gradually encroaches upon the space devoted to the rest of the story and the sound track adds parasitical noises, a computer's clicking sound that interrupts the assistant's litany. The film represents the internal border as a sort of narrative stamp: the story disappears under the layer of documents or stamps as if an immigration officer had superimposed his mark of authority over Xavier's life story.

Because the border changes, border crossing occurs in different places and the rules that one used to abide by are no longer the same. This, contrary to what the official discourse would have us believe, does not necessarily mean that it is easier to enter, to become an insider. Practices of cohabitation and expectations about norms, assumptions about solidarity and alliances are radically redefined and become more chaotic, more unpredictable. Just as the new European subjectivity that emerges out of Xavier's experience turns him into a messy subject, the reality that he experiences resembles his chaotic self. Like him, Europe is messy: "C'est le bordel" (It's a right mess).

But the colloquial word is not clearly derogatory. As one interviewer puts it: "Clearly that word is the key to understanding Klapisch's take on a changing Europe. 'Of course, Europe is a mess,' he says. 'Just as life is a mess. But I try to put a positive spin on the word. [...] I like to live in a multicultural, melting-pot environment. Because the idea of unifying everything leads to fascism'" (Brooks 2003). His conviction is reflected in the film both metaphorically and through storytelling practices especially at particularly symbolic junctions, when Xavier moves on to a different stage, a different place or a different level. When he tries to get accepted as a housemate (when he crosses the border into his new temporary home that he will, himself, name "the Spanish Inn"), a chaotic border forms in front of him and incorporates him as a subject. Because he ends up being the film's narrator, that moment also coincides with the birth of the film itself.

The fact that this border is deterritorialized makes crossing it chaotic. Xavier does not know what to expect and his future housemates, who are busy selecting among the numerous applicants, are rather poor imitations of border

---

[7] "Les frontières déterritorialisées dont Balibar souligne à juste titre l'émergence sont, au contraire, des lieux d'intense frottement" (Crowley 2002, 65).

guards. At first, the scene reminded me of a passage in *Monty Python and the Holy Grail* (1975) where Arthur and his knights have to cross the bridge over the gorge of Eternal Peril and must answer the bridge keeper's ridiculous and unexpected questions (from "What is your favorite color?" to "What is the capital of Abyssinia?" [Rosello 1997, 109]). Here, the messiness of the protocol is indicated by the fact that no proper ritual is in place. The students, who did not know that a border would have to be crossed, improvise and choose a pastiche of another genre with which some of us are familiar: the job interview. They end up collectively turning into a parody of a badly prepared interview panel or rather a chaotic hybrid between the interviewer, the immigration officer or the examining board member.

Before the camera even reveals the scene, we hear the voice of a woman who will be one of Xavier's future housemates. As long traveling shots scan the cityscape, we hear Wendy's voice apologetically stating: "This isn't a trial or anything." Except that, of course, the selection process is both a trial and "anything." The rules are not any clearer than the game. Some of the panelists ask questions that others resent or at least comment upon, suggesting that they are inappropriate and irrelevant. Tobias, the criticized interviewer defends his position by means of self-referential explanations of why he chooses a certain line of questioning, drawing a self-portrait that calls attention to his own subjectivity instead. This relegates the test to the background and re-empowers Xavier who now becomes an amused observer. At that moment, even narrative options are interrupted and instable. Xavier moves out of the position of intradiegetic character and applicant or supplicant to a different narrative plane: from within the story, he is curiously silent as an interviewee but as the writer that he finally became, he chooses to intervene as a first-person narrator and his voice over crosses all the generic and fictional border that he encounters in his European experience. We hear his narrative voice cover the chaotic discussion between the other protagonists:

> J'ai tout de suite adoré cet endroit. J'aurais donné n'importe quoi pour qu'ils m'acceptent ici. Le bordel qui habitait là ressemblait totalement à celui qui m'habitait depuis toujours. C'était comme si leurs engueulades c'était celles qui avaient lieu dans ma tête en permanence depuis que j'étais tout petit.
> (I immediately loved the place. I would have done anything to be accepted there. The mess that lived there was the exact replica of the mess that has always lived within myself. It is as if their rows had been taking place inside my head, constantly, ever since I was a kid).

Once Xavier is indeed invited to join the crew of the "Spanish Inn," the chaotic crossing of this chaotic border allows him to enter a space but it is never really clear what type of citizenship he has gained, which characteristics, duties or rights are now his. This becoming-a-member, this pseudo naturalization is shown to be just as complicated as the ritual that precedes it. What is supposed to be inside the chaotic border is another type of chaos.

As a result, solidarities within that space no longer resemble the kind of networks that the traditional citizen of the old nation state envisages. The members of the international group that live in and constitute *L'Auberge espagnole* are no more bound by a clear set of values than by a principle of jus soli or jus sanguini. Throughout the film solidarity between the European heroes occurs almost spontaneously, on an ad-hoc basis that is neither the result of common values nor the consequence of carefully mobilization and planning. The ideals advocated by the characters' behavior are difficult to articulate and they have nothing to do with the recognizable grand narratives of Western democracies (freedom, equality or even peace). A tendency to protect the other's sexual desires and some level of experimentation with modestly unorthodox types of relationships is the closest they get to a rationalized agenda.

From an international policy perspective, solidarity is often assumed to be the by-product of an imagined shared national identity. Elsewhere is the land of the others, often barbarians, sometimes enemies. Joan of Arc would not function as a national myth if the French and the British had not constructed each other as mythical enemies. Even when the protocol of encounter is positive, for example when the Germans and the French become the narrative elements of a remarkable story of reconciliation, the distinction between two peoples, two states and two nations is preserved. I am suggesting that in order to feel reconciled with "the Germans," the "French" have to first assume that their fundamental basis of solidarity would still primarily, instinctively be with other "French" people. Differences between states are still perceived as more obvious than differences within states, or, another way of saying this is that narratives of national solidarity are a question of national identity. In *L'Auberge espagnole*, the old national narrative is mocked and denounced as an obsolete, old fashioned and destructive set of stereotypes.

Only one character in that first film consistently relies on that pattern and he is the exception to the rule. In the first film, he is an outsider, a visitor. As Wendy's brother, he comes from England and stays with the group for two weeks. William, who is constructed as the voice of national stereotypes, seems immune to chaotic representations. For him, each student represents one country, Alessandro is supposed to me as messy as Italy, Tobias is supposed to be as tidy as Germany and William does not even hesitate to bring up Hitler as the reason why trains are always on time in that country. An Englishman who does not speak one word of Spanish but still explains to Soledad what Spaniards are like, he infuriates everyone and puts an end to conversations. The result of this type of border thinking has consequences on the communication patterns that he is capable of utilizing. His refusal to acknowledge chaotic borders and chaotic subjects kills the story and stops the turbulent flow of words between the housemates.

While all the characters constantly talk with each other, he can never have a real dialogue with the other protagonists. As one of the students notices, his privileged form of communication is the "monologue," a long and monotonous litany of preconceived bits of information about Germans, Italians, Spaniards etc. While *L'Auberge espagnole* brings differences together, his articulation of what he thinks is the nature of the difference (the clear-cut border between people that resembles the border between their states of origin) creates physical and linguistic fragmentation. For example, offended by his generalizations about Spain and his literally barbaric imitation of fake Spanish or fake French, Soledad, the Spanish character, simply gets up and leaves the room. Later, outraged by his allusion to Hitler as the symbol of German organization, Tobias orders him out to his room and then asks to talk to Wendy, in Spanish, leaving William alone beyond the language boundary that he—alone—is incapable of crossing, chaotically or not.

On the other hand, William reinstates, within his own language, the old traditional frontier between the national and the foreigner who speaks, supposedly with an accent. He imitates what he believes to be a German accent or a French accent, but fails to convince others that standard English is or should be the norm. When the national language is the assumed mother tongue of the citizen who resides in the country, linguistic inadequacy is often expected to be the migrant's lot. In France, the French speak French. Any other combination is the beginning of a minority situation that normative interpretations soon read as anomalous. As Kristeva reminds us in *Strangers to Ourselves*, the foreigner makes barbaric noises, the barbarian does not communicate adequately.[8]

In *L'Auberge espagnole*, the binary system that places a clear border between the linguistically competent national and the accented other no longer functions. In this film, the opposition between the migrant who must learn the dominant language and the national who already masters the mother tongue (that is also the national language of the fatherland) disappears because the status of language has changed as drastically as the other type of borders. William is clearly the undesirable exception to the rule in this film where language is one of the most obvious redefined borders. The story is not only multilingual itself[9] but constantly crossing over between languages and also

---

[8] Kristeva refers to Homer's use of "barbarophone" and suggests that he coined the word to imitate the sound made by incomprehensible forms of language: "bla-bla or bara-bara" (Kristeva 1988, 75).
[9] See the intricate code that had to be adopted to account for the presence of different languages in the subtitles: a different font has been used depending on whether the

between media (translations, subtitles, visual references to dictionaries: for example the voice over reads outloud the definition of a "Spanish inn," pointing out, as if by chance, that "reading" is like what happens in a Spanish inn, i.e. you read or you eat what you brought to the table).[10] The characters speak to each other sometimes in English, sometimes in Spanish and sometimes in French. Their dialogues are subtitled in French or in English.

Intradiegetically, the presence of several simultaneous linguistic systems translates as a chaotic flow of information or noise that the characters always fail to control properly. In the flat, students put up with a permanent level of inadequacy. The fact that no European language dominates is not an obstacle to constant conversations even if the keyword, in the Spanish Inn, is approximation. Multiplicity is the norm to the extent that at least seven national languages are represented but multilingualism is both a given and an illusion: the students all speak more than one language, at least one language beside their native tongue, but they are not perfectly or even almost multilingual. Their competence in the others' languages is often limited if not minimalist. Danish is not part of the film's picture, Italian is marginalized and so is German. Three languages dominate, from a quantitative and qualitative point of view: Spanish functions as a lingua franca because they are all trying to learn that language for personal reasons. The idea that they should speak Spanish because they are in Spain is not a priority: the students live in a micro-territory (the Spanish Inn) rather than in a state called Spain. Even Barcelona is not treated as a quintessentially "Spanish" as the discussion about whether courses should be in Spanish or in Catalan demonstrates. Even "Spain" is not a good enough reason to assume that Spanish is the default language. The flat does not function as a subset of Spain, it functions as an allegory of a process of discovery of multilingualism, not as a picture of success or failure, but of the difficulties that such a situation creates for the protagonists. In the "Spanish" inn, the unwritten linguistic policy is that a constellation of languages coexist and each is used on an ad-hoc basis.

At times, an attempt to organize chaos leads to the creation of tactical borders that expose, rather than solve, the problems they encounter. For example, a list of basic phrases in different languages is posted next to the phone in case one of the students' friend or parents calls in a language that the person who picks up does not master. The system hardly works, creating the equivalent of noise and static on a line. When Wendy desperately tries to read a French sentence that she does not understand, she cannot control the effect of

---

characters use Spanish, English, French etc... Creative renditions of barbarisms also had to be invented.

[10] The quote is attributed to Malraux. See also the relationship to Erasmus as a historical character but also as a hallucination.

the sort of echo that her own linguistic production generates. She does not correctly appreciate the chaotic feedback that she is getting in response to her mispronounced French words and appears shocked to hear Xavier's mother use what she believes to be the F. word, incapable as she is to decode the French colloquial abbreviation for university: "fac." As spectators, we know that it is the case because Wendy (not Xavier's mother) actually says "fuck" aloud, thinking that she is repeating what she has heard, but in fact volunteering the idea through a chaotic (though conventional and well-known) effect of mistranslation. The misunderstanding is probably funnier than what would have been said had the two characters communicated. Imperfect as they are, these tactics often replace dialogues that would only be conventional chitchats with productive moments of chaotic misunderstandings that make the story a more interesting narrative. The camera does not show us the mother, which symbolizes the failure of the dialogue, and the comic episode emphasizes the deterioration suffered by any language when a mechanical translation is attempted. A gimmick that was supposed to help characters cross the linguistic barrier (the answer that is supposed to be predictable) leads to more chaos as it creates the space where empty repetitions fail and repetitions with a difference only make the misunderstanding more acute. Just as William's empty iteration of stereotypes forces the dialogue into a monologue, the dictionary or tourist book principle effectively highlights the meaninglessness of supposedly predictable conversations within the same language.

Here, no identifiable agency tries to prevent subjects from crossing a pre-existing border: they change in their relationship to each other as they move more or less painfully in and out of several languages. Chaos reigns, for a long time, producing remarkable results and sometimes radically changing the character him or herself. For example, the issue of unpredictability and temporality to which *L'Auberge espagnole* alludes, is taken up again and developed in *Les Poupées russes*. In that second film, William reappears as the character who brings the others together again when he plans to get married and invite them all. In the second film, Klapisch has made him evolve into a sensitive language learner. At the beginning of his chaotic linguistic and subjective transformation, the initial contact between the technician that he has become and the Russian dancer with whom he is about to fall in love seems to be a replica of the "tourist book" scene in *L'Auberge espagnole*.

At first, language plays a minimalist role in their relationship and eyesight is the only meaningful sensory medium between them. He does not speak the language of the Russian ballerina who dances on the stage below. A specialist of lights, he controls what has to do with visibility and invisibility but any linguistic communication is ruled out. They "saw" each other for a while but could not speak. William explains to Xavier that the dancer then returned to

Russia and we could assume that the story had ended there, just like the conversation between Wendy and the writer's mom in *L'Auberge espagnole*. Klapisch, however, adds a temporal dimension to the chaotic linguistic border.

It takes William one year to learn not "the" language but enough words to make his declaration to his beloved. Naturally, the meaning of the few sentences that he utters is immensely enriched by the determination with which he pursued the linguistic challenge. The crossing of the national border, in this case, is not the issue. The film does not take the point of view of the undocumented migrant. On the other hand, even if no political will tries to keep William out, even if Russia is presented here as the allegorical possibility of an expanding Europe, the border that William must cross is neither here nor there, it is inscribed in time, as an unfinished and difficult process. It takes time, effort, and a patience and humility that the first part of the story had not made the viewer expect from William, the manufacturer of stereotypes.

In both films, the border, the territory, the language and the subjects are all entangled in the same chaotic structure. The key words are misunderstanding, an emphasis on degrees of extremely rudimentary knowledge. At the same time, there is a generally high level of casual acceptance regarding linguistic ability. No one masters the other's language and that is acceptable. What is original about this context is that linguistic incompetence is expected to be everyone's lot. It is encoded as the norm rather than the exception. Consequently the crossing of that chaotic border, i.e. the process of language acquisition, also changes drastically. It permeates every other activity, it becomes a way of life rather than a self-contained moment in a high school student's schedule (the so-called language class). Instead of language being a border that the subject must cross by gradually mastering more and more skills, the subject is the border through which language flows or not. As Yves Citton suggests in his exploration of membranes and borders in Europe, it might be possible to "concevoir le vivant, non pas comme un être entouré d'une membrane, limité par une frontière (semi-perméable) qui nous distingue et nous unit à notre environnement, mais comme un être dont l'essence singulière consiste en une membrane, en une grille de (se)lection" (imagine living organisms not as a being surround by a membrane and contained by a semi-permeable boundary that both links us to and separates us from our environment but as a being whose the specific essence is to be a membrane and selection grid) (Citton 2005).

The characters move in and out of several languages simultaneously, with little regard for what is supposed to be the new European ideal of "one mother tongue plus two" foreseen by official commissions.[11] In Europe and especially

---

[11] See the work done by the "European commission responsible for Education, Training, Culture and Multiculturalism." In March 2004, in Brussels, Ján Figel, speaking on behalf

in France, linguistic policies have always tended towards centralization and the erasure of minority languages. Calling them "patois" was one way of ensuring their minoritization. Even after the metropole lost its prestige as the colonial center, the ghost of the primacy of one national language sometimes haunted newly decolonized states. The fact that the French language carried such symbolic power may explain why a country like Algeria should reject multilingualism to better eliminate French from the realm of possibilities instead of welcoming the problematic but rich coexistence of say Arabic, French and Berber. Europe does not seem tempted to come up with a European idiom that would supercede national languages but on the other hand, the current linguistic situation no longer simply collapses nations and linguistic borders. The half idealistic half bureaucratic dream of translating every single language into every other language so that the twenty-five states can have their say in their own language is not reflected in everyday practices. Europe can neither adopt the kind of centralizing slogan that was the mark of previous nationalistic linguistic policies (where the uniqueness of the official language is thought to symbolize the integrity of the sovereign state), nor pretend that all the languages will coexist in a great festive multilingual party where everyone will speak their own language and everybody else's.

English is never demonized in the films. It is shared, it is Wendy's native language but they all understand it even if mastery varies, the script making no attempt to correct Alessandro's faulty grammar or Tobias's relatively idiosyncratic use of adjectives. No unique language emerges that we could call a new creole and no attempt is made as creating a new European tongue on the model of the other national languages. In other words, the theoretical principle that may be seen as work when people try to learn Esperanto is not implemented here. The hesitant, often garbled attempts at speaking another language is shared by all as a process. The learning of Spanish does not make Spanish the dominant native language that will make all the other students feel dominated in terms of linguistic mastery. Inaccuracy is the norm, a high threshold of tolerance for what is not perfect is acceptable.

---

of the commission, discussed the different types of multilingualism that he sees emerging in Europe: "It rapidly became apparent to me that there are in fact two sides to multilingualism. The first is what one might term societal and concerns the European citizen in his everyday life. The second dimension is institutional multilingualism which is the dimension you are here to discuss today. But they are two sides of the same coin. Multilingualism is clearly an asset to anyone and I am sure that I do not need to expand on that here in the company of so many highly accomplished specialists. That is of course why the Commission's target for language learning is summed up in the expression 'mother tongue plus two'" (Figel 2005).

How and more importantly when, or why does one learn a language in this film? The characters do not learn Spanish because they moved to Spain (as would be the case, for example, for Moroccan or Albanian migrants who seek jobs temporary jobs). It is the other way around: they came to Spain in order to learn a language. At first then, the language itself functions like a product, something exterior to the characters, which can be acquired, purchased. In Xavier's case, the job search is even presented as a most traditional, even old-fashioned typical form of cronyism. Because his father knows someone at Bercy (the Ministry of Finances) he is made aware that a graduate project revolving around Spain's economy will earn him a job in the foreseeable future, Xavier is practically promised a position provided his Spanish improves. An old boy's network is thus at the origin of what will in fact turn out to be a radical point of discontinuity.

In the meantime, the need to learn Spanish is almost treated as a disembodied skill, it is the equivalent of an insider's tip. Like a desirable stock, the language is implicitly treated like a merchandise. Like those commodities advertised as more authentic when they come from a given nation (Italian olive oil, Dutch tulips), Spanish language is a readily available product. Predictably perhaps, and this is why Klapisch is described as a Europtimist, this rather crass definition of the language as product is not stable: eventually, language will flow through the subjects and be added as one the different chaotic facets of the overall experience. The way in which the students seek to acquire that cultural capital is a process that will redefine the boundaries between commercial transactions and national education and perhaps more importantly, the boundaries between what they think is important and what is part of their identity and what is not. On the one hand, the old assumption according to which learning the language is either a sort of luxurious humanities pursuit that one has to defend with pragmatically-minded students goes out of the window. Languages are Europe's new big business: if Xavier learns Spanish, he is to be offered a job in the prestigious Ministry of Finances, the so-called "cruise-ship" (paquebot) with a wonderful view over Paris. On the other hand, what happens on the ground is that this new vision of language as a commodity that can be imported is rejected by the film in favor of chaotic multilingualism, a high threshold of tolerance for linguistic approximation and a strong desire to learn and understand others' life stories in spite of the difficulty of the enterprise.

In the end, it is clear that Xavier does get the job that he was promised but he renounces the security and boredom of a well-paid administrative position. Language or rather languages will be his raw material. It is not clear which language is the film's language. French may dominate in purely quantitative terms but the viewer is obviously expected to at least understand some English, some Spanish and the language that each character uses in their conversation with each other does not always correspond to their own origin or their point of arrival (the traditional metaphor of language departure and language of arrival that translation adopts is thus redrawn and redefined).

With its constant emphasis on hesitation, and false beginnings,[12] the film suggests that the imaginary geography of Europe is no longer readable through traditional linear narratives of departure and arrival, insider and outsider, citizen and foreigner. In order to suggest the crucial importance of accepting, as the norm, what seems to be a highly uncomfortable level of friction, messiness, rudiments, Klapisch represents his European hero as a young, confused individual whose subjectivity (and therefore identity as an autobiographer) is the chaotic result, rather than the cause, of his travels and border crossing. The other lands, Spain or Russia, are not exoticized and the heroes are neither ethnographers nor tourists.

Xavier's self-referential attempts at writing about something that remains barely comprehensible even to himself provides the spectator with a vision of an identity that we are invited to consider as representative of what a certain European subject might become.[13] At the same time, the films do not take the experiment seriously. Xavier's own relationship to writing, to his life, to his desires is always treated with humor. No European grand narrative of peace, harmony or democracy replaces the old-fashioned national constructions. It is a fanciful project that ends up having very serious implications, which does not mean that the resulting narrative is treated as a new authoritarian grand narrative. The first film spells out that the experiment is limited in time and space. This is not an allegory of the construction of Europe, this is an example of how self-contained episodes, with their open-ended lessons, their emphasis on messiness, rudimentary knowledge, and experimental storytelling practices that have a "to be continued" quality to them are the best possible way of representing the construction of a twenty-first century European "mess."

A "chaotic border," then, has been defined as the complicated, messy yet not completely haphazard combination of subjectivity, territory and narrative operations that results from a film's attempt to describe the ways in which contemporary Europeans think of and therefore negotiate the borders that used to surround nation states.[14] It would be imprudent to argue that all European

---

[12] See the first two chapters starting with a plane taking off, the end of the film that ends up being a loop, and the self-referential references to computer writing.

[13] See reservations about the number of students who benefit from the program.

[14] When we talk about "chaos," two great semantic fields open up: on the one hand, we make gestures in the direction of chaos theory and of its more or less poetic re-appropriations by poets such as Edouard Glissant. Here the emphasis is on the existence of an immensely complex structure that tends to be dismissed or ignored because our tools of calculation and prediction are imperfect. The notion of a fractal graph that

borders are systematically chaotic or becoming chaotic due to the reconfiguration of the supranational community. Theoretically, it may not be absurd to suggest that even when the most traditional (nation)-state line exists, the closer one gets to the actual line of demarcation, and the more difficult it is to define the qualitative moment of discontinuity that it is supposed to materialize. Borders perform difference at the same time as they symbolize it. But in 2005, it may well be politically irresponsible to talk about the "borders" within and around Europe as if they were interchangeable. Yet, stating that the reinforcement of outside supranational borders goes hand in hand with some level of de-bordering within Europe already presumes that the same type of object is undergoing a different type of evolution while it might be more accurate to posit that we may need different words to refer to different phenomena. That is a gesture that Klapisch helps us avoid. An African migrant who is physically stopped and sometimes literally disintegrated by his or her encounter with some form of hostile border (the liquid walls of the Mediterranean or the barbed wires that surround the non-European European enclaves of Ceuta and Melilla)[15] is the tragic version of what happens when our collective imaginary enforces the distinction between inside and outside, the border and the body. And yet, insisting on the existence of qualitatively different borders is a political agenda in itself. A border that is strictly policed by immigration patrols and physically materialized suggests the will to minimize rather than enhance the chaotic elements that are theoretically at work in any border zone.

In other words, imagining chaotic borders is easier if a story takes place within Europe and if a narrative focuses on what is now perceived as internal European borders. Recent films have offered spectators stories or units of

---

makes it quasi impossible to decide whether a point is in or out, and of an order that parades as disorder is part of this analysis. I also understand "chaos" as a strategic way of naming what some power wants to tame and organize (through policing for example). In this case, we are meant to recognize "chaos" as something negative and unnecessary, as the contemporary image of primordial disorganization and shapelessness, something that imagine happened before the introduction of a grand organizational plan that literally put things into place, i.e. create borders. Both fields are themselves chaotically linked in and as borders in this text.

[15] In October 2005, six immigrants who were trying to force their way across the border at Melilla were killed by the members of a Spanish border patrol. The tragedy made it perfectly clear to the general public that European borders are not necessarily physically located around Europe. Melilla and Ceuta are "enclaves" which may link them to the "continent" in at least theoretically chaotic way, but the issue of transgressing or entering was treated as a perfectly clear matter of yes/no, life/death by both immigrants determined to cross and border patrols bent on stopping them. For a series of short articles on that border, see *Le Monde*, especially Ferenczi (2005) & Chambraud (2005).

stories that make it more challenging to decide how a subject is positioned in the presence of a chaotic border: a chaotic border renders the opposition between in and out less relevant but also makes it more difficult for a reader to distinguish between the territory and the body, or between the defining of the border and the practices that proliferate as the result of its existence. This type of imaginary work will produce forms of cultural knowledge and representations that will eventually have repercussions on what we mean by borders within or around Europe, but also within stories or more exactly storytelling practices (what counts as fiction or what counts as stating the facts), within or around units of cultural information (what is a national stereotype, what counts as a fact or an unprejudiced observation).

Works cited

Balibar, E. 2001. *Nous citoyens d'Europe. Les frontières, l'état, le peuple.* Paris: La Découverte.
—. 2004. *We, the people of Europe? Reflections on transnational citizenship.* Translated by J. Swenson. Princeton: Princeton University Press.
Brooks, P. 1984. *Reading for the plot: Design and intention in narratives.* New York and London: Oxford University Press.
Brooks, X. 2003. Interview with Cédric Klapisch: Eurostar and the europudding. *The Guardian*, (Thursday May 8). <http://film.guardian.co.uk/interview/interviewpages/0,6737,951803,00.html > consulted 2.13.06.
Chambraud, C. 2005. Les forces marocaines admettent avoir tiré, à Mellila, lors d'un assaut de clandestins qui a fait six morts. *Le Monde* (October 8): 2.
Citton, Y. 2005. Créolectures et politiques membraniques. *Multitudes* 13 September <http://multitudes.samizdat.net/>
Crowley, J. 2002. La frontière n'est plus ce qu'elle était. Review of Etienne Balibar's *Nous, citoyens d'Europe. Les frontières, l'état, le peuple.* Paris, La Découverte. *Critique internationale* 15 (avril): 64-69.
Ferenczi, A. 2005. L'Afflux d'immigrés force l'Europe à revoir sa relation à l'Afrique. *Le Monde* (October 8): 2.
Figel, J. 2005. Multilingualism: a vibrant and dynamic idea in an enlarged E.U. SCIC Universities Conference, Brussels, 4 March.
http://europa.eu.int/rapid/pressReleasesAction.do?reference=SPEECH/05/136&format=HTML&aged=0&language=EN&guiLanguage=en
Klapisch, C. 2005. L'Europtimiste. *Télérama* 2892 (15 June).
<http: //cinema.telerama.fr> (Consulted 9.18.05).
Kristeva, J. 1988. *Etrangers à nous-mêmes*. Paris: Fayard.

Mazierska, E. 2001. Travelling to the margins of Europe. *Kinema* (Fall). <http://www.finearts.uwaterloo.ca/juhde/mazi-012.htm> (Consulted 2.13.06).

Pratt, M.L. 1992. *Imperial eyes*. New York and London: Routledge.

Rosello, M. 1997. Interviews with the Bridge-Keeper. *Poetics of the Americas: race, founding, and textuality*. Edited by B. Cowan and J. Humphries. 105-122. Baton Rouge: Louisiana State University Press.

Tourné, I. 2005. Interview with Cédric Klapisch. Le Monde selon...Cédric Klapisch (20 June) <www.routard.com> (Consulted 9.18.05).

CHAPTER TWO

BORDERS AND BRIDGES
IN THE FILMS OF FATIH AKIN

JANIS LITTLE SOLOMON, CONNECTICUT COLLEGE

Much of the literature on minority film starts with the presumption that it has not received enough serious attention from the public or the cultural establishment. This argument is difficult to sustain in the case of Fatih Akın's filmmaking; his critical and popular success speaks German with a Hamburg and a Turkish "accent." It seeks, however, to demonstrate connections more than contrasts between the two nationalities, cultural traditions and life styles that contribute to Akın's own background, outlook on life, and to his self-understanding as a filmmaker. He seems determined to bring Hamburg to Turkey as well as Turkey (insofar as it can be represented by Istanbul, a clearly Europeanized city) to Hamburg (and Germany/Europe).

Akın—a self-taught filmmaker (Kreitling 2004)—is the most visible and successful of the numerous minority directors working in Germany today. Born in 1973 in Hamburg-Altona to Turkish parents, he studied visual communications at the Hamburg *Akademie der bildenden Künste*, and continues to identify himself with Hamburg and make most of his films there. However, Istanbul plays a significant role in most of his films as well. Perhaps for this reason, borders and barriers, but also connections such as bridges and travel are central to his films on both the literal and figurative level.

When Akın won the Golden Bear at the Berlin International Film Festival in February 2004 with *Gegen die Wand* (*Head-On*), the German press immediately claimed it as a "German" film and lionized the director as a godsend for the German film industry. The following year he was chosen as a member of the jury at two of the most important international film festivals, Berlin and Cannes.[1] This is an unusual phenomenon for a young minority director and a clear sign of the major impact his filmmaking has had within Europe, not just

---

[1] He had previously served on the Berlinale jury in 2001, following the success of his road movie *Im Juli* (Grund 2004).

Germany. Akın's films thus present a high-profile example of how minority filmmaking situates itself in the contemporary cultural landscape of Germany, Europe, and beyond.

This article will examine the three feature films that Akın has both written and directed, *Kurz und schmerzlos, Im Juli,* and *Gegen die Wand*, all of which present something like a transnational imaginary, in which literal and figurative border crossings are continually negotiated. They exploit ethnic and national stereotypes for comic effect at times, but invoke neither an exclusionary sense of ethnic/national identity nor of "Otherness." Their primary concern seems to be that of bridging differences. These films also can serve as examples of the extent to which the concept of "national cinema" has lost currency as a meaningful category within which to discuss contemporary European cinema. They are rooted in distinct spaces, and feature characters who belong to these spaces, which are defined as regional rather than national. The appeal of the films extends far beyond their regional locale to audiences aware of a transnational reality.

Kurz und schmerzlos (Short Sharp Shock)

A case in point is Akın's first feature film, *Kurz und schmerzlos*, made in 1998. It was not distributed in the United States, regrettably, and is currently available only on a German DVD in PAL format. It was shot on a low budget (one million DM) and co-produced by a small Hamburg production company, *Wüste Filmproduktion*, and *Zweites Deutsches Fernsehen*. The regional governmental agency *Filmförderung Hamburg* provided a production subsidy on the basis of Akın's script and the recognition he had received for two short films, *Sensin, du bist es!* (1995) and *Getürkt! (Weed,* 1996). *Weed* won several awards, including the prize for the best short film at the Chicago International Film Festival in 1997, and *Sensin* won the Audience Award at the Hamburg International Short Film Festival the preceding year. Although *Kurz und schmerzlos* was not a big box office success with 80,000 admissions (Tews 1999), it did very well in festivals and garnered a number of awards.[2] Later that year, this critical success helped inspire a catchy headline, "The New 'German' Film Is 'Turkish'?" as the media took note of the rise of several successful second generation Turkish-German directors.[3]

---

[2] Outstanding Feature Film, German Film Awards 1999; Best Young Director, Bavarian Film Awards 1999; Special Prize for Actors, Locarno International Film Festival 1998; Best Actor (Mehmet Kurtulus), International Thessaloniki Film Festival 1998.

[3] Tunçay Kulaoğlu, "Der neue 'deutsche' Film ist 'türkisch'?: Eine neue Generation bringt Leben in die Filmlandschaft." *Filmforum* 16 (Feb./Mar. 1999): 8-11. Quoted by Mennel (2002).

Kurz und schmerzlos is a formulaic genre film set in Hamburg-Altona, which is presented here as a seedy, multicultural neighborhood populated mostly by first and second-generation migrants and run by various rival gangs. Akın said the story could as well be set in Paris or New York as Hamburg, but the tension among the ethnic groups in the film is closely linked to the experience of the *Gastarbeiter* nationalities in Germany and specifically in the milieu of Altona.

The main characters are three young men with a history of living on the wrong side of the law. The opening sequence introduces them individually, labeled by national origin and accompanied by visual vignettes for each. Gabriel (Mehmet Kurtulus), a Turk, is being released from prison and is first slapped, then embraced by his father; he intends to stay out of trouble, save money and make a fresh start in Turkey where he imagines an idyllic life on the beach renting boats to tourists. Costa (Adam Bousdoukos), a Greek, is seen breaking into a car to steal a computer; Gabriel later convinces him to find a job, but Costa hasn't a clue about what he wants after Gabriel's sister dumps him. Bobby (Aleksandar Jovanovic), a Serb, is being thrown out onto the street by his uncle in reaction to the news that Bobby wants to work his way up in the Albanian instead of the Serbian mafia; he dreams of fame and the fast life of a mafia lieutenant.

Thus, it is clear from the outset that these young men live among boundaries established by family expectations, religious traditions, and national prejudices. The ethnic groups mentioned inhabit the same physical space, i.e. the multiethnic neighborhood of Altona, where they are somewhat uneasily careful to maintain separate linguistic, religious and ethnic identities and values, especially in the older generation. Only among the young men and women do we see friendships that reach across ethnic identities on the basis of affection and shared interests. But they also share a common cultural heritage of traditional, restrictive gender roles, a barrier that cuts across all their ethnic traditions and is in conflict with the presumed liberationist ethic of the German society within which the groups live.

Muhamer, the mafia boss and brothel owner, sees in Bobby's bravado and charm a younger version of himself and takes him on, even though he's a Serb. But Bobby learns the hard way that he's not so tough when the gun deal he was responsible for goes sour, and his boss comes looking for him. Costa's naive attempt to avenge Bobby's death ends with his own death from a savage knifing. Finally, Gabriel does manage to kill Muhamer and avenge the deaths of both of his friends, but at great cost. His ethos of honor, based on male bonding, destroys his own chance of happiness with Alice and also his dream of earning enough money in Hamburg to establish his own small business in Turkey. It is symptomatic that the trio's choice of entertainment on an evening together is a

Kung Fu movie, though de Palma's *Scarface* would have been Bobby's choice. Their adherence to an international code of machismo is their downfall.

Ethnic barriers are thus crossed repeatedly in the course of the film narrative, but ultimately with tragic consequences. The four non-German ethnic groups represented regard one another with an underlying suspicion that can erupt in violence. This is suggested from the beginning by the blurred scenes of gang fights under the opening credits. This potential for violence is finally fulfilled in the bloody demise of three of the four men, though ethnicity is only a contributing factor in these deaths, not the primary one.

The friendship and camaraderie of the three young men, as well as several cross-cultural romances (Costa and Gabriel's sister Ceyda; Ceyda and Sven; Bobby and Alice; Alice and Gabriel), seem to suggest that it is possible for the younger generation to cross the "borders" of inherited ethnic distrust. But in the end a heady brew of ambition, machismo, conflicting loyalties, and bad luck brings about a tragic ending and erases any hope of transcending cultural barriers. Ceyda's relationship with Sven might be unaffected by those events, but its importance in the film is minimal except in its effect on Costa. The same is true of Gabriel's relationship with Alice, which he breaks off, seeing it as a betrayal of Bobby and the indirect cause of his death. As the lone survivor, he leaves on the next plane to Istanbul to escape the consequences of his violent act and his feelings of guilt over his romance with Alice.

Alice (Regula Grauwiller) and Ceyda (Idil Üner) are friends and partners in a small business making and selling jewelry. Both appear to be independent, liberated women who reject traditional restrictions on their freedom. Alice breaks up with Bobby over his affiliation with the brothel owner and misogynist Muhamer. Ceyda dumps Costa because he is a loser. But neither Ceyda nor Alice have any say in the ill-considered decisions of these men, as the ethnic cultures represented do have one fatal thing in common: unthinking adherence to the ideals of male honor, which trumps any relationship they might have with women.

Kurz und schmerzlos has been read by scholars in the context of transnational film genres, especially the mafia crime film in the manner of Martin Scorsese's *Mean Streets* and de Palma's *Scarface,* or Kung Fu movies.[4] This lineage is referenced directly in the scene where the three buddies watch a

---

[4] Gemünden (2004, 185) mistakenly refers to "Al Pacino's struggle to fit into U. S. society as a Cuban (in *Mean Streets*)," rather than to this actor's role in de Palma's remake of *Scarface*. Mennel discusses several German films, including this one, in the context of the "ghetto-centric" film, emphasizing their common reliance on the codes of conduct valorized by the "outsider" male to valorize their heroes. In a 2003 interview with Amin Farzanefar, Akin says the film oriented itself on John Cassavetes and the early Scorsese (Akin 2003).

video of *Drunken Master*, a Jackie Chan movie, and then talk about Bobby's idol—Al Pacino in *Scarface*. In interviews, Akın deliberately placed his film within that transnational tradition when it was released, and bragged that the Italian-Americans needed 70 years to begin making their films, whereas the German Turks were ready after one generation (Nicodemus 2004). This film established Akın as a force within the German film world, enabling him to secure funding for further projects over the next few years: *In July* (2000), *Denk ich an Deutschland—Wir haben vergessen zurückzukehren* (*We Forgot to Go Back* [2001])[5] and *Solino* (2002). It also earned him the gratitude of some colleagues for making this kind of genre film "possible" again in Germany, as one young director publicly stated at the 2005 Berlinale.[6]

Akın not only directs, but typically writes his own scripts as well. This is the norm in Germany due to the nature of the federal and regional subsidy systems, which allot funding based on a combination of previous box office and festival success and the script submitted for consideration, usually written by the director. *Solino* (2002), set in an Italian migrant milieu and scripted by Ruth Toma, is the sole exception for Akın so far. Each of the three feature films he has written begins in Hamburg and moves either figuratively or literally to Istanbul. In *Kurz und schmerzlos,* Istanbul is present only as an image on a travel bureau poster, standing in at first for the dream of a new start in an idyllic "homeland." But at the end, when Gabriel is running away from the mess he made in Hamburg, Istanbul takes on the character of a self-imposed exile from love as well as a refuge from retribution, thus constituting a reversal in the definition of "exile."

Akın's second feature, the charming romantic comedy *Im Juli* (*In July*), features a complicated road trip through Eastern Europe that ends in Istanbul, under the bridge over the Bosporus, while the last part of *Head-On* is actually set in Istanbul. His latest film, *Crossing the Bridge: The Sound of Istanbul*, is a music documentary filmed entirely in that city; it is devoted to an exploration of contemporary Turkish music and its connections to European and American popular music as well as to traditional Turkish and Romany idioms.[7]

---

[5] I have been unable to view this film produced for television about Akın's family, which originally intended to return to Turkey, but instead established roots in Hamburg.

[6] The filmmaker Tilman Zens expressed this view at a screening of his film *Such' mich nicht* in the "German Film" series at the 2005 Berlinale.

[7] While this film does not visually begin in Hamburg, it does begin conceptually in Germany, with Alexander Hacke, the film's narrator and Berlin-based bassist and leader of the avant-garde Berlin band *Einstürzende Neubauten,* arriving by taxi in Istanbul from the airport to explore the international musical crosscurrents of contemporary Istanbul.

Im Juli (In July)

Akın himself is clearly very much aware of making films within a transnational practice, as we can see from the fact that he explicitly placed his gangster film in a line of descent from Scorsese and thus from a larger body of Italian-American films that has assumed the status of a transnational genre. But he also views his work in the context of German cinema and is actively involved in public debates over institutional support structures.[8] Introducing *In July* at a press screening at the 2001 Berlinale, he insisted—in English: "*Im Juli* is a *German* film. It was made in Germany. It was shown here in German theaters."[9] This last statement is not self-evident. The fact is that it is hard to find films produced in Germany in German theaters outside of Berlin and a few other large cities; even in those places, there are few venues for German films, because American productions dominate the German market. In 2004 German films achieved their highest share of the domestic market in well over a decade, and that was a mere 20%! Akın's *Gegen die Wand* was popular, though by no means the most visited German film production of the year 2004 (Rodek 2005).

But Akın was right to call *In July* a "German" film. Its stars (Moritz Bleibtreu and Christiane Paul) are well-known German actors, especially Bleibtreu of *Run Lola Run* fame, who also co-starred in *Solino*. Turkish-Germans Mehmet Kurtuluş and Idil Üner (Gabriel and Ceyda from *Kurz und schmerzlos*), play supporting roles. The film chronicles a journey from Hamburg through Eastern Europe to Istanbul, but it really concerns the cultural and educational journey of Daniel Bannier (Bleibtreu), its protagonist, from an uptight "German" attitude to greater awareness of the world around him and a more relaxed and cosmopolitan state of mind—a kind of cinematic *Bildungsroman*, as it were. One reviewer titled his piece "Auf der Straße zu mehr Gelassenheit" ("On the Road to a More Relaxed Attitude!") (Rodek 2000). By insisting that *In July* was a German film, Akın, was, I believe, claiming for himself the right to tell "German" as well as "ethnic," comic as well as dramatic tales. He could, however, with equal justification have placed the film in the tradition of Hollywood romantic comedy, the Shakespearean comedy of mistaken identity, as he suggests in an interview on the German DVD, or even the American or German road movie. In a 2003 interview he adds Kusturica and French adventure films of the 60's to the models for this film (Akin 2003).

---

[8] Cf. articles in *Die Welt* by Rodek ("Kommentar," 2004), Hanauer (2004) and Hentz (2004) on the decision of the Hamburg Senate in June of 2004 to cut the funds for support of film production by half. Akın and Wim Wenders were among those in the Hamburg film industry to criticize this move and help restore the bulk of the funding.

[9] Quoted by Gemünden (2004, 180), who goes on to speculate why Akın might have insisted on calling the film German, without coming to a definitive conclusion.

Actually, *In July* takes a common theme of immigrant writing—the annual summer vacation pilgrimage of guest workers and their families from Germany to Turkey along the route once designated as E-5, and turns it on its head. In this film four characters make their way to Istanbul. The journey that comprises the heart of the movie, however, is made not by Turkish guest workers, but by two young Germans in a borrowed jalopy that breaks down in Bavaria. They continue on their way as hitchhikers, as stowaways on a Danube barge, and in stolen vehicles, both together and singly. All this is told as a flashback after Daniel manages to hitch a ride in Bulgaria with a German Turk driving from Berlin to Istanbul in a new Mercedes, who has an unusual load (a corpse) in the luggage compartment!

The problem of how to transport a deceased family member whose visa has expired from Germany back to Turkey, without being arrested, is a recurring motif in "migrant" literature, and usually functions as a macabre and tragic-comic way of dramatizing the insecure legal status of the migrant and his divided loyalties between tradition and modernity.[10] The corpse in this opening sequence is a red herring, however, suggesting that Isa, the Mercedes driver, is a criminal. Only near the end do we learn that it is his uncle's body.

Interestingly, it is the two Germans, Daniel and Juli, who resort to car theft, illegal border-crossings, and other questionable activities in order to reach their destination without financial means. Daniel is a nerdy high school physics teacher in his probationary year, Juli a vaguely bohemian street vendor with a crush on him. She manages to sell him a "magical" ring embossed with a Mayan sun image, promising him that his "true love" will be wearing the same image. When he meets Melek, a beautiful young Turkish woman, that night at a street festival, she is wearing such a symbol; thus he believes he has found his destiny. She, however, is flying to Istanbul the next morning, where she is to meet a friend the following Friday at noon under "the bridge." This is Daniel's reason for driving to Istanbul. Juli had of course intended for him to see *her* wearing a "sun" symbol at the street festival, but comes too late. She is so disgusted at the failure of her plan that she decides to fold up shop and take the first ride she gets the next morning. Naturally it is Daniel who stops to pick her up. The trajectory of the film thus involves Daniel's relentless, though continually frustrated quest to reach Istanbul in time to meet Melek, while Juli tries her best to divert him from this goal and make him realize that *she* is his "true love." It is quite an entertaining romp, complete with a sexy ex-Yugoslavian temptress who sedates Daniel and steals his passport and money in Hungary. It turns out finally that Melek is actually Isa's girlfriend and Daniel realizes that he really likes Juli after

---

[10] The best-known work of this type is the novel *Europastraße 5* (1981) by Güney Dal.

all. The two couples drive on further south on a joint vacation trip, paired off traditionally by ethnic background.

Even from this thumbnail sketch, it is apparent that *In July* was designed to appeal to both German and Turkish, as well as international audiences. And indeed it was a German-Turkish-Hungarian co-production. The film follows a classic comedic structure of mistaken identity; the socio-economic circumstances and behavior of its German and Turkish-German characters confound traditional expectations; and stereotypes of crime and corruption in Eastern Europe are not tendentious, but presented as spoofs and over-the-top satire. After many misadventures Daniel leaves behind his rule-bound identity as a cute but clueless and rather rigid German pedant, and morphs into an emotionally aware man who is able to engage life as it presents itself to him. The romantic liaisons of German to German and Turk to Turk reassure both groups that their identities will remain intact regardless of whether they live side by side or in relatively homogeneous neighborhoods (cf. Isa's description of his family's neighborhood in Berlin, where his uncle felt so much at home that he didn't go back to Turkey when his visa expired). It is also noteworthy that no family responsibilities or backgrounds are presented for the German characters, while filial duty makes it an absolute obligation for Isa to smuggle his uncle's body from Berlin to Istanbul. This risky exploit also earns him the status of a hero with the man in charge at the Turkish border crossing. This film is certainly "German," as Akın stated, but at the same time it is "transnational" in terms of its narrative appeal, implications and inter-textual references. On a purely visual level, Daniel's comical attempt to propel his car across a river is reminiscent of the opening sequence of Wenders' 1976 film *Im Lauf der Zeit* (*Kings of the Road*). The concern with borders resonates in that film as well, but the satirical tone of Akın's border crossings evidently has a closer connection with the 1999 Turkish film *Propaganda* by Sinan Çetin (Göztürk 2002, 255). Somehow Daniel and Juli both are able to cross all the borders, even after Daniel has suffered the loss of his passport and cash. The geographic markers of national territory thus present themselves as immaterial, silly, and arbitrary, though highly regulated. Even rivers turn out to be insubstantial barriers, as they can be traversed in a "borrowed" canoe, if not in an air-borne car! The Bosporus, however, and the bridge that traverses it receive a thoroughly serious, even majestic, treatment as both boundary and link between and Europe and Asia.

Gegen die Wand (Head-On)

Head-On, Akın's most celebrated film, won the top three prizes for fiction films at the Berlinale in February 2004—best film, best actor, and best actress. In June it swept the German Film Awards with five prizes (best film, direction, actor, actress, camera); in December of that year it won the European Film Prize in Gold (Best Director, Best Film) against strong competition, and in 2005, the National Society of Film Critics named it best foreign film, to name just the most prominent awards. This is a stunning record for any film, and it was a truly sensational event in Germany, especially since this was the first *German* film production to win the Berlinale's Golden Bear in *eighteen* years.

The press reaction in some quarters was even slightly reminiscent of the surge of national pride when Germany won its first post-war world soccer championship in 1954! This was especially true in Hamburg, where he was welcomed home as a "dyed-in-the-wool" native son (*"einen waschechten Hamburger"*) by the Senate (Stahlberg 2004). The conservative bastion of Munich was less enthusiastic (Göttler 2004). Since minority artists have in the past often found themselves marginalized in the German "cultural establishment," it was fascinating to see the success of this film celebrated so explicitly as a national victory in an international arena. Within weeks Akın was being called a "national institution" (Engels 2004) and hailed as the pivotal figure of a broad-based turnaround in the fortunes of "German film" as a commercially viable as well as an artistically accomplished enterprise.[11] This appropriation of *Head-On*'s success for the "German" cinema, despite its largely Turkish-German and Turkish cast and milieu,[12] might seem ironic in light of Akın's earlier need to insist that *In July*, with its German stars, was a "German" (and not a "minority?") film.[13] And yet, he was still being asked the identity

---

[11] See, for example, Rodek ("Ein Kino der süßen Stückchen," 2004; "'Gegen die Wand' ist durch die Wand," 2004; 2005); Nicodemus (2004); Theil (2004).

[12] The cast included Birol Üner as Cahit Tomruk, Sibel Kekilli as Sibel Güner, Catrin Striebeck as Maren (Cahit's partner for recreational sex), Güven Kirac as Seref, Meltem Cumbul as Selma, Demir Gökgöl as Sibel's father, Aysel Iscan as Sibel's mother, and Cem Akın as Sibel's brother.

[13] After his triumph at the Berlinale, Akın expressed impatience with the constant questions by journalists as to his feelings of national identity. Asked in a press conference why he preferred to feature "*Gastarbeiter*" in his films, he replied that that word did not exist in his vocabulary and that the "chauvinistic" question belonged in the last century. "*Wir sind Deutsche...ob Ihnen das nun passt oder nicht*" (Junghänel 2004). On the one hand he calls himself a "Deutsch-Türke," but on the other he stresses the fact that he was born and educated in Germany and is a "German director." In an interview with Frank Junghänel and Anke Westphal in the *Berliner Zeitung* magazine section (Akin, "Ich zelebriere so ein Seemannsleben," 2004), the interviewers stated that in Turkey *Gegen die Wand* was being regarded as a Turkish film. Akın replied that he believes every good film reflects the condition of the society from which it comes, and that for that reason *Gegen die Wand* was a German film, without question. He called the film his reaction to "all these" discussions: the EU, the head scarf issue, problems of integration.

question in some interviews, and expressed impatience with the seeming reluctance of some in the media to regard him as a "German director" (Junghänel 2004; Westphal 2004; Akin, "'Ich bin ein deutscher Regisseur,'" 2004).

In any case, the film's arresting and desperate story of a passion awakened and then thwarted, its darkly comedic elements, and the high-voltage, no-holds-barred performances of its stars were major factors in its impact on both audiences and critics everywhere. Its formal qualities are also impressive, however. Akın creates a sharp contrast to the violence of his narrative and its break-neck pace by introducing it and segmenting its course with a series of static musical interludes of varying length, but always with the identical visual set-up. These pieces show a group of Romany musicians (led by Selim Sesler with Idil Üner as uncredited vocalist) in long shot as they perform traditional folk music on the banks of the Golden Horn, an arm of the Bosporus, against the picturesque skyline of Istanbul. These extra-diegetic interludes add an exotic or folkloristic element to the film narrative (Akın even compares them to a "kitschy postcard"), but he also sees them as "Brechtian." Like Brecht's technique of the alienation effect, the interludes foreground narrative agency and break the gritty realism of the action. And somewhat like the chorus in classical Greek tragedy, they provide a distanced, stylized reflection and indirect commentary on the painfully out-of-control lives of the protagonists, projecting their passion into a "timeless," balladesque dimension. These scenes also suggest from the very beginning that Istanbul will be the film's destination, an existential alternative to the brick wall of the film narrative's opening sequence, into which Cahit deliberately drives his car at high speed. Istanbul represents an escape from, though not a resolution of, the conflicts that drive both protagonists to attempt suicide.

The perspective of the film is largely that of the male protagonist, Cahit (Birol Ünel), but the events are propelled by the familiar theme of oppressive patriarchal restrictions on female sexual and personal freedom to protect the "honor" of the Turkish family. The space represented by the family also constitutes a "territory" with very distinct borders and guards. Sibel and Cahit meet in a psychiatric clinic after their respective failed suicide attempts. She has slit her wrists in an attempt to break out of the prison of her family, mistakenly believing her father and brother will relax their control of her behavior when they see she is serious about living on her own. She decides her only real chance to escape is to enter a sham marriage with a Turk, and when Cahit initially refuses to help her, she immediately slashes her wrist again to demonstrate just how desperate she is to free herself at any price.

The film thus rather surprisingly reproduces images of family relations consistent with stereotypes of Turkish culture that are still widely held in

German society, and this may well have been a factor in its broad appeal.[14] Stories of daughters disowned by fathers and subjected to physical violence, or even killed, by their brothers or uncles for bringing dishonor to the family, and of wives married off without choice and literally imprisoned in the home, have for decades been staples of the representation of Turkish family and gender relations in films by German and Turkish directors alike.[15] Unfortunately, these are not mere stereotypes. Incidences of "honor" killings of young Turkish women by male family members are still occurring in Germany. And in real life, Sibel Kekilli, the actress who played Sibel, was disowned by her own family, her photos burned by her father, just as in the film, after the German tabloid *Bild* publicized the fact that she had once worked in "adult films" (Nicodemus 2004; Wewer 2004).

The theme of needing to break out or cross the boundary of restrictive family custody is not exclusively a female issue, however. It is repeatedly voiced in interviews with young Turkish-German artists of both sexes, including Akın, as part of their own experience, though not in the tragic mode (*Gegen die Wand* DVD interview with Feridun Zaimoğlu). Despite his opposition to tradition, he stresses that he criticizes from a position of respect (Akin, "Interview with Fatih Akin," 2004). It is in this sense of rebellion against overly restrictive familial customs that *Head-On* subjects the conventions and rituals around Turkish courtship and marriage to broad satire. By recruiting Cahit for a sham marriage, Sibel subverts the cultural requirement that she marry a Turk in order to leave her parents' house, since his *sole* qualification to be her husband is his Turkish birth. A friend agrees to masquerade as his uncle, the obligatory older male relative who has to accompany him to ask the bride's father for her hand on his behalf and establish his family "credentials." In a hilarious scene, they have to lie about the nature of his job and "manufacture" a persona to fit the demands of tradition. Akın pokes fun at these conventions as empty, anachronistic formalities; one would have to be blind not to notice that things are not as they seem, but Sibel's father seems concerned only with whether the chocolates

---

[14] In one of the few German reviews that voiced reservations about the film, Tilman Krause (2004) expresses astonishment over the image of the "traditional Turkish milieu" presented in the film, which he compares with "*jener unduldsamen, borniertenAntihaltung, wie sie herzulande vermutlich zuletzt um 1970 Standard war.*" He goes on in the vein of a critical assessment of German mass culture to imply that Turks are becoming the victims of the darker sides of the German consumer society they live in. In other words, this is an argument from the vantage point of endangered traditional values. I am less convinced that the attitudes Krause attributes to the 1970s are so uncommon today.

[15] E.g. *40m2 Deutschland* (1985), the work of the Turkish director Tevfik Baser, or Hark Böhm's *Yasemin* (1988).

Cahit has brought contain any alcohol. Her brother is suspicious, but goes along anyway.

This is not the only example of the film's critical stance toward Turkish-German patriarchal conventions. Cultural hypocrisy around sexuality is lampooned in the couple's obligatory visit with the family some months after their marriage (itself a highly comic scene). The intercut sequence features a scene in which Sibel's brother and cousins invite Cahit to visit a brothel with them and almost beat him up when he asks them why they don't f*** their wives. They are outraged that anyone would dare use that word to refer to sex with *their* wives. Meanwhile the wives are quizzing Sibel about the erotic techniques of her husband and complaining about the clumsy incompetence of their own men in such matters as oral sex.

In a reversal of German stereotypes regarding the oppression of women in Turkish culture, Selma, Sibel's cousin from Istanbul, is represented as a thoroughly independent, Western-style career woman. She is divorced and focused on climbing the corporate ladder and keeping fit by working out, rather than seeking casual sexual encounters and amnesia through drugs as Sibel does. This reinforces the generally positive or at least neutral representation of Istanbul in the film by suggesting that Turkish diaspora culture is much more rigidly patriarchal and resistant to change than urban society in Turkey. Several journalists referred to the film's role in bringing such matters to open discussion in the Turkish community (Heun 2004; Zander, "Not der Zweisamkeit," 2004; Zander, "Das wird die Türken schockieren," 2004). Sibel, who is still seeking stimulants of every kind, finds Selma's values contemptible, and even throws her careerist emancipation up to her as the grounds for her divorce. These middle-class liberationist values are meaningless to Sibel, for despite her destructively promiscuous behavior, she judges Selma from the perspective of a traditional patriarchal definition of femininity (she works as a hairdresser in the Hamburg sequences). She has crossed some boundaries, as well as geographic borders, but remains imprisoned by others.

Of course, Sibel's scheme to liberate herself by pretending to stay within the borders of the patriarchal structure misfires. The two spouses start to exhibit jealousy toward one another and actually fall in love. As a result, Cahit goes to prison for manslaughter and Sibel flees to Istanbul to escape being murdered by her brother. But she nearly dies there after she becomes bored with the prospect of working in a menial job Selma has offered her in the hotel where she is employed. Climbing the corporate ladder does not appeal to her, so she goes back to drugs and makes another desperate suicidal gesture, which almost succeeds when she provokes a brutal attack by street thugs. When they rendezvous years later, after Cahit's release from prison, Sibel, who had promised to wait for him, has a child and is living with its father, the taxi driver who rescued her after finding her bleeding to death in the street.

Although Akın's script had originally ended with the lovers together again, (*Gegen die Wand* DVD interview) there is no "happy end" for this grand passion. Both Cahit and Sibel seem to have learned something from their pain, and will likely survive and lead more serene lives than they did in Germany, but they are essentially in exile, refugees from irreconcilable intercultural and interpersonal conflicts. As Akın noted in a Deutsche Welle interview, Turkey is a foreign country to them. Their "returns" are a response to dashed hopes marked by defeat, as was Gabriel's return to Istanbul in *Kurz und schmerzlos*, and Cahit's ultimate destination is unclear (Akin, "Interview with Fatih Akin," 2004).

To return to the question of what the media appropriation of the film as "German" might mean, I want to suggest some additional perspectives on the reception of *Head-On*. First, it is significant, as noted above, that the film aligns itself with a secular critique of what are widely perceived as anachronistic, misogynist tendencies and a desperate adherence to tradition within Turkish-German culture. I believe this was essential to its success, as it coincides with prevailing views in German society and validates the attitudes of educated, "progressive" young Turkish-Germans as well. In this sense, the film does present a "German" perspective, and Akın himself identifies with this rejection of rigidly "Turkish" values and expectations, as he makes clear in the interview included on the German DVD. These restrictive attitudes and values constitute figurative territorial "borders" that are self-imposed or imposed within the family "prison." On the other hand, the film also validates and respects Turkish culture itself by showing some understanding for Sibel's family and by representing Istanbul and social relations there in a generally positive light, aside from the universal problems of drugs and crime that plague all large cities. In this sense *Head-On*, like Akın's other films, can be seen as a "cross-over" film meant for Turkish as well as Turkish-German and German audiences, recognizing "difference" even as it moves across borders.

Further, films exist not only in a cinematic or artistic sphere, but in political contexts as well, and in the case of *Head-On*, the most relevant context certainly is that of Turkey's bid for admission to the European Union, i.e. to be considered part of Europe. Films such as this that represent Turkish-Germans and Turks automatically participate in some way in the discourses surrounding this controversial European issue. At least one journalist made this connection quite explicit in Dec. 2004, just before Akin received the European Film Prize; he wrote that if *Head-On* won, it could "send a signal" to the EU-Commission, which was meeting the following week to decide whether to begin negotiations on Turkey's admission to the European Union! (Zander, "Europa entdeckt sich selbst," 2004). As we know, they did decide in the affirmative, though the ultimate outcome of those negotiations is still far from settled. Akın himself had previously expressed his impatience with the repeated delays in beginning those negotiations (Akın 2003).

Another aspect of coverage on the film was the direct or implied critical comparison of *Head-On* with the "low voltage" productions of domestic directors and their usual themes of bourgeois ennui, misery, and consumerism, which apparently have little appeal at home or in the international marketplace. This is an opinion shared by the well-known, articulate, and incendiary second-generation Turkish-German author and media star Feridun Zaimoğlu (who fully merits the designation "Young Turk!"). He stated:

> We have fire and rage in our hearts. We're not content to tell boring, middle-class stories. Ours are about blood, honor, the ultimate love, all or nothing (Quoted in Theil (2004)).

Such a boast may be an effective marketing strategy, but it also runs the risk of promoting Turkish-German culture as "primal" and exotic, as "Oriental," in other words. It thus would tend to perpetuate the assignment of cultural difference and "otherness" to minority cinema and/or literature.

I propose that the metaphor of the bridge, which plays a significant role in the spatial imaginary of Akın's cinema, is an appropriate supplement to that of border-crossings. The image of the bridge over the Bosporus that physically *connects* Europe with Asia is of central importance in three of Akın's films: *In July*, *Head-On,* and most recently, *Crossing the Bridge: The Sound of Istanbul.* Airports and planes constitute an additional and related motif in each of the three films discussed here. Air travel bridges the two continents and renders the many barriers presented by national borders meaningless. A case in point would be the ease with which Melek makes the journey from Hamburg to Istanbul by air in the film *In July*. This stands in sharp contrast to the trials and tribulations of Daniel, Juli, and Isa, who travel by land and are subject to the strictures still imposed by national territorialities. It is striking, however, that in *Head-On* the shot of Selma's plane arriving at the Hamburg airport foregrounds a chain-link perimeter fence. It thus could appear that she is entering a restrictive, fenced-in zone, which seems to correspond to the critical representation of traditional patriarchal attitudes of the Turkish diaspora by Akın, Zaimoğlu and others.

From a pragmatic point of view, there is no doubt that simply by virtue of language, location, and means of production, cultural artifacts produced in Germany by ethnic minorities are "German." The thematic content of these works also reflects the contemporary reality of multi-ethnic society in most German cities, despite official statements that Germany is *not* a "land of immigration." But I would argue that it is misguided to view minority film as "belonging" to a single national culture at all. Akın's films are neither "German" nor "Turkish," but rather an expression of an intercultural, transnational sense of identity that is both regional and multinational. Their narratives foreground border-crossings of a comic as well as tragic nature, crossings of physical, ethnic, familial, legal, artistic, and cultural boundaries. The ultimate intent, it seems to me, is to establish bridges that are traversed in both directions, not one-way traffic.

The fact that Akın's filmmaking does not meditate on German "national identity" or "coming to terms with the past," might also be a factor in its favorable reception, coming as a "breath of fresh air," to quote the title of one piece (Theil 2004). The sub-heading of another piece even noted the fact that *Head-On* won the European Film Prize "without Nazis" (Rodek, "'Gegen die Wand' ist durch die Wand," 2004). It seems that minority filmmakers may enjoy a certain advantage in this regard, a freedom not commonly available to native Germans, as no one can expect them to process the crimes of an era when neither they nor their parents were German citizens or residents.[16] They are thus not subject to what was until now an implicit obligation for "German" filmmakers with international ambitions to deal with the burden of national guilt over the atrocities of World War II. To be sure, the immigrant experience of working and living in Germany added a new chapter to a troubled past, but it is one that most minority filmmakers seem able to address without casting the Germans as victimizers. Their films deal more with conflicts within their own subculture.

Finally, I would like to propose that in explicitly claiming Akın's film as "German," at least some critics were welcoming the proof that a "German" film can and should be a potentially "transnational" film.[17] This appropriation reflected an intense desire to reconnect German filmmaking to a broader, international cinematic practice, as in the Weimar era and to a lesser degree in the New German Cinema, whose engagement of "Hollywood" was both critical

---

[16] Some minority authors do engage this issue, though few so directly as Zafer Şenocak, who makes it integral to his novel *Gefährliche Verwandtschaft* through the mixed Jewish/German/Turkish heritage of his protagonist. See the discussion of this work by Andreas Huyssen (2003). Huyssen cites an essay by Şenocak that "raises the question of how Turkish-Germans or second-generation Turks can migrate into German history" (from his *Atlas of a Tropical Germany*). See also Leslie Adelson (1997; 2000; 2001).

[17] The *Spiegel Special Die Deutschen: 60 Jahre nach Kriegsende* (No. 4 2005) entitled its section on film "Wunder auf der Leinwand" (Miracle on the Screen) as a tribute to the phenomenon of revived international interest in German films. This turnaround started with *Lola rennt* (1998) and seemed at a high-water mark with two German films nominated for the Oscar in 2004 (*Der Untergang* and *Die Geschichte vom weinenden Kamel*), in addition to Akın's successes. See also Alanyali (2004).

and productive. Under the title "Inspiring Differences," a Hamburg journalist (Poschardt 2004) called attention to the enormous *potential* that the cultural talent of ethnic minorities represents for the future of German cinema. Citing the model of Hollywood and American culture in general, with its creative energy and innovative mix of ethnic and racial influences, the author saw precisely this process at work in the rising fortunes of young minority directors in Germany. Although American cultural and economic hegemony is often cited as a threat to national cinemas in discussions of globalization, Akın and many other minority artists[18] are more likely to see American cinema, and other elements of American pop culture such as jazz, rap, and hip-hop in a positive light, as inspiring models for a potential shift from an *exclusive* national to an *inclusive* transnational cultural practice in Germany, but still rooted within a specific region and the local atmosphere and mores. Again, this can be seen in the context not only of "border-crossing," but of "bridging," which establishes traffic in both directions, or "taking flight" above the ground of binding territorialities, effectively denying the dominance of hegemonic relations in contemporary cinema and cultural production as a whole.

Works Cited

Adelson, L. 1997. Minor chords? Migration, murder, and multiculturalism. In *Wendezeiten Zeitenwenden: Positionsbestimmungen zur deutschsprachigen Literatur 1945-1995*. Edited by R. Weninger and B. Rossbacher. 115-129. Tübingen: Stauffenberg.

—. 2000. Touching tales of Turks, Germans, and Jews: Cultural alterity, historical narrative, and literary riddles for the 1990's. *New German Critique* 60 (Spring-Summer): 93-124.

—. 2001. Against between: A manifesto. In *Unpacking Europe: Towards a critical reading*. Edited by S. Hassan and I. Dadi. 244-255. Rotterdam: NAi Publishers.

Akın, F. 2000. *Im Juli*. Ismaning, Germany: Eurovideo DVD.

—. 2001. *Kurz und schmerzlos*. Hamburg, Germany: Universal Picture GmbH. DVD.

—. 2003. Migrantenkino heißt jetzt Mittelmeerkino: Der Filmregisseur Fatih Akin sieht die ethnische Emanzipation der Einwandererkinder vollendet. Interview by A. Farzanefar. *Berliner Zeitung* (Aug. 9) http://www.berlinonline.de/berlinerzeitung/archiv/.bin/dump.fcgi/2003/0809/feuilleton/0006/index.html

---

[18] Cf. Yasemin Yildiz (2004) for a perceptive discussion of Zaimoğlu's language and cultural stance.

—. 2004. Interview with Fatih Akin. Interview by E. Volodina. www.DW-World.de. *Culture & Lifestyle* (Feb. 14). http://www.dw-world.de./dw/globalsearch/0,266,00.html

—. 2004. "Ich bin ein deutscher Regisseur": Interview mit Berlinale-Sieger Fatih Akin. Interview unsigned. *Die Welt* (Feb. 16). http://www.welt.de/data/ 2004/02/16/238247.html

—. 2004. Ich zelebriere so ein Seemannsleben. Interview by F. Junghänel and A. Westphal. *Berliner Zeitung* (Mar. 13). http://www.berlinonline.de/berliner-zeitung/archiv/.bin/dump.fcgi/2004/0313/magazin/0002/index.html

—. 2004. *Gegen die Wand.* Hamburg, Germany: Universal Pictures GmbH. DVD.

—. 2004. *In July.* Port Washington, NY: Koch-Lorber Films DVD.

—. 2005. *Crossing the bridge: The sound of Instanbul.* Hamburg, Germany: Itervista digital media DVD.

—. 2005. *Head-On.* Strand Releasing & Bavaria Film International DVD.

Alanyali, I. 2004. Raus aus der Multikulti-Ecke:; Vergesst Kopftuch und Gastarbeiterliteratur: Künstler aus der Türkei gewinnen für Deutschland Preise. *Die Welt* (Aug. 17). http://www.welt.de

Dal, G. 1990. *Europastraße 5.* Aus dem Türkischen von Carl Koss. München: Piper Verlag. 1st edition: Hamburg: Buntbuch-Verlag, 1981.

Engels, J. 2004. Die seltsame Rückkehr des Berlinale-Siegers Fatih Akin. *Die Welt* (March 8). http://www.welt.de/data/2004/03/08/248122.html

Gemünden, G. 2004. Hollywood in Altona: Minority cinema and the transnational imagination. In *German pop culture: How "American" is it?* Edited by A. C. Mueller. 180-189. Ann Arbor: University of Michigan Press.

Göttler, F. 2004. Im Kino: Der Berlinale-Gewinner "Gegen die Wand." *Süddeutsche Zeitung* (Mar. 10). http://www.filmzentrale.com/rezis/gegendiewandfg.htm

Göztürk, D. 2002. Beyond paternalism: Turkish German traffic in cinema. *The German cinema book.* Edited by T. Bergfelder, E. Carter and D. Göktürk. 248-256. London: BFI Publishing.

Grund, S. 2004. Das Hamburger Filmwunder. *Die Welt* (Feb. 16). http://www.welt.de/data/2004/02/16/238461.html.

Hanauer, F. 2004. Film-Prominenz demonstriert für Fördergeld. *Die Welt* (Dec. 14). http://www.welt.de/data/2004/12/14/374510.html

Hentz, S. 2004. Produzenten kritisieren Kürzung der Filmförderung. *Die Welt* (Dec. 2). http://www.welt.de/data/2004/12/02/368294.html

Heun, S. 2004. In der Türkei leben die Frauen freier als in Berlin. *Die Welt* (Mar. 17). http://www.welt.de/data/2004/03/17/252432.html

Huyssen, A. 2003. Diaspora and nation: Migration into other pasts. *New German Critique* 88 (Winter): 147-164.

Junghänel, F. 2004. Pressekonferenz. Identitätsfragen. *Berliner Zeitung* (Feb. 2). http://www.berlinonline.de/berliner-zeitung/archiv/.bin/dump.fcgi/2004/0213/feuilleton/0033/index.html?keywords=fatih%20akin;every=1;utf8=1;mark=fatih%20akin;start=40

Krause, T. 2004. "Gegen die Wand". *Die Welt* (Dec. 18). http://www.welt.de/data/2004/12/18/376048.html

Kreitling, H. 2004. Fatih, der Sieger. *Die Welt* (Feb. 16). http://www.welt.de/data/2004/02/16/238247.html

Mennel, B. 2002. Bruce Lee in Kreuzberg and Scarface in Altona: Transnational auteurism and ghettocentrism, in Thomas Arslan's *Brothers and Sisters* and Fatih Akin's *Short Sharp Shock. New German Critique* 87 (Special Issue on Postwall Cinema) (Autumn): 133-156.

Nicodemus, K. 2004. Ankunft in der Wirklichkeit: Mit Fatih Akins *Gegen die Wand* siegt das deutsche Kino über die deutschen Träume von einer Leitkultur. *Die Zeit* (9). http://www.zeit.de/2004/09/Berlinale-Abschluss

Poschardt, U. 2004. Inspirierende Unterschiede. *Die Welt am Sonntag* (June 20) This two-paragraph piece is no longer available through the www.welt.de archive site.

Rodek, H. 2000. Auf der Straße zu mehr Gelassenheit: Das wundervoll entspannte Road Movie "Im Juli" des Hamburger Türken Fatih Akin. *Die Welt* (August 24). http://www.welt.de/data/2000/08/24/578284.html

—. 2004. Kommentar: Gegen die Wand. *Die Welt* (June 19). www.welt.de/data/2004/06/19/293360.html

—. 2004. Ein Kino der süßen Stückchen: Nach dem künstlerischen Erfolg stellt sich für den deutschen Film auch der kommerzielle ein. *Die Welt* (Sept. 24). http://www.welt.de/data/2004/09/24/336820.html

—. 2004. "Gegen die Wand" ist durch die Wand. Durchbruch auch ohne Nazis: Das neue deutsche Kino gewinnt den Europäischen Filmpreis und zieht Zuschauer in den USA. *Die Welt* (Dec. 13). http://www.welt.de/data/2004/02/16/238257.html

—. 2005. Surprise: Ein Traumjahr. Ein Kanon der Regisseure, die dem deutschen Kino 2004 einen Publikumsrekord bescherten. *Die Welt* (Feb. 7). http://www.welt.de/data/2005/02/07/459578.html

Stahlberg, B. 2004. Senat ehrt einen "waschechten Hamburger." *Die Welt* (Mar. 6). http://www.welt.de/data/2004/03/06/247321.html

Tews, H. 1999. "Ich habe die Bilder dazu im Kopf und im Bauch": Shooting-Star Fatih Akin startete auf St. Pauli die Dreharbeiten für seinen Film 'Im Juli' mit Christiane Paul und Moritz Bleibtreu. *Die Welt* (July 23). http://www.welt.de/data/1999/07/23/636609.html

Theil, S. 2004. A breath of fresh air: With their passion and anger, Germany's creative young immigrants are revitalizing the country's cultural scene. *Newsweek International* (Mar. 15) Cited from on-line archive of *AICGS-Advisor* (Mar. 19 2004). http://www.aicgs.org/analysis/c/theil031504.aspx

Westphal, A. 2004. Ein Goldener Bär für zwei Nationen. *Berliner Zeitung* (Feb. 16) http://www.berlinonline.de/berliner-zeitung/archiv/.bin/dump.fcgi/2004/0216/politik/0007/index.html?keywords=fatih%20akin;every=1;utf8=1;mark=fatih%20akin;start=40

Wewer, A. 2004. "Ich will nur Freunde sehen": Der 54. Deutsche Filmpreis feiert die Rebellen des deutsch-türkischen Liebesdramas "Gegen die Wand." *Die Welt am Sonntag* (June 20). As with the Poschardt piece, this article is no longer available online.

Yildiz, Y. 2004. Critically "Kanak": A reimagination of German culture. In *Globalization and the future of German*. Edited by A. Gardt and B. Hüppauf. 319-340. Berlin/New York: Mouton de Gruyter.

Zander, P. 2004. Not der Zweisamkeit: Die deutschen Beiträge II: Sibel Kekiklli spielt in Fatih Akins "Gegen die Wand" ihre erste Filmrolle. *Die Welt* (Feb. 12). http://www.welt.de/data/2004/02/12/236152.html

—. 2004. Das wird die Türken schockieren. *Die Welt* (Feb. 13). http://www.welt.de/data/2004/02/13/236765.html

—. 2004. Europa entdeckt sich selbst: Heute wird in Barcelona der Europäische Filmpreis verliehen – der erste in der erweiterten EU. *Die Welt* (Dec. 11). http://www.welt.de/data/2004/12/11/372929.html

CHAPTER THREE

PERMEABLE BORDERS IN *NOTRE MUSIQUE*

JEHANNE-MARIE GAVARINI, UNIVERSITY OF MASSACHUSETTS-LOWELL

> The writing of a text presupposes the existence of a fine net of relationships binding the different threads that weave within it. Everything converges: outside events, personal experiences, moods, journeys, chance occurrences—all randomly mix with reading, fantasies, images, thanks to an *ars combinatoria* of encounters, correspondences, memory associations, sudden illuminations, alternative currents (Juan Goytisolo 1994, 11).

Reminiscent of cubism in which fragments and disjunctions are seamless parts of the final collage, Jean-Luc Godard's films are allusive; they present questions from multiple viewpoints, yet provide few answers. A veteran of crossing borders between documentary and fiction, Godard has developed and refined his technique since the early days of the Nouvelle Vague and *Cahiers du cinéma*. His latest film *Notre Musique* (2004) is a stunning example of his editing mastery. Using his now well-known signature-style, Godard weaves images from graphic arts, visual arts, advertising, and the cinema in an intensely layered film rich with symbolism. In addition to the high aesthetic quality of its images, *Notre Musique* blends music and philosophical texts in an extraordinary sound track. Borrowing from literature, philosophy, and consumer culture, Godard's films evoke Marcel Duchamp's readymades. Similarly to early twentieth century artists who appropriated cultural signs and altered their meaning by making objects and text contingent on their environment, Godard integrates found texts and images in his films. These juxtapositions create unexpected associations. In *Notre Musique*, he cites a plethora of writers whose texts are not only quoted, but also transformed through his montage and re-contextualizing process. This destabilizes acquired notions of authorship and blurs the boundaries between literature, philosophy, and cinema. The cited texts are at times repeated and translated into different languages, thus adding another thread to Godard's tangle of ideas. In this on-going exploration of form, he blends the realm of cinema and that of reality until they become indistinguishable. This is done sometimes fluidly, sometimes in a syncopated manner that stresses the drama and lack of coherence of emotions, memory, and mental representations. This permeability between documentary and fiction emphasizes the strong role cinema plays in our understanding of reality and the construction of history.

Modeled after Dante's *Divine Comedy*, *Notre Musique* opens with a remarkable editing tour de force. "Forgive us our trespasses as we forgive those who trespass against us," implores the voice over as rolling images of charred, shot, stabbed, and dismembered human bodies, propel us into the film. This disturbing found-footage collage brings forth Godard's vision of "Hell," the first "Kingdom," as he calls the three separate chapters of *Notre Musique*. This violent opening sequence comments not only on human beings' extraordinary potential to imagine and commit atrocities against one another, but also on their constant need to create images that depict their destructive instinct. Through his somber examination of the atrocities of war, Godard brings our attention to his particular language, the language of cinema. Cinematic representation itself makes up his vision of "Hell." Fulfilling human beings' desire for violent spectacle, cinema, like dreams, brings to the surface repressed fantasies. It becomes the symptom of human obsessional neurosis. Cinema is the social mirror that reflects back on our barbarian behavior. Resembling the passing shadows of Plato's cave, the flickering images of films projected in the darkness of the movie theater dispense *our* repressed knowledge.

> Le principe du cinéma: aller vers la lumière et la diriger sur notre nuit, notre musique (The principle of cinema: Go towards the light and shine it on our night, our music).

Although this multifaceted cinematographic essay cannot, and should not, be reduced to a single interpretation, *Notre Musique*'s three "Kingdoms" evoke the psychic apparatus of psychoanalytic subjectivity. The first "Kingdom," the "Kingdom of Hell," suggests the unspeakable Lacanian real (Lacan 1998).[1] The representation of war constitutes a residue of the raw and unprocessed human death instinct. "Hell" is the act of making images which, when our words fail, come back to haunt us like a traumatic memory that cannot be recounted. Cinema shows the impulsive character of our compulsion-to-repeat when acting out our murderous instinct through conflicts and wars. The obsessional quality

---

[1] "The real is that which always comes back to the same place –to the place where the subject in so far as he thinks, where the res cogitans, does not meet it" (49). In *Notre Musique*, war is the unthinkable, the unnamable. It comes before language; it is without language.

of the repetition corresponds with what we don't want to remember and therefore need to leave out of the histories we construct. What comes back to haunt us in cinema is our repressed memory.

The blurring of boundaries between documentary and fiction is carried over in "Purgatory," the second—and longest—sequence of *Notre Musique*. "Purgatory" re-enacts the European Literary Encounters, a conference that took place in Sarajevo in 2000. Godard, playing himself, is invited to the conference to give a talk on the relationship between image and text. He meets writers, poets, journalists and students who communicate sometimes directly, sometimes through translators in a chaotic multi-lingual atmosphere. Their exchanges are profound, yet the film resonates with a confusion of tongues. Far from creating a utopian Neoplatonic vision of European unity, Godard's "Purgatory" is the "Kingdom" of disorganized multi-language communication. It mirrors today's global world, a world where borders are eroded by inexhaustible international exchange, yet a world torn apart by wars and conflicts.

If Godard's "Hell" is the realm of images and cinematic representation, his "Purgatory" focuses on verbal communication, text, and language. Most of the characters in the film are multi-lingual; several of them are split between multiple places, living in linguistic exile. Ramos Garcia (Rony Kramer), a translator, speaks French, Hebrew, Russian, Spanish and Portuguese. Judith Lerner (Sarah Adler), a young Israeli journalist who has come to Sarajevo to make better sense of the conflict in her own homeland, communicates in French, throughout the film although she also speaks several other languages. Godard's "Purgatory" resembles a contemporary Tower of Babel. The different languages people speak create obvious divisions among Europeans who sometimes have to rely on translators to communicate. Creating bridges across linguistic divides, translation brings people together in spite of separation and differences. The translator's decoding of texts is instantly converted into new words. Continuously digesting and giving new form to ideas, translators become cogs in the wheel of communication. Further, according to Walter Benjamin, translation is a form in itself. Beyond fidelity to the original language, Benjamin argues that translation liberates the language imprisoned in a text by re-creating the work and supplementing it (Benjamin 2004, 253-263). Speaking about translation and elaborating on the concept of the supplement developed by Walter Benjamin, Jacques Derrida (1985) writes:

> ...the translator must assure the survival, *which is to say the growth*, of the original. Translation augments and modifies the original, which, insofar as it is living on, never ceases to be transformed and to grow. It modifies the original even as it also modifies the translating language (122).

Europe, as depicted by Godard, is the ground for multiple language cross-fertilizations. This multiplicity of languages creates rich and multi-layered communication within the complex European cultural environment.

Documentary filmmakers transpose information and actual events into the visual language of cinema. This process supplements and adds to the reality they represent in a way that can be paralleled with linguistic translation. By restaging the European Literary Encounters, Godard not only documents the Encounters, but he also goes a step beyond documentary film. In *Notre Musique,* he blends in a fictitious narrative openly supplementing what actually took place at the conference. This believable, yet unfaithful documentation of the conference allows him to erode our idea of Truth by adding a layer to the original events and weaving in his own agenda. In this way, the language of cinema supplements reality by adding, subtracting, transforming, and translating. Inevitably, the film's distribution beyond the borders of francophone countries, will create another supplement to the original through the use of subtitles.

The ambient chaos of languages in Godard's film exposes a linguistically and culturally complex Europe. With the landscape of today's Bosnia-Herzegovina as background for Godard's "Purgatory," viewers are left to wonder what sins Bosnians, along with other intellectuals gathered at the conference, are expiating in Sarajevo. The wounds of the Bosnian War are ever present and, although not referred to directly, Sarajevo's abandonment by European powers during its siege is clearly implied. Thus the film depicts a fragmented and two-tiered Europe and indirectly casts doubt on the concept of European unity.

Godard's "Purgatory" might take the physical appearance of today's Bosnia-Herzegovina; however, curiously *Notre Musique* overlooks Bosnians. Aside from a few shots of the streets, including open markets and city trams, *Notre Musique* shows very little of postwar life. Remnants of the conflict are present in the shell of the bombed out Sarajevo library and in the scattered images of burnt buildings, tombs and bullet holes. At times viewers can hear sniper shootings interlaced in the soundtrack. This creates a certain doubt as to whether the streets of Sarajevo still echo with the sounds of war, or possibly whether these noises belong in the collective memory of people visiting Bosnia. The André Malraux Center that organized the Literary Encounters was created by Paris-Sarajevo-Europe, a solidarity association, born during the siege of Sarajevo. A symbol of resistance, this cultural institute's mission is to renew ties between Bosnia, France and Europe. Foreign scholars have come to the Encounters in Sarajevo to seek answers to their intellectual queries; nevertheless, Godard's lens gives out a dim picture of the life of Bosnian intellectuals themselves. Their country used as background for the Encounters—and Godard's film—Bosnian students listen somewhat passively to the filmmaker's lecture. Godard addresses the dialectical relationship between shots and reverse shots to explain the two faces of Truth and deliver other aphorisms about the dual nature of every concept in Western culture. In the meantime, he gives the viewers no real sense of post-conflict Bosnia or of the climate during the current reconstruction. Very little is shown of Bosnia, its people, its thinkers, or its culture. No explanation is given on how Bosnia is dealing with the wounds of war. Bosnia does not speak for itself in *Notre Musique*; it is simply reduced to a purgatory for European intellectuals. Although they certainly appear well-intentioned, the conference participants have nonetheless temporarily transformed Bosnia into their philosophical lab.

This brings the viewer to wonder whether Godard could have overlooked the lack of representation of Bosnians in his film; or quite the opposite, whether *Notre Musique* could be an intended letter to absent Bosnians. Jean-Luc Godard is undoubtedly aware of the voice of the oppressed, as his film—an ode to losers of conflicts—makes clear. In a long interview by the young Judith Lerner, Godard gives voice to the Palestinian poet Mahmoud Darwish who addresses the power imbalance in the Israeli/Palestinian conflict. About the absentees Darwish states:

> The Trojan victim speaks through the mouth of the Greek Euripides. Troy did not tell its story.... and I wanted to speak in the name of the absentee, in the name of the Trojan poet. There is more inspiration and humanity in defeat than there is in victory.

In *Notre Musique*, Bosnians become present through their absence. At times, it seems that Israeli and Palestinian intellectuals might be used as surrogate for Bosnians who curiously are left out, and minimally participate in a conference on their own soil. Godard does not specify the reason for Bosnians' exclusion from the literary world. Bosnians become the ghostly supplement to the conference, its implied lack.

Additionally, in *Notre Musique* Bosnia is undeniably seen from a French viewpoint. Despite the multilingual cast, French is the main language of the film. *Notre Musique* subtly draws attention to the awkwardness of the French presence in Sarajevo. A reception at the French embassy illustrates the typical surreal quality of foreign bourgeois crowds when they are displaced. The French ambassador's entourage parades drinking champagne in a scene with unequivocal neo-colonial overtones.

In another instance of France occupying center stage in postwar Bosnia, the off-screen voice of Gilles Pecqueux—the French engineer who, at the time the film was made, was in charge of rebuilding the sixteenth century Mostar Bridge blown up during Croat and Muslim clashes in November 1993—echoes within the stones of the bridge recovered from the bottom of the river. He is discussing the symbolic reconstruction of the bridge in the face of pain and guilt with Judith who is leafing through *Entre Nous,* a book by Emmanuel Levinas (1998).[2] Watching Pecqueux's feet stepping through the maze of stones, marked some in red, others in black, viewers hear his voice explain how they were identified and numbered according to their original placement. The exhumed remains of this important historical landmark look like catalogued specimens from a lost civilization. In this intimated graveyard, the obsessional quality of the recovery work appears like a vain attempt to cancel out the bodies forever lost in the war. While Pecqueux talks about the bridge as the two faces of a multiethnic country, its destruction inevitably illustrates the shattering of the bond between Bosnian Muslims, Serbs and Croats. If cinema is the mirror through which Europe—like a Lacanian "body-in-pieces"—searches for unity, *Notre Musique* does not provide the cement that will re-assemble the fragments and hold the pieces together. In the Sarajevo that Godard depicts, France is a leading force whose presence is conspicuous. The integration of Bosnia in Europe is still mythical and the opening of borders is reduced to unilateral exchange. Bosnia is not an equal partner but a country in need. In the meantime, old European powers linger and still occupy center positions. The dialectic of a visible and strong French presence in relation to the absence of Bosnian representation discussed above is uncomfortably haunting in *Notre Musique.* The silence of Bosnians is akin to the silence of their ghosts. In Freudian terms, this silence resurfaces, by way of the film, as a "return of the repressed." It corresponds with the symptomatic shame associated with the abandonment of Sarajevo by European powers during the war.

Beyond a Europe contained within its geopolitical borders, the film reflects on Europe as part of a broader world forever scarred by wars and its colonial past. In a magnificent and surreal scene in the destroyed Sarajevo library, three Native Americans make an incongruous appearance. More symbols than developed characters, the three denounce Columbus and the White man for the exploitation of Native Americans as well as the destruction of their culture to a white scribe. This silent clerk takes notes without engaging with the three Native Americans despite their telling him that it's about time they come face to face. He does his job without questioning while people, flowing in and out of

---

[2] While the reconstruction of the Mostar Bridge has been used as a symbol for the reunification of Bosnia, Godard interlaces Levinas's text to address the idea of Otherness in relationship to the ethnic conflicts that tore apart the former Republic of Yugoslavia. For Levinas, the face of the Other establishes ethical responsibilities and represents the prohibition to kill. Traveling back and forth between the two banks of the Neretva River before focusing on the turquoise surface of the water that mirrors Mostar's historical buildings, Godard's camera alludes to differences, otherness, and the continual responsibilities and guilt inherent in human conflicts.

the frame, bring books and pamphlets to his table. Occasionally whispering words in his ear, they also take documents from the table and add and subtract from a huge pile of discarded books on the floor. In the beginning of the sequence, the cool tone of the light in the destroyed historical library, whose windows were shattered during the war, create a wintry environment. However, beautiful bonfires illuminate the background, warming up the ambient blue hues and the chill of the scene. Typical of Godardian dialectic, the fires do not just dispense warmth. Whether evoking the Spanish Inquisition, the Nazi era, or the more recent attacks on the Harry Potter series in the United States, the juxtaposition of piles of books and fires is not without reference to the long worldwide history of book burnings and auto-da-fé. At the end of the scene when an older woman who could be Bosnian, her head wrapped in a headscarf, brings her own book to the table, the clerk is gone. The inkbottle and the pen are left without a note taker. Again, Bosnia seems left out of the writing of History, the official text.

The three Native Americans also manifest in a strange scene near the destroyed Mostar Bridge. As Judith is trying to take a photograph of them leaving in their pickup truck, the magic of editing replaces the three Native American's contemporary western clothes with traditional attire. Thus they appear to her, and to the viewers, like a hallucination, one of them on a horse, the other two standing near the bridge in full ceremonial regalia. Judith's act of taking the photograph temporarily stops the momentum of the film and disrupts the linearity of this cinematic sequence. Facing the camera, poised, the three Native Americans become an iconic image, layered with symbolism accreted through centuries of representation. Although this is not footage of an actual photograph, Godard stops the fleeting quality of the moving images by immobilizing his actors in a static and frozen apparition. This suggests the long dialog between sculpture and dance, still images and motion pictures, photography and cinema. Evoking sepia-tone photographs from the past, Godard's Native Americans become a postcard. Reminiscent of the suitcase of photographs Michel-Ange and Ulysses bring back home as spoils of war in *Les Carabiniers* (1963),[3] the Native American characters are at once transformed into folklore, memorabilia, and a historical monument.

A few seconds prior to the Native Americans' metamorphosis, Pecqueux stated that in Sumer, people used the word "after" to talk about the past, and they used the word "before" to talk about the future. Applying this concept,

---

[3] In this anti-war film, the main characters, Michel-Ange and Ulysses, are not particularly bright. Godard uses them to denounce the idiosyncrasies of consumer society and modern capitalist culture. In particular, Godard interweaves graphic images and photographs to expose how advertising, tourism, and cinema use the illusions created by representation as brainwashing tools.

Godard creates temporary disruption in the sequential order through momentary non-chronological montage of the shots. Further, the disruption takes hold of the history of representation itself. Not only does Godard bring the viewers back to a time when sepia images preceded the cinema, he also uses the transmutation of the three Native Americans from characters to idealized images to reverse the order of things. In the western history of portraiture, idealized representations—such as Giotto's thirteenth century figures—preceded individuated Renaissance portraits that depicted individual features. From speaking subjects, Godard's three Native American characters are transformed into a static image. The powerful statements they delivered in the library are gone. Godard creates a time warp by silencing them and stripping them of their individuality. Their symbolic representation creates a split between their image and their voice.

In their temporal and geographical displacement, the three Native Americans resemble western representations of the "Indian" forever etched in the European Imaginary by Western movies as well as popular culture and literature. Beyond the geographical borders of the North American continent, Europeans have projected and vicariously identified with the mythical "Indian" in whom they see a symbol of a possible return to a pre-civilized life in harmony with nature. For instance, a New York-based husband-and-wife team Andrea Robbins and Max Becher have thoughtfully documented this kind of fantasy in *German Indians,* a series of photographs shot at the Karl May Festival in Raedebul, Germany. This yearly event celebrates the birthday of Karl May, a popular nineteenth century German novelist who wrote about the American West although he apparently had never visited the United States. During the weeklong festival, Germans gather from all over the country and dress up as Native Americans reenacting their traditional lifestyle. Beyond the bizarreness revealed in the photographs of these German "tribes," Robbins and Becher draw their viewers' attention to the political significance of the festival. In the exhibition catalog, Robbins and Becher explain that the Nazis identified with "the Indian" whom they understood as "noble savage and as the victim of a modern, corrupt, overly-intellectual world," and further "while Hitler was researching American Indian reservations as models for concentration camps, he made his generals carry around volumes of May's writings" (Robbins and Becher 2000).

Notre Musique's three Native Americans are trapped in purgatory along with intellectuals, young and older. They are trying to understand the meaning of life and death, power, the horrors of war, empire, and greed. According to Jacques Le Goff (1988, 86-92), the notion of purgatory appeared in 1190 in *Saint Patrick's Purgatory,* a treatise written by an English Cistercian. Le Goff explains that in medieval purgatory, the souls of the dead awaiting a possible remission of their sins witnessed passive souls being tortured and attacked by aggressive demons. In *Notre Musique,* possibly punished for challenging God through their constant quest for knowledge, intellectuals dwell in "Purgatory." Being exposed to wars and their representations might be the torment they have to endure while transiting on earth. These questioning beings are caught in the loop of human culture that endlessly reproduces the same models: war, atrocities, quest for knowledge, and desire to change the world. Like Sisyphus, new generations replace the old, endlessly generating the same questions but finding few answers.

Godard's protagonists dwell in purgatory except for Judith Steiner and Olga Brodsky (Nade Dieu). Judith's character is developed according to the rules of traditional narratives. Her presence throughout "Purgatory" fulfills the viewer's need for continuity. Nevertheless, Godard breaks away from traditional cinematic form by having Judith's voice narrate over the images of the "Kingdom of Hell," the film's first chapter. Her off-screen and disembodied voice seems to be observing human beings on earth as they subject each other to torture and the atrocities of war. Although—or probably because—Judith bears the name of the iconic Jewish heroine who cut Holofernes' head, her voice-over questions how there can still be survivors on earth considering human beings' "habit of cutting each other's heads off." Because she uses third person pronouns, Judith does not appear to be a part of that life on earth. It sounds as if she were watching human beings from some other place.

Olga appears toward the middle of the "Purgatory" sequence during Godard's lecture on image and text. She is a young Franco-Russian Jewish woman searching for philosophical Truth. At the end of the "Purgatory" sequence, Godard gets a phone call from Olga's uncle announcing that she took a Jerusalem cinema hostage asking if anyone in the audience would join her onstage for peace. Instantly shot, her body is recovered along with her bag in which she was carrying books, her sole weapon. Despite her fear of suicide admitted in an earlier scene, Olga finds her passport to the world of the dead and liberation from her earthly purgatory in the symbolic books. Although guided by Virgil through hell and purgatory, it is Beatrice who guides Dante in heaven. A contemporary Beatrice, Olga might be showing the path to heaven to Godard himself. A few shots earlier, Godard's goodbyes at the Sarajevo airport take place under a prominent sign of a yellow question mark. Immediately after, he sits in the airport café, a red and conspicuous "Lucky Strike" ad framing the shot. Could Olga's eschatological travels between life, death, and eternity, provide answers to Jean-Luc's own questions about the afterlife? The curious cross-language relationship between the filmmaker's and his actress's last name (*God* (ard) and *Dieu* which signifies God in French) might not be just accidental. This tongue-in-cheek association brings together the masculine and feminine principles as the Idea of God in this apparently godless paradise.

Godard intentionally creates confusion between Olga and Judith who look alike and whose voices are somewhat difficult to differentiate. Both beautiful idealists, these two young women stand at the opposite ends of the psychological spectrum, Judith is utopian and full of life, while Olga is gloomy and mysterious. Although *Notre Musique* is open to interpretation, these two women could very well form the two sides of a same personality or represent the continuum between light and darkness, the body and the soul, life and death. Indeed, there are several clues that lead the viewers to believe this might be the case. When Olga is seen entering the "Kingdom of Heaven," she is alone and her voice-over repeats lines from a previous scene: "There are two people side by side...(pause) I am next to her ...(pause) I never saw her before...(pause) But I recognize myself...(pause) It is...(pause) like...(pause) an image."

This leads the viewers to question what imago the pronoun "her" refers to. Could it be Judith? Godard does not give clear answers; and this monologue, in which the script repeats itself, remains mysterious. The previous scene where these lines were heard followed the apparition of the Native Americans to Judith near the Mostar Bridge. Olga emerged from a very hazy shot, walking down a city street. After the blurry long shot, the lens focused on a close-up of her face and her voiceover delivered these same lines. The transition from the Mostar Bridge to the hazy image of the street suggests that this might have been a premonitory dream, or a sort of psychic projection into Olga's future, her afterlife. Of course, bridges have throughout the centuries symbolized the passage from this world into the other world. A bridge replaces the "*passeur*" who in some legends carries the souls from one world to the other; and Godard seizes the symbol to create a complete blurring of boundaries between one scene and the other, Judith and Olga, dreams and representations, the body and the soul, the future and the past, life and death.

A magnificent landscape creates the idyllic background of *Notre Musique*'s "Heaven," where Olga lands in her corporeal body. A mix of sounds from nature and dramatic music accompany her as the camera follows a rushing river running through this peaceful land. The combination of images and sounds is mesmerizing. The aesthetic quality of this sequence suggests the presence of higher spiritual powers in nature. The afterlife evokes dreams more than western representations of paradise; it looks familiar and reassuring. Nevertheless, Olga's journey in "Heaven" takes her to a fenced area guarded by armed United States Marines. The use of Marines as keepers of heaven's gates mirrors the global political climate. This might be an ironic comment on the current United States president's claim to his special relationship with God.[4]

---

[4] Godard has had a long love and hate relationship with the United States and its culture. He often comments on the United States' position as a political, economic and cultural superpower. He is particularly vocal about the domination of Hollywood cinema that he

Heaven's gate is a checkpoint where Olga shows her arm to a soldier who gestures as if stamping her wrist. This resembles play-acting in children's games. No words are exchanged as Olga goes through the empty metal frame. Godard does not clarify why her blank wrist is her entry document. Olga is noticeably alone in magnificent nature until she goes through the checkpoint. Inside the gates, young people frolic in a state of happiness. At one with nature, they read, play, and abandon themselves in leisurely activities. These images are reminiscent of representations of the Greco-Roman Golden Age when neither hatred nor war was known as people lived in perpetual bliss, enjoying permanent youth and love for one another. In the last scene of the film, Olga walks to the beach of a lake where a young man is sitting eating an apple. Gesturing for him to move over, she sits in his place and proceeds to repeat Eve's original transgression by biting into his apple.

The complexity of Godard's "Heaven" comes from Olga's transformation in the last "Kingdom." Her life on earth ends alone, alienated from everyone. Asking for solidarity, her statement for peace is unheard in the Jerusalem cinema. Nobody steps forward to join her in her symbolic action. Her passage into the afterlife is alone as well. Beyond the idea of pleasure, her initial entering "Heaven" evokes the Lacanian concept of *jouissance*.[5] Olga appears in a pure state of harmony with herself and nature, she is freed from her past and her future. However, just like *jouissance* always implies desire and its lack of satisfaction, Olga's delightful solitary journey is short-lived. Her pleasure is already tied with future pain. Soon after experiencing "Heaven's" initial state of bliss, Olga enters the military compound.

Thus, "Heaven" seems divided into two stages. Before Olga goes through the gate, "Heaven" resembles the Lacanian Imaginary.[6] Speechless for the most

---

denounces, for instance in *Histoire(s) du Cinéma* (1998), as destructive of all European cinema.

[5] This concept that keeps evolving throughout Lacan's oeuvre holds the impossibility of reaching an ideal state of pleasure. *Jouissance* is desire for desire's sake. In its impossibility to be attained, *jouissance* contains its own limits; it implies lack and the idea of death. Lacan also refers to jouissance as a mirage "which is only accessible to the Other" (Evans 1998, 8). This is epitomized in *Notre Musique* by the joyful and carefree young people Olga witnesses playing with one another.

[6] Lacan's early work focused on the register of the Imaginary. This was developed in relationship with his research on the mirror stage. The mirror gives the child a sense of bodily unity. This exterior image provides a sense that the self is not only an individual subject separate from its environment, but also the object of another's gaze. The child understands himself or herself through this specular double that establishes the relationship to otherness. Simultaneously, the child enters the realm of the Symbolic Order that will allow him or her to create his or her reality by conceptualizing and naming it through language (Lacan 1977, 1-7).

part, Olga appears to be going through the pre-language realm of fantasies where conscious and unconscious images get formed. During this pre-subjectivity stage, Olga is in a state of suspension. She is an idealized representation of purity. An image of human narcissism, Olga, just like saints and other virtuous souls said to dwell in heaven, represents the human need for ego ideals. But her original state of bliss and satisfaction is an illusion that dissipates as soon as she encounters other people. The Marines' presence implies that the harmonious atmosphere inside the fence is possible because people are artificially parked and guarded. Human beings' vulnerability, their constant search for control over their lives through language and the Law of a symbolic Father—as represented here by the presence of United States soldiers, the self-declared world police—become the painful counterpart to *jouissance.* This puts an end to Olga's timeless and carefree journey. As she encounters other people inside the fence, the mirror image she finds in their alterity initiates the sense of loss that will lead her to bite into the apple. Experiencing lack and desire, she will be sent back to the realm of signifiers, the speech and language-based Lacanian Symbolic Order, Godard's "Purgatory."

Although encoded with rich content, the meaning of the last section of *Notre Musique* is far from being fixed. What is certain is that Godard refuses to have a traditional ending. The words "*Fin*" or "The End" do not magically appear on the screen to conclude the story and send satisfied viewers home. The film provides neither cinematic nor eschatological closure. Instead, Olga's biting into the apple sends the viewers back to their myth of origins. Along with her, they remain trapped in Godard's Möbius strip, his endless cinematic loop. Although Godard visually separates the three "Kingdoms" by framing them with black transitions and inter-titles, the film is a continual philosophical circle, a borderless narrative that takes its viewers on a circular ride.

Influenced by Hegelian dialectic, Godard constantly opposes conflicting ideas in his films. Positing everything in relation to its opposite, his analytic system breaks down traditional boundaries by refuting binary structures and highlighting the dependence of each category in human taxonomy on its own duality. The film's script repeatedly states that truth has two faces. Thesis and antithesis, like certainty and uncertainty are combined in *Notre Musique.* Preserving and reconciling these opposing forces, *Notre Musique* becomes the synthesis of conflicting elements that are absorbed into the narrative. Propagating like waves, Godard's ideas form concentric circles. They ripple, swell, and billow endlessly bringing new tides of emotional and intellectual associations.

Using nonlinear editing, *Notre Musique* dissolves cinematic conventions of time and temporality. Disrespectful of sequential time as well as traditional formulas of narrative constructions, the last "Kingdom" also represents the beginning. Temporal borders appear like a useless convention. As stated several times throughout the film: "*Before* is *After*." *Notre Musique* blends the present, the future, and the afterlife erasing the division between the world of the living and that of the dead. Bodies and voices appear and disappear, at times leaving the viewer unsure of whom they belong to. They travel in space and time apparently unencumbered and unburdened by the weight of their earthly corporeality. *Notre Musique* is an amalgam of myth, visions, dreams, projections, memory, representation (both literary and cinematic), and history. Dissolving the borders between reality and cinema, form and content merge in Godard's montage.

Faithful to a style developed in earlier films, Godard brings to light the presence of the filmmaker. Playing himself, his own performative act in front of the camera positions him as both a protagonist existing within the diegesis, and the author of the film. This *mise en abîme* further erodes the border between life and cinema. Nothing seems contained or even containable in Godard's film. The constant collapse of categories exposes the limitations of the artificial divisions within traditional classification.

In an interview with Katherine Dieckmann in 1985, Godard states his lack of belief in geographical borders that physically and ideologically delineate countries: "I've always been crossing borders. I belong to two countries, even if I have only one passport, Swiss" (Sterritt 1998, 173). This going back and forth between Switzerland and France might have allowed Godard to identify with the position of outsiders. Following his lack of personal identification with any one motherland, he remains critical of European policies. This film does not present any kind of utopian vision of post-Dayton Europe. Whether Bosnia-Herzegovina will officially integrate the Union or not, Godard subtly reminds the viewers that Bosnia was abandoned by European powers during the Balkan War. Ten years later, as war criminals like Radovan Karadzic and Ratko Mladic still have not been captured, Bosnia-Herzegovina remains one of the poorest European countries with a forty percent unemployment rate. The interests of Bosnians weigh little next to global capital in an ever-expanding Europe.[7]

---

[7] In fact, the interests of the whole Balkan region have been a low priority for Western European powers historically. Petar Ramadanovic denounces the self-centered attitude of Western powers during the war in former Yugoslavia. According to Ramadanovic, Western strategy changed after a shell hit the Markale Marketplace in Sarajevo, killing eighty people. This event prompted the first NATO military action not because the West suddenly cared for the people of Bosnia, but more likely, because the massacre was interpreted by the West as "the unimaginable happening again." Ramadanovic further states that: "in Bosnia in 1992, the West was no longer encountering what it saw at the beginning of the war—the age-old animosities between Balkan tribes—but an event from its own past, namely, the Holocaust. This identification of the West's past with the

In Christian allegory, purgatory is a step toward the purification of souls. By making his protagonists dwell in purgatory, Godard suggests that their lives are suspended in a transitory state. Although God might have punished human beings by creating a multitude of tongues, the atonement of languages and the human struggle through the difficulties of interpersonal communication could be a step toward redemption. The *Divine Comedy* used ideas from Aristotle, patristic theology, and thirteenth-century scholastic debate to educate and elevate Dante Allighieri's countrymen. Similarly, still adding to the school of thought started by André Bazin and the writers of *Cahiers du cinéma,* Jean-Luc Godard's films are a tribute to cinema as a powerful form that can contribute to building a better world. *Notre Musique* confirms that Jean-Luc Godard is not only a poet who forms the most unexpected visual and intellectual associations; he is also a great thinker whose ideas are solidly grounded in philosophy. Nevertheless, always faithful to his own style, Godard raises questions but does not clarify critical points. Although *Notre Musique* intimates the lack of interest of Western powers in getting involved in the horrific siege of Sarajevo, Godard's silencing of Bosnians is open for interpretation and can be perceived as ambiguous. While Godard claims throughout the film that the voice of the victims is more important than that of the winners, *Notre Musique* maintains values untouched by postcolonial discourse. For instance, although Dante had radical ideas for his time, his condemnation of the prophet Mohammed to hell, and Godard's use of the *Divine Comedy* as a model for *Notre Musique*, might be a sensitive matter for Bosnian Muslims who endured ethnic cleansing during the war. This could be interpreted as Godard's alignment with hegemonic Western European ideology. Furthermore, two other writers emerge and provide subtexts for *Notre Musique*: Juan Goytisolo the Spanish author of *Quarantine* (1994)[8] and Ibn Arabi, a 13th-century Muslim Sufi philosopher whose portrayal of the afterlife influenced both the *Divine Comedy* and *Quarantine*. Goytisolo appears in person reading some of his own texts in *Notre Musique*. However, the reference to Ibn Arabi is lost in the film's complex intertextual weave. In the early nineteen nineties, Jacques Derrida, reflecting on the construction of a post-wall Europe, ponders on the prospect of a new European subjectivity. Europeans are caught in a double bind. On one hand, they are obligated to defend the idea of Europe, but they also have to imagine a Europe of difference. Contrasting the

---

Balkan present, and the ensuing guilt and trauma of (non)intervention, were the dogs that the West actually introduced into the Bosnian war" (Ramadanovic 2005, 351-364).

[8] *Quarantine* is a multilayered experimental novel. According to Islam, after death, the soul goes on a forty-day journey before reaching its final resting place. In a way that resembles the soul's travels, the narrator of *Quarantine* is going through the isolation needed to write the very novel we are reading. With Desert Storm Operations as background, the novel explores the agony of war, death, and the creative process.

hegemonic position that Western European countries, and France in particular, have occupied during the colonial and modern era with the need for newer models, Derrida (1992) states the double obligation of Europeans:

> The injunction in effect divides us; it puts us always at fault or in default since it doubles the *il faut,* the *it is necessary:* it is necessary to make ourselves the guardians of an idea of Europe, of a difference of Europe, *but* of a Europe that consists precisely in not closing itself off in its own identity and in advancing itself in an exemplary way toward what it is not, toward the other heading or the heading of the other, indeed–and that is perhaps something else altogether– toward the other *of* the heading, which would be the beyond of this modern tradition, another border structure, another shore (29).

Although sometimes ambiguous on critical issues, Jean-Luc Godard always looks on the other side of power. An expert in dialectics, he keeps analyzing the duality of social and historical forces. The plight of Bosnians in the nineteen-nineties as much as that of Vietnamese people in the nineteen-sixties and seventies is a major subject for Godard who, since his early films, made a habit of scrutinizing what Derrida calls "the other *of* the heading." An uncompromising and revolutionary thinker, Godard remains a rebel who gives a voice to under-represented groups of people. The formal and conceptual permeability of borders in *Notre Musique* nears dissolution. Trafficking in the underworld of Hades and the unconscious, Godard, like Charon, Dante's irascible old ferryman, embarks us on an introspective journey. Always generating new ideas and new form, Godard's images and relentless questions could be the thrust that steers our boat in the direction of that "other heading," and shows us the suggested other shore.

Works Cited

Benjamin, W. 2004. The task of the translator. In *Selected writings: 1913-1926.* Vol. 1. Edited by M. Bullock and M. W. Jennings. 253-263. Cambridge: The Belknap Press of Harvard University Press.

Derrida, J. 1985. *The Ear of the other: otobiography, transference, translation,* translated by A. Ronell and P. Kamuf. Edited by C.V. McDonald. New York: Schocken Books.

—. 1992. *The Other heading: reflections on today's Europe.* Translated by P.-A. Brault and M. B. Naas. 29. Bloomington: Indiana University Press.

Evans, D. 1998. From Kantian ethics to mystical experience: An exploration of jouissance. In *Key concepts of Lacanian psychoanalysis.* Edited by D. Nobus. New York: Other Press.

Goytisolo, J. 1994. *Quarantine.* Translated by P. Bush. Normal: Dalkey Archive

Press.

Lacan, J. 1977. *Écrits: a selection.* Translated by A. Sheridan. New York: Norton.

—. 1998. *The seminar: Book XI, The four fundamental concepts of psychoanalysis.* Edited by J.-A. Miller. Translated by A. Sheridan. New York: Norton.

Le Goff, J. 1988. *The Medieval imagination.* Translated by A. Goldhammer. Chicago: University of Chicago Press.

Levinas, E. 1998. *Entre Nous: On thinking of the other.* Translated by M. B. Smith and B. Harshav. New York: Columbia University Press.

Ramadanovic, P. 2005. Simonides on the Balkans. In *Balkan as metaphor.* Edited by D. I. Bjelic and O. Savic. 351-364. Cambridge: MIT Press.

Robbins, A. and Becher, M. 2000. *German Indians: Karl May Festival and Cologne Karnival.* http://www.ybca.org/archive/trythison/try_ldeeper/german_indians_deep.htm.

—. *Try this on: Exhibition catalog.* San Francisco: Yerba Buena Center for the Arts.

Sterritt, D., ed. Godard in his fifth period. In *Jean Luc Godard: Interviews.* Jackson: University Press of Mississippi, 1998.

PART II:

MAPPING NEW BORDERS: GENRE, CO-PRODUCTIONS, AND TECHNOLOGY

CHAPTER FOUR

BORDERS IN/OF THE BALKAN ROAD MOVIE

NEVENA DAKOVIĆ,
UNIVERSITY OF ARTS, BELGRADE

> I am never sure of the reality of what I see, if I have seen it only once; I know that until it has firmly established its objective existence by impressing my senses and my memory, I am capable of conscripting it into the service of a private dream. In a panic I said, "I must go back to Yugoslavia, this time next year, in the spring, for Easter" (West 1942).

Balkan Roads and Borders

Throughout the centuries, migrations, journeys, travels, mobility, and nomadic life were and still are an intrinsic part of Balkan life and history. The journeys are made in search of daily bread, the myth of a promised land, or a new beginning. They have been delayed, if we compare them to the rest of Europe, because the Balkan countries' borders opened quite late. Sometimes, these journeys delve into history and collective memory in search for identity, roots, or a past that defines the present. The Balkan wars set on the road the new wave of refugees who were escaping from the spreading political chaos and ensuing poverty. All of these journeys, real and imaginary, are narrativised in the Balkan road movie.[1] It inevitably encompasses border crossings spatio-geographically (*Valkanisateur* [1998] by S. Goritsas; *In July/Im Juli*, [2000] by F. Akin; *Journey to the Sun/Güneşe yolculuk* [1999], by Y. Ustaoğlu), temporally (including the past reminiscences in *Underground/Podzemlje* [1995] by E. Kusturica and *Dust* [2001] by Milcho Manchevski) or both (*Ulysses' Gaze/Vlemma tou Odyssea, To* [1995] by T. Angelopoulos). Some of these journeys are more abstract, revealing the borders between classes or social groupings (urban vs. rural in *Premeditated Murder/Ubistvo s predumišljajem* [1995] by G. Stojanović) and between ethnicities (diaspora stories in *Escape* [2004] by D. Lungulov and *Head On/Gegen die Wand* [2004] by F. Akin; or

---

[1] For more detailed systematizations of the journey, traveling, and border crossing as related to "accented cinema," see Hamid Naficy (2001, 222-289).

stories about refugees and émigrés in *Sjaj u očima/Loving Glances* [2003] by S. Karanović). Their complex structure and intricate mapped-out trajectories allow the inscriptions of a number of metaphorical or symbolical meanings. Journey as a modernist trope references coming-of-age stories, big mythical adventures, frontier adventures, identity quests, and the search for the Proustian *temps perdu*.[2] These premises delineate a three-pronged approach. It is concerned with the journey as the metaphorical quest for identity and with the cinematic text as the articulation of the essential feeling of Balkaness. Finally, it attempts to profile the interrelatedness of the journey, narrative structure and cinematic genre trespassing.

The concept provides a double definition of the Balkan road movie. Literally, it is understood as the narrativization of journeys across Balkan space and time, which reflects the redrawn regional geographical borders and its spatial (re)imagining. Metaphorically, the Balkan road movie is the narrativization of the different searches for identity and journeys of self-discovery. The moments of border crossing mark the (ex)change of identity extending back in time to the period of the "mythomoteurs" (Stoianovich 1994, 303).[3] It also marks the changes of genre and the motif is not surprisingly found in comedies (*Valkanisateur*), adventure films (*Dust*), historiographic metafiction (*Underground*), war films (*Pretty Village, Pretty Flame/Lepa sela lepo gore* [1996] by S. Dragojević), dramas (*Hotel de Lux/Luxury Hotel* [1992] by D. Pita), and in social realist films (*Tirana, Year Zero/Tirana année zéro* [2001] by F. Koci).

The aim of this paper is twofold. First, I explore the Balkan road movie as genre, studying its formula, constitutive elements, and borders. Second, I analyze the ways in which the various border crossings along the journey shape the meaning of Balkan identity, or Balkaness at its core. The theme of Balkaness—as a nucleus of national, cultural and regional identities—is negotiated among numerous identities (gender, religion, and class, for example). Simultaneously, the Balkan road movie is constructed through cinematically-articulated prolonged arguments among different ethnicities, between the past and the present, the Balkans and Europe, between official and mythical history, and among various social groupings.

Since the majority of Balkan cinematic production from the 1990s onwards can be included in this analysis, my close reading of two paradigmatic narratives

---

[2] For journey, borders and frontiers as tropes in Hollywood cinema (1930-1990), see Robert B. Ray (1985).

[3] The term used by Stoianovich is coined by Anthony Smith (1986) to designate the basic myth or narrative set of symbolic values, identity constituents (memory, language, territory). "It is a defense of a 'particular' mythical claim, of a nature so precious as to demand any sacrifice to defend it" (Parsi 2005).

will be enriched by a number of comparative cinematic references. As case studies, the films *Valkanisateur* and *Dust* mark the opposing poles of the genre's range. In the film *Valkanisateur*, two men from the Balkans/insiders, travel across space, moving from Greece and across the Balkans, to end up in Switzerland. Along the journey, as they imperatively remap the region in geopolitical terms, they discover that their own identities are built on the opposition of Balkan(isation) vs. Europe(anisation). The second film, *Dust*, belongs to the subgroup of the Balkan travelogue, which depicts the revealing journey's experience of the foreigner/outsider—the Western traveler in the Balkans. According to Dina Iordanova (2001), this specific narrative is characterized by three elements. First, it deals with the number of plots positioned in the Balkans. Second, it perpetuates Western-made stereotypes and discards the very option of criticizing the Eurocentric construction of the world. Finally, it confirms the controversial positioning of the Balkans as "geographically part of Europe, but conceptually excluded from the European cultural space" (56).[4] The journey in *Dust* occurs mainly through time, in the mapping of the Balkans as a mythical domain. The identities of the foreigners and the natives are constantly (re)shaped through the genre premises of the western, which eventually restructure the *mythomoteur*. Strong genre hybridization—evident also in *Valkanisateur*—and numerous references and citations testify to textual self-consciousness and create meta-cinematic layers. Both films are polygeneric, multilingual texts of intercultural sensibility as well as rich interpretative fields. The dense intertextuality and intertwined layers of metaphorical, mythical, symbolic meanings are made not only with the intention of imagining the region, but also of explaining and familiarizing the Balkans for a heterogeneous international audience.

Cultural Thematisation of the Journey

The raising of questions of identity in the Balkans, national identity in particular, has been supported by the occurrence of theoretical and historical

---

[4] Iordanova (2001) claims: "First, the distinctive travelogue-type narrative structure is characterized of a large number of 'Balkan' plots. Second, by submissively accepting instead of critically challenging a narrative structure, which inevitably positions and constructs them as objects of the Western traveler's gaze, recent films from the Balkans that aim to address the current troubles of the region largely cater to traditional stereotypes. By doing so, Balkan film remains uncritical and fails to recognize the controversial effects of the Eurocentric construct. Third, this lack of critical examination provides grounds for wider speculation about the paradoxical positioning of the Balkans as geographically part of Europe, but conceptually excluded from the European cultural space" (56).

factors. The postmodern theories of changing, fluctuating, non-stable and multiple identities—founded upon the Saussure-Barthes's theories of language, sign, and meaning and the Althusserian-Lacanian paradigm as well as the construction of identity through and in the texts—arrived in the Balkans only in the late 1980s.[5] At the same time, the resurgence of the concern with national identity resulted in the political and ideological destabilization of the region. While national identity was *sine qua non* for the formation of the nation state as the ultimate aim of the former Yugoslavia wars, the post-modern theories of identity became part of an attempt to rationalize the haunting and escalating nationalism.

In film theory, identity formation is explained by general schemata based upon Lacanian theories of the endless interplay of gazes. Identity is discovered only in relation to the Other. The process of Othering works through the gaze exchange, between us and the (small/Big) Other, that is, between the subject and object of the gaze. The constitutive gaze in road movies is ascribed to the traveler through the landscapes. For the local, he is the big Other/subject of the gaze, the norm in relation to which every object exposed to the scrutinizing gaze, is (mis)recognized. His gaze thematizes the issues of culture, identity, and nation. But the Othering involves both parties as confirmed by the gradual change of the engrained stereotypes used by the normative Other. The change of the vision (of the Balkans) enables both an analysis of "the stereotyper" and its "deconstruction" (Stam 2000, 21). It confirms the identity recognition to be played out by the Big Other as the subject of the gaze.

Depending on whether the traveler is a native or a foreigner to the region, Mete Hjort (2000) discerns two types of narrative development—thematisation of the nation/region and consequentially of the (national/regional) identity:

> The theme of nation [...], arises when the elements that are constitutive of banal nationalism are consistently flagged in the course of the narrative. The theme is typically topical in nature, and as a result, it tends to be subordinated to themes of the perennial type. [...] The explicit thematisation of the nation tends to involve one of two approaches: monocultural hypersaturation and intercultural contrast. [...] The thematisation of a nation, particularly in the case of hyper saturation, tends to promote opacity in international contexts, for local, topical and nation-specific thematic elements are likely to be only partially comprehensible in other national contexts. The risk of opacity that accompanies topical schematizations of specific nations in international contexts can, however, be somewhat mitigated

---

[5] For insightful comments about the Althusserian-Lacanian paradigm, see Noel Carroll (1988, 65-74).

by the more inclusive intercultural approach which is by far the most common incarnation of the theme of the nation (16).[6]

In other words, Hjort delineates the representational strategies of the theme of the nation and their effects. Bearing in mind the targeted audience and the desired transparency of the thematisation, the nation could be represented through a number of banal and locally understandable elements. In this way it achieves the self-representation for itself while not being concerned with the transparency for the outsiders that do not know much about local history or customs. If oriented toward an international audience, filmmakers are more prone to portraying the nation through universal elements, comparative structure, and perennial topicality, which offers simply another variation of the known schemata and situations in the local context painted in a stereotypical way.

The narrative about the people from the region traveling around the region is clearly monocultural thematisation, which is characterized by "hyper saturation, use of specifically cinematic techniques and dialogue to flag national elements" (Hjort 2000, 111). According to Hjort, on the other hand, intercultural thematisation "uses contrastive cultural elements" (113), whereas the contrast is created between the gaze of the outsider, as the bearer of the normative Western standards, and the wild, exotic and murky Balkans.

By Othering the Balkans, the foreigner (mis)recognizes his own identity and arrives at a cathartic experience. He finds new meaning in life when confronted with the suffering of the local population in the war-torn, ruined, or simply impoverished country. The figure of the Balkan person, on the other hand, offers a more complex analysis. He/she is involved in his/her self-definition, with a confirmation, denial or subsequent reversal of the common stereotypes. All ingrained features (barbarism and regressive moves, for example) are reread (noble savagery, return to paradise lost) and fused into a positive image. This redefinition of identity develops along two lines. First, it explains and naturalizes Balkan identity and the region for and by the gaze of the Outsider. Second, being also self-recognition, it inverts the prejudiced outsider's image.

The best of the narratives play upon the thematisations of the nation as mutually-converting. If the narrative manages to use the gaze of the Balkan hero (as the subject) (1) who in some way is estranged from the homeland (he returns from diaspora in *In July*); (2) who travels to the previously unseen parts of the country (*Journey to the Sun*); or (3) who "travels" into the past (*Ulysses' Gaze*,

---

[6] Mette Hjort's (2000) explores the ways national cinema thematises the nation. He proposes several models: perennial and topical themes (linked to M. Billig's "banal nationalism" [1995]) as well as monocultural and intercultural thematisation of the nation.

Underground) then the monocultural becomes intercultural. In *Journey to the Sun*, a boy from Istanbul accompanies the dead body of his friend to the forbidden Kurdish regions near the Iraqi border. In *Ulysses' Gaze*, a modern Ulysses travels around the Balkans visiting the devastated city of Sarajevo, reinforcing it as a mythical site and one of collective memory. *Cabaret Balkan/Bure baruta* (1998) by G. Paskaljević) shows an unrecognizable and derealized Belgrade scape that acquires mythical underworld dimension. In *In July,* a young, Turkish man travels from Germany to Turkey, crossing all the Balkan borders. The reverse version of intercultural thematisation is seen in the narratives depicting the first encounters of Balkan immigrants with lands of promise. Turks encounter Switzerland in *Raise der Hoffnung/ Journey of Hope* (1990) by X. Koller; Romanians meet Paris in *Asphalt Tango* (1993) by N. Caranfil, and Serbs experience America in *Someone Else's America/ Tudja Amerika* (1995, d. G. Paskaljević).

Balkanisateur in the Conquest of Europe

Balkanisateur exemplifies successful manipulation of thematisations in deceivingly light comedy. In the third film of Greek director, Sotiris Goritsas, whose oeuvre generally exploits the motives of journey and/or schemes for getting rich. The heroes of the film *From the Snow* (*Ap to Hioni*, 1993) are Albanians who travel to Greece looking for a better life. In *V/Balkanisateur*,[7] two friends travel to Bulgaria and Switzerland, hoping to make money from the difference in foreign exchange rates.

Balkanisateur is a combination of an amusing and easygoing narrative, good photography, and effective *mise-en-scène*. In genre terms, it brings together the diverse traditions of social drama, road movie, buddy movie and national mentality-driven comedy that play upon a wide array of Balkan stereotypes. The story begins in a continental village, near the Greek-Bulgarian border, when the *gasterbaiter*'s stories of getting rich quickly inspire a pair of friends, Janis and Fotis, to try their luck. After discovering the money exchange scheme that should bring them the desired profit, they embark on a journey to Switzerland. The road leads through Bulgaria, via Zurich and back home. Their little plan fails, but their journey brings unexpected gain. It becomes the road to maturity, friendship, and the accomplishment of the mission of Balkanization.

The various border crossings (Greece-Bulgaria, Bulgaria-Switzerland) simultaneously outline the patterns of changes of identity, genres, and

---

[7] The film is cited under the titles *Valkanisateur* and *Balkanisateur* depending on the language. The Serbian translation *Balkanisateur* successfully draws up the main point of the film: the ways the two guys balkanize everyone.

thematisations. The first part of the story is worked out through the monocultural thematisation between the villagers/insiders, and the estranged ex-insider. The home setting, shown through banalities of the forsaken Balkan province—*kafana*, ethno music, dusty roads, poverty, and the stalemate atmosphere—is a non-typical Greek village, far from the sunny islands and the coast. The villagers, sinking under the burden of local, inland traditions, dream about the glamour of the big world. Reminiscent of the Balkan mood of Chekhovian inertia, these characters hardly do anything but make idle plans. Janis and Fotis are common ethno(stereo)types—Balkan patriarchal macho and lazy guys full of unrealistic ambitions. The motivation for action is provided by the stories of the rich *émigré*. The narrative, nevertheless, does not evolve toward intercultural thematisation because the point of view of the *émigré*—in spite of being denaturalized—is not demarcated as different. Although an outsider's perspective, his stance is full of nostalgic benevolence that makes it closely resemble an indigenous perspective. He understands, defends, and does not judge.

In the second part of the journey, as they pass through Bulgaria, the narrative develops into monocultural thematisation in a broader sense, or intercultural thematisation *stricto senso*. If we accept the Balkans as one entity, homogeneous-in-diversity, then within its borders, we find a monocultural thematisation or "othering" within one regional, supranational community. One nation is othering the other Balkan nation, but the differences do not escape the confines of regional identity. Intercultural thematisation is established by the fact that these are not simply two nations from the same region, but two nations marking the poles of Balkan identity. The misunderstanding and cultural differences are present to assure the charm of a paradoxal Balkaness. Mediating between East and West, Greece has always had a particular status. It is the country on the barbaric fringes, as well as the cradle of European civilization that reinforces its superiority vis-à-vis the rest of the peninsula.[8] If the Balkanized Greek village is taken to be paradigmatic, then one confronts inter-Balkan othering. If the image of two Greek guys in under-developed Bulgaria is understood as paradigmatic, it is a Europeanized Greece and the film represents intercultural thematisation. In their journey through the Balkan darkness, Janis and Fotis, being representatives both of Balkan(isateur) and Europe(anisateur) contribute to the overall duality of structure. As Europeanisateurs, they feel superior in intercultural othering. As Balkanisateurs, they complain about the miserable work of the monks Kyrillos and Methodios in Bulgaria. Though they are pan-Balkan educators, they had not succeeded in the expected

---

[8] About the particular split or dual position of Greece, see also Shohat and Stam (1994, 55-58).

(monocultural) unification of the region. A case in point: Fotis asks a Bulgarian, Vasili, whether he's Greek, Vasili answers "ne" which means "no" in Bulgarian, but "yes" in Greek.

The Bulgarian picaresque narrative is seen through the filters of mainstream cinema and with deep mistrust. Made of ethno-comical episodes depicting the wild realm, it shows both the land of primitivism and the heart of Balkanism. The threshold of civilization contains the scenes of the untamed Balkan wedding in the middle of nowhere, with a pregnant bride and an indigenous lifestyle. Bulgaria is shown to be some fifty years or so behind the West, which confirms the notion of Balkan jet lag. In the seminal book, *Imagining the Balkans*, Marija Todorova (1997) claims that the delayed development of the Balkans sufficiently explains the dominant pejorative attitude and ensuing denigrating stereotypes. Looking at the Balkans, the West sees its own past that it would like to forget. It sees the dawn of civilization or the last home of barbarism. Traveling through Bulgaria, lagging behind developed Greece, Janis and Fotis travel back in time, revisiting the 1950s in their homeland. The space acquires a temporal dimension, as time materializes into space.[9]

Although they approach the border, the two friends actually never travel through the former Yugoslavia and the rest of the Balkans. The narrative and editing ellipse brings them directly to Switzerland. While the road leads to a promised Heaven, the gradual introduction of contrastive elements builds up the intercultural thematisation. The Swiss landscapes are pastoral, neat and clean, like glossy consumerist ads disturbed only by the anachronistic, unshaven *gasterbeiter* faces traveling in bumped cars. As they encounter the national banalities of a different kind—green pastures, pretty sugared houses, empty and smooth roads, cows and bells, dreamy valleys—they begin to suspect the bitter truth about their improper presence.

The cultural contrast further develops through the appearance of other characters from the Balkans. The first people Fotis and Janis encounter in Switzerland are their regional and "traditional" enemies. When they hit the stopped car in the middle of the road, they initially think that the driver is Serb. However, he turns out to be a Turk driving a van full of women and crying children. The Turkish man is willing to help the Greeks out of solidarity as indigenous intruders in the heart of Europe. The Balkan nations themselves create a new "crystallized, collective image" (Todorova 1997, 122) of the Balkan population, which tends to erase the internal differences and smooth out the mutual conflicts. This "crystallized collective image" is not the knot of blunders and prejudices that confirm the "lack of differentiation" created due to

---

[9] Compare with "films can convey what Mikhail Bakhtin calls 'chronotopes,' materializing time in space, mediating between the historical and the discursive" (Shohat and Stam 1994, 102).

the ignorance and disinterest of the distant observer. Rather, it is an attempt in polycentrism that "globalizes multiculturalism. It envisions a restructuring of intercommunal relations within and beyond the nation-state according to internal imperatives of diverse communities" (Stam 2000, 271). The Balkan nations outside the Balkans alter their relations, emphasizing their shared characteristics. In the new imaging, historical enemies, oppressors and oppressed, Turks, Greeks and Serbs will get together of their own free will, mistakenly and confusingly alike and repositioned toward Europe. In the next village, the Greek friends meet "real" Swiss people. Two brothers—European versions of Janis and Fotis—owners of the little hotel, have different opinions about how and whether to help them. One wants to help them in exchange for money, while the other refuses on principle. In the end, the more xenophile brother gives them spare parts for free.

The role of the meeting point is assigned to Switzerland. It stands for the heart of Europe, the headquarters of international institutions (Geneva), a central and neutral spot of the Old Continent. It brings together European opposites in a number of surprising and unpredictable situations. In the hotel, the Greek friends meet a group of European tourists sightseeing in Switzerland. The relaxed atmosphere is helped by the wine and the sounds of diverse music. Throughout the film, the music played articulates "ethnic heterogeneity" (Shohat and Stam 1994, 223) and changing power relations. In Bulgaria, the ethnic background music is pervasive; there is gypsy music at the wedding and finally Bulgarian versions of western popular music from the seventies. In the Swiss hotel the evening begins with Sinatra's "Something Stupid," that is to be replaced by *bouzouki* and *sirtaki* as the romance grows stronger. As the Greek melodies invade the atmosphere, the hotel lobby converts into a make-believe romantic summer in Greece. Janis and Fotis romance the women who come from France and Germany, countries that form the new European axis.[10] Hence, their national provenance also stands for different models of European culture: "kulturnation" (Germany) and "European civilization" (France). Implicitly, the choice of the successful romance marks the more successful conceptualization of European relations. More tolerant, the Europe-loving French girl (fittingly named Marianne, the symbol of the French Republic) goes back with the charming Southerner, Janis. On the other hand, Fotis remains faithful to the woman he left behind, which goes against all the typecasting of the Southern

---

[10] The previous experience with the women they met by accident in Bulgaria was quite different. Two Bulgarian "ladies of the night" use the Greeks to get a rich dinner in a decent hotel. Later, instead of staying in the hotel, they take them to their home. One couple makes love in a separate room behind a closed door, while the other is supposed to do the same by the side of the blind grandmother in a grotesque and frustrating situation.

macho womanizer-*gastarbaiter*. Although a Europeanized Greek, Fotis nevertheless refuses German-shaped Europe, i.e. he refuses German national culture. For him, as a fan of European Greece, ancient Greek civilization is a model superior to all others.

The denouement of their adventure is expectedly tragic-comic due to language misunderstandings. The Greeks based their plan on the exchange rate given in American cents, while in reality the exchange rate was in Euro cents. Janis and Fotis are doomed losers, yet only a few minutes later, they achieve even bigger and unexpected gains. Back on the Greek border, they realize that their external journey was paralleled by an internal one. They mature and adopt a more serious outlook on life, as the film's narrative fulfills the basic demands of a *bildungsroman*. After the last youthful adventure, they return home to familiar customs. Fotis is happily reunited with his pregnant wife. Maria decides to stay with Janis in Greece. Sorting out their romantic relationships brings them emotional satisfaction. However, maturity involves social recognition, which comes later. Making big money or getting a serious job are yet to come. But, after many temptations and trials, they are, at least, ready to accept the responsibilities of adulthood and to face life's problems in their homeland. Harmony is restored both through the establishment of marriage/relationships and through the innovative gaze they cast on their village after their voyage through multicultural Europe.

The journey confirms and strengthens their friendship and turns into the contemporary Balkan version of the "buddy-body" movie. The term is coined for the films in which the romantic comedy's couple is replaced by the contrastive pair of male buddies.[11] Simultaneously, the romantic harmony of the marriage turns into a harmony achieved through male bonding. Janis is a free, easy-going bachelor who melancholically envies the married, pessimistic, and serious Fotis who is afraid of life. The very first shot of the film, the interior of *kafana*—which they own and run together—defines their relationship.[12] At first, it attempts to be a kind of Las Vegas attraction with Western music; a few shots later it is reshaped as the local joint with *sirtaki* and little profit. Further, the appropriation of the Western buddy pattern is refined through the added contrast

---

[11] The gender difference is rewritten in terms of race, age, social status, position, philosophy in *Tango and Cash* (1989) by A. Konchalovsky, *Lethal Weapon* (1987) by R. Donner and *48 Hours* (1982) by W. Hill). For more films, see Cynthis J. Fuchs (1993).

[12] *Kafana* is the local version of the restaurant, pub and coffee shop. It is a place for a quick drinks and long conversations. It is a place to eat and enjoy supper mainly with local, ethnic food and entertainment. For more information, see Mattijs Van de Port (1998, 117-207). Sometimes he translates the term as "bar" or "Gypsy" bar that is only a vaguely correct translation.

of the Balkanisateur/ Europeanisateur. Janis is very confident that the Balkan mentality will effortlessly outsmart the normativized West because customary law and resourcefulness will triumph over written law. He is the incarnation of Balkan narcissism, a superiority complex of the half-tamed barbarogenius that inverts typical European (Western) racism. The Balkan type manages to bring a bit of Europe into the borderline region. He is the one literally "taming" the French passion and bringing Western Europe to the traditional Balkan borders. Quite appropriately, the quest for Europe is resolved through emotions and not through political means or any other logic.[13] It is announced from the very beginning by the cohesive gendered translation of cultural contrasts. The Balkans represented by two men is a male, patriarchal principle that wins over a female principle embodied by the European women. Balkanisateur has accomplished his mission by balkanizing Europe. Popularizing Balkan's way (and its way to Europe), he has repositioned the Balkans within a European framework. Fotis is more cautious since his character provides an ever-skeptical reading of the narcissistic self-imagining. He is both tolerant and respectful toward European law. He suspects that there is the proverbial "catch 22" lurking in every rule that may favor the Balkans. He is the Europeanisateur of the Balkans who realizes that Balkan otherness is sufficiently Europeanized already.

The Mythical Optique

My analysis of Milcho Manchevski's most recent film *Dust* (2001) as the case study for the Balkan road movie reveals it as the opposite of *Balkanisateur*. It is read as a multicultural and intercultural transposition of the western that, in return, rewrites a mythical version of the Balkan history by depicting the foreigner's journey through Balkan history, past and present. A system of comparative, intertextual, and multimedia references in the portrayal of the events, the region and people assures the perennial treatment of Balkaness. Balkaness and the pertaining new version of *mythomoteur* are seen as something that "resonates across historical and cultural/national boundaries" (Hjort 2000, 106). Introducing Balkan models and Balkaness as identity confirms the discrete but constant process of the Balkanization of the world.

---

[13] Compare with *Nešto izmedju/Something in Between* (1982) by S. Karanović as a "portrayal of a young American woman journalist, who, in a brief six-week stay in Belgrade, finds herself caught 'in-between' her sexual and sentimental attachments to two Yugoslav men who are best friends. At a deeper level, the film explores the ambivalent posture of Yugoslavia, herself trapped 'in between' political tensions of East and West and the cultural and economic collision of North and South" (Goulding 2002, 175).

Dust is a two-layered narrative. One narrative line is situated in present-day New York and the other in pastoral Macedonia at the beginning of the 20th century. In the contemporary beginning, a young African-American man named Edge robs an apartment in New York. Angela, the old lady, owner of the apartment, unexpectedly wakes up. But instead of calling the police, she begins to tell her life story, holding Edge at gunpoint. When she ends up in the hospital, Edge keeps visiting her and the storytelling continues. Angela dies and Edge carries on the telling of her story. Angela's life story represents the distorted western. In the "wild, wild West" in the very last years of the century, two brothers—Luke and Elijah—fall in love with the same woman—Lilith. The Cainesque Luke runs away from the family *ménage à trois* and ends up in Macedonia, becoming the bounty hunter. Instead of hunting for the rebels and money, he joins the Macedonian freedom fighters in their battle against the Turks. Elijah, the Abel-like brother, follows Luke in search of revenge. Luke dies saving the rebels, while Elijah takes the small Macedonian baby-girl with him to New York. The baby is Angela, the storyteller. Back in the present, Edge finishes telling the story and finds himself inserted into the same ongoing remembrance story. The entangled narrative unravels as the road veers from New York-Wild West across to the Atlantic-Wild East. In temporal terms, it shuffles between present and past. It departs from the present, goes back to the end of the 19th century and the beginning of the 20th century and ends in the realm of myth. In terms of genre, it interweaves road movie, western, and its mutation Eastern. Rare genuine western elements are left as such; the majority of them are given as strange and defamiliarised, while western and Balkan road genres convert into historiographic metafiction. According to Linda Hutcheon (1996, 178-208), historiographic metafiction is equally occupied with the representation/rewriting of history and with the search for the history of representations. *Dust* ventures into the past, offering its mythical image; it mirrors the past in the present; it constructs tradition and articulates Balkaness through the evoked history of imagining and performance. The text tightly knits together historical explorations of the western and Balkan history; it also includes the history of its (fictional) representation (through hybridized genres). The western displaced in the Wild East as Macedonia that accommodates archetypal imagery of the paradise lost becomes Easterner. The endless Balkan freedom fighting, at the turn of the 19th and 20th centuries, is translated into the western conquest of new territories. Luke is a conqueror rediscovering the Golden Moments of the legendary Wild West made out through the evocation of the highlights of the genre's history.

Metafictional dimension and intertextuality are nested in the confluence of western elements from the different phases of the genre's developments (classical and super western) and its variations (spaghetti western). Excessive violence is shown with graphic naturalism—which is the trademark of Packinpah—and the baroque *mise-en-scène* of Sergio Leone. Furthermore, Manchevski consciously and neatly, like Anthony Mann, uses composition and symbolism of the landscape and costumes to emphasize morality of the biblical-like story of revenge, catharsis, redemption. His heroes ironically wore white and black hats, wandering through bucolic settings to confront the enemies in the spaghetti's festive scenes of Hawksian iconography and mounting tension (silent parts with dripping blood; tossing of the coin). The western brother/buddy competitive relationship is again *déjà vu* in the films of Mann (*Winchester 73* (1950); *Bend of the River* (1952); *The Naked Spur* (1953)), John Ford (*My Darling Clementine,* (1946)) or Hawks (the western trilogy). Luke, the lonely and brave man with a shadow from the past (*Shane* (1953) by G. Stevens), comes to the rescue of the rebellious village (*The Magnificent Seven* (1960) by J. Sturges*, Wild Bunch* (1969) by S. Peckinpah). The multiple genre's reflections are rather discreetly found in the New York narrative part. The gold coins, in jackpot manner, flow from the refrigerator when Edge looks at the photos that help him understand the Balkan mystery. They are the money Edge was seeking. They are hidden treasures usually searched for in westerns like *The Treasure of Sierra Madre* (1948) by J. Huston or *Mackenna's Gold* (1969) by J. Lee Thompson.

As the regional genre variation, the Eastern genre is not gastronomically titled (although it has been referred to as the *baklava* western as well as the Byzantine western at times) as the more common: spaghetti, *kraut*, *paella* or *borsch* western. It is labeled in geographical (East/ern) or period terms (Byzantine) that underlie the natural, evolutional displacement of its narrative. Already with Packinpah and Huston, the western moved toward Mexico, toward a new century and new themes. In *Dust*, the film moves toward the "West of the East," into the Balkans at the height of colonization as the genre's last frontier. Arriving in Paris, Luke goes to the cinema and watches newsreels. In the block showing exotic countries and people is the short film, *The Visit of the Sultan Rašid V to Kumanovo and Skopje* (1905), which is about the visit of the Ottoman Emperor to the "colonial" Balkans. Made by the Manaki brothers, Greek-Macedonian cinema pioneers, it is one of the very first preserved films from their legacy—the same legacy Harvey Keitel tries to locate in the *Ulysses' Gaze*. During the projection, the short film is preceded by the intertitle "Macedonia—Jewel in the Crown of the Ottoman Empire" equating the relationship between Macedonia and the Ottoman Empire with the colonial relationship between England and India. Macedonia is the oriental "jewel" in Sultan's "crown" as India was for the British Empire, while the film converts into a cinematic trope of colonization.

The Balkan travelogue, in this case, is the journey through time, shifting between the present in New York and the Balkan past. The narrative is relocated to the 20th century while the hero encounters historical figures. The insertion of the fictional characters within a verified historical context is done in a lucid way, similar to *Zelig* (1983) by W. Allen, *Forrest Gump* (1994) by R. Zemeckis or *Underground*. On the ocean-liner, in the pseudo-authentic footage—made as old black and white film news—Luke meets Freud and Einstein. Upon arriving in Paris, he sees Picasso. A while later, the audience sees Angela on the photos with Tito. Another time frame is built through an elaborate web of Biblical allusions and references. The very title quotes funeral service words "ashes to ashes, earth to earth, dust to dust." The dialogue is replete with lines from the Old Testament and the New Testament, while the characters have Biblical names—(Prophet) Elijah, Luke (Gospel according to Luke but also Luke as Lucky Luke of the comics) or Lilith (female demon who drowns). Angela is angel and saint protector of repentance and remembrance. The other names are generic or vocational like in the early Christian community—Teacher, Grandpa.[14] The symbolic iconography evokes Judas's kiss; gold as payment for betrayal and disappointment; meanings clustered around water—death and (re)birth of the soul, sin and purification.

The changed western keeps the traditional function of the mythologisation of the past/history. The Balkan past is revised according to the command "when history becomes myth, print the myth!" (*The Man Who Shot Liberty Valance* [1962] by J. Ford). Elegiac, glorified, and ideologically naturalized memories in an eternal rephrasing become the Eastern. The mythologizing perspective is assured by Luke whose bewildered gaze, finally identifies the Balkan skirmishes and battles in terms of the Western Armageddon fight between good and evil. The shiny cowboy is the ethical corrective in the Balkan conflicts, otherwise shown to be like the legacy of spaghetti westerns and narratives of the Mexican revolution. Macedonian heroes are equally driven by the lust for gold (*Duck you Sucker!/Giù la testa,* [1971] by S. Leone), prone to violence without firm coda as they are zealous freedom fighters (*Viva Zapata!* [1952] by E. Kazan). "The Othering" in the other direction makes the Balkans an ennobling experience for Luke. He is changed and regains his lost idealism. Arriving in Macedonia, he sides with the rebels and their nominal moral imperative "do not kill for gold, but kill for ideals." Angela proudly claims "Luke never killed a man without a good reason." The savage realm gives the dignifying aura to the Wild West outlaw, providing the most positive version of Balkanization. The concealed gold coins are symbolic countervalue of the hidden Balkans that make possible

---

[14] As the only contemporary character, Edge is named functionally. He marks the edge(s) between the story lines and chronotopes but also unites them.

all cathartic events. Thus, the Balkan gold is not cursed, but rather connects time, spaces, nations, and cultures. Only after discovering the gold, Edge can step from New York, via Angela's mesmerizing memories into his rewarding Balkan adventure. He is the new actor on the Balkan stage of remembrances and foretelling.

In spite of jumping back and forth between centuries, the narrative time is not a linear one, but rather a circular one. Manchevski's concept of time in *Before the Rain* (1994) is "The circle is not round, time never dies." In *Dust,* it is explained as "The centuries do not follow up each other but coexist like parallel universes," floating in the mists of time. Linear time bends and buckles into a circle. Its trajectory is paved with the repetition of the *déjà vu* events and rituals in different contexts.[15] The bowing of time is endorsed by the style of Medieval Orthodox Metaphysics founded upon the revived medievalism which combines Byzantine, Orthodox, national mythical and Biblical elements. Its constitutive elements are iconography, legends, and religious symbolism that visualize the historicized *zeitgeist*, thus contributing to the perennial imagining of the theme. The film contains the beautiful aerial views of churches scattered across hilltops and barren hillsides. The decisive confrontation takes place in front of the fresco of the *Judgment Day*. The souls that are weighed and judged give the western duel an orthodox spiritual allure. When Neda takes dying Luke into her arms, the film shot paraphrases the Serbian painting "The Girl from Kosovo." It is like a *tableau vivant* from a medieval episode considered the *mythomoteur* of the Serbian nation. It is saturated with the ideals of martyrdom, sacrifice, victimization, injustice, and suffering.[16] Secular defeat at Kosovo Polje is reread as a glorious moral victory and spiritual reward, insuring that future generations will follow the example. The defeat changed into destined victory is a myth that lies at the heart of the Balkans, casting new light on the purpose of Balkan history for eternity.

The narrativisation of the past and the search for identity are the all-inclusive motives set by the film's motto—questions: "Where does your voice go when you are no more? What do we leave behind? Is it the story of our lives? Is it how others remember us? Is it the children we leave behind? Or the material

---

[15] The time of the past is spatially accommodated in obvious metaphors of Balkan films: it is underground (*Underground*), a tunnel (*Pretty Village, Pretty Flame*), and bucolic imaginary (*Dust)*.

[16] The famous legend quoted in Rebecca West's novel-travelogue *Black Lamb and Gray Falcon* (1942), tells about the prophet Elijah who turns into a gray falcon flying from heavenly Jerusalem to Kosovo on the eve before the 1389 battle. Arriving at Kosovo, the bird asks emperor Lazar—Serb's leader—to choose between earthly and heavenly kingdom. Instead of the earthly, Lazar chooses the heavenly one, thus invoking eternal, spiritual salvation and worldly, physical defeat.

records such as movies and photographs? Is it only the ashes in the urn? Is it the Dust?" (*Dust*). Answering these questions, the film provides pure pleasure from complex storytelling about collective memory. The film also offers a diasporic/traveler memory shaped in multiple narrative voices and a web of gazes. Their audio-visual growth is structured in concentric circles. The central gaze belongs to Luke, through whose eyes we encounter the rustic sights for the first time. The central part—the flashback—is mediated by Angela's storytelling.[17] The images accompanying her narration—in the heavily-accented, rough, and trembling voice—are probably the ones projected on the memory screen in her head.[18] The new time and landscapes seen initially through Luke's eyes, then through Angela's and finally through Edge's, explode into the mythical realm. Edge, at first a passive listener, becomes increasingly involved in the story and ends up displaced by its narrative. The intercultural thematisation grows as the process of Othering widens. At the beginning, Luke and Elijah stand for the number of binarisms—white/black, nature/civilization, West/East, New/Old World, Old/New Age. Upon Luke's arrival to the Balkans, the meaning of traditional western dichotomies (Kitses 1969)—Individual vs. Community, Nature vs. Culture, West vs. East—is contextually enriched. With Angela as manipulative narrator, the story is expanded to include the present vs. the past, female vs. male; urban vs. rural, diaspora vs. indigenous; colonizers vs. colonized. Edge's character embodies the oppositions of ethnicity, race, age and class.

The Balkan travelogue narration is the grid which maps the various representations and performances of Balkaness. The film links the consensual imaginings of the Balkans from different periods into rewritten *mythomoteur*—versions of the past and foretelling for eternity.[19] The Byzantine terms are

---

[17] As pointed by Svetlana Slapšak (2002), "Angela, as her Greek name indicates, is a messenger, a bearer of stories, [...] Angela is a messenger of the world of dead and the world of memories."

[18] Compare with the problematisation of the narration in the film *Letter from an Unknown Woman* (1948) by Max Ophuls analyzed by G. Wilson (1986): "Whenever a fiction film includes a verbal narration of past events by a character who is supposed to have witnessed them, and the import of this telling is conveyed on the screen in a flashback, there is a potential question about how the flashback is to be construed [....] I it that the shots in the flashbacks are meant as a sort of 'visual translation' of the verbal narrators' assertions? [...] Or is it that the flashback depicts, from its own proper perspective the *actual* occurrences that the narrator then claims to be describing" (105).

[19] A persuasive example of the ways past determines and is repeated in the present is given in Manchevski's answer to the question whether Luke stands for NATO: "He's not NATO, because the script was written before NATO came to have their fun in the Balkans, [...] But once the bombing happened, [...] it was impossible to ignore it. We had it in the back of our minds. Everything you see influences you, even subconsciously. I

superimposed with western ethical and mythical concepts and the historical framework of the Balkans. As a construct, the Balkans rest upon their metaphysical and mythical qualities, emblematic of the narcissistic self-imagining and the spreading of Balkanization as a spiritual revelation for the foreign traveler.

On the Balkan Trail

The instabilities of the genre (Balkan road movie) and (Balkan) identity are mutually enhancing and supportive. Their normative work and inscription reshape the cinematic texts as they are being permanently cinematically remapped in the process. The dialectic practices delineate the widening specter of the notions of Balkaness. Thorough their collaboration, they succeed in "rooting"—together with the work of chosen context and imposed interpretative framework—the signified Balkaness as an ever ambivalent and changeable "floating signifier." The articulation of Balkaness occurs through genre contamination as well as through the intertextual, palimpsest, and postmodern performance of cinematic texts. The genre constantly spills over its established borders, becoming contaminated by the elements of a coming-of-age psychological drama, a national historical narrative, an ironic myth. Its unstable existence remains on the verge and in the margins, since border crossings symbolise the ever-changing views toward the Balkans, which is embodied in its fluctuating relationships with Europe and the West. The Balkan road movie read as metaphor stands for the essential Balkaness defined in comical, mythical, topical, perennial, monocultural or intercultural ways. The multilayered text crossing through time figures Balkaness through knotted allusions, imitations, dense pastiche, or references to images and performances established in other arts, genres, epochs and cultural contexts.

But regardless of the mode, the wandering quest along roads and borders ends with the restoration of Balkaness. Initially problematized, Balkaness is seen in a new way and/or often exalted. Read from different perspectives, exhibited in different genres, narratives, chronotopes proliferating in the web of gazes, and (re)visions, Balkaness seems to both undergo Europeanisation (of the Balkans) and perform Balkanization of the world. The Westernization of the Balkans as well as the (positive) inspiring Balkanization of the world mark the

---

guess I was a little more careful in portraying the fact that Luke is absolutely ignorant of what's going on" (Holley 2001). Manchevski, thus, explains how his concept of Luke's character was influenced by the NATO bombing i.e. by the similarities and differences between the position and "intervention" of NATO and Luke and the Balkans. Unlike NATO that intervened with clear conscious, decision and reason Luke was blissfully ignorant about the real situation.

poles of the cubistic visualization that offer the pleasure of permanent change and multiple, and diverse border crossings.

Works Cited

Barthes, R. 1977. *Image-music-text*. London: Fontana/Collins.
Billig, M. 1995. *Banal nationalism*. London: Sage Publications.
Carroll, N. 1988. *Mystifying movies: Fads and fallacies in contemporary film theory*. New York: Columbia UP.
Fuchs, C. J. 1993. The buddy politic. In *Screening the male: exploring masculinities in Hollywood cinema*. Edited by S. Cohan and I. R. Hark. 194-213. London and New York: Routledge.
Goritsas, S. 1998. *Valkanisateur*. Greece/Bulgaria/Switzerland: D. Herodotou.
Goulding, D. J. 2002. *Liberated cinema: The Yugoslav experience, 1945-2001. (Revised and expanded edition)*. Bloomington and Indianapolis: Indiana UP.
Hjort, M. 2000. Themes of Nation. In *Cinema and nation*. Edited by M. Hjort and S. MacKenzie. 103- 117. London and New York: Routledge.
Holley, D. 2001. Milcho Manchevski film explores a timeless "dust" swirling in the Balkans. *Dust: Essays*.
http://www.manchevski.com.mk/html%20en/essays_dust.html (accessed January 03, 2006).
Hutcheon, L. 1996. *Poetika postmodernizma*. Novi Sad: Svetovi.
Iordanova, D. 2001. *Cinema of flames. Balkan film, culture and media*. London: BFI.
Kitses, J. 1969. *Horizon's West*. London: Thames and Hudson/BFI.
Manchevski, M. 2001. *Dust* UK/Germany/Italy/Republic of Macedonia: Lions Gate Films.
Naficy, H. 2001. *An accented cinema: Exilic and diasporic filmmaking*. Princeton: Princeton UP.
Parsi, V. E. 2003. Civic identity without national identity? Political identity in a new and challenging global context. In *The essence of Italian culture and the challenge of a global age*. Edited by P. Janni and G. F. McLean. http://www.crvp.org/book/Series04/IV-5/chapter_xi.htm (accessed December 11, 2005)
Port, M. V. 1998. *Gypsies, wars & other instances of the wild: Civilisation and its discontents in a Serbian town*. Amsterdam: Amsterdam University Press.
Ray, R. B. 1985. *A certain tendency of Hollywood cinema 1930-1980*. Princeton: Princeton UP.
Shohat, E. and R. Stam. 1994. *Unthinking eurocentrism: Multiculturalism and the media*. London and New York: Routledge.

Slapšak, S. 2002. Luke Balkanwalker shoots down Corto Maltese: Milcho Manchevski's *Dust* as an answer to the Western cultural colonialism. *Dust: Essays.* http://www.manchevski.com.mk/html%20en/essays_dust.html (accessed January 03, 2006).
Smith, A. 1986. *The ethnic origins of nations.* Oxford: Basil Blackwell.
Stam, R. 2000. *Film theory: An introduction.* Malden: Blackwell Publishers.
Stoianovich, T. 1994. *Balkan worlds: The first and last Europe.* New York: ME Sharp Inc.
Todorova, M. 1997. *Imagining the Balkans.* New York and Oxford: Oxford UP.
West, R. 1942. *Black lamb and grey falcon. A journey through Yugoslavia.* London: Macmillan. http://knigite.abv.bg/en/rw (accessed January 02, 2006).
Wilson, G. M. 1986. *Narration in light: Studies in cinematic point of view.* Baltimore and London: The John Hopkins UP.

CHAPTER FIVE

SPANISH CO-PRODUCTIONS: COMMERCIAL NEED OR COMMON CULTURE? AN ANALYSIS OF INTERNATIONAL CO-PRODUCTIONS IN SPAIN FROM 2000 TO 2004

ALEJANDRO PARDO, UNIVERSITY OF NAVARRA

Co-productions have been a typical formula in most of the European film industries since the mid-1950s. With some ups (1960s) and downs (1980s), European countries have developed these collaborative efforts quite regularly, in the spirit of sharing costs and risks as well as multiplying the domestic market size. As globalization has multiplied the possibilities of trade and exchange between cultures, the European audiovisual policy has intended to draw tighter the ties among different countries. As a consequence, the number of international co-productions in Europe has increased annually. Nowadays, as much as 34.8% of the feature films produced in the main five Western European countries are internationally co-produced films.

In this sense, it is not a coincidence that recent times have witnessed a renewed interest in studying the "international co-production phenomenon" both as a competitive strategy to confront Hollywood domination as well as an issue related to "national identity" and "crossing-border" cultures (Hoskins et al. 1997, 102-103; Eleftheriotis 2001, 47-53; Wayne 2002, 33-45; Jäckel 2003, 59-65; Everett 2005, 7-14; Miller et al. 2005, 173-212; Elsaesser 2005, 485-513). In other words, co-productions are a key confluence point between economic strategies and multicultural implications, as Miller et al. (2005) underlines:

> Co-production marks an important axis of socio-spatial transformation in the audiovisual industries, a space where border-erasing free-trade economics meets border-defining cultural initiatives under the unstable sign of the nation (209).

On the one hand, from the economic and financial perspectives, co-productions have clear advantages for film producers in Europe, such as pooling or sharing of financial resources, access to a foreign government's incentives and subsidies or even to favorable tax schemes, access to a broader market (those of their co-production partners and those of third-country partners), exploitation of comparative production cost advantages in different countries, learning from partners' know-how, access to foreign locations and even enriching from cultural exchange (Andersen 1996, 349; Hoskins et al. 1997, 104). On the other hand, some disadvantages must be taken into consideration as the need for wide appeal stories, increased cost incurred for co-ordinating the project, loss of control and cultural specificity, possible inflationary effects, use of different languages and some times irreconcilable cultural differences (Andersen 1996, 349; Hoskins et al. 1997, 105-106). Moreover, the co-producing formula can also have positive and negative effects as a multicultural platform. Since it helps to widely spread and share different cultural backgrounds, it can also endanger national identity. Using Miller et al.'s words,

> International co-production policies simultaneously inscribe and destabilise national descriptors of cultural value. As a practice of international cultural collaboration, co-productions call into question national measures of cultural identity, but reinscribe them in treaty language that struggles to specify national cultural preservation. Co-production marks a site of transformation in cultural scale, from the local and national to the regional and global (Miller et al. 2005, 177).

Or as Santaolalla points out referring to the current new order, "globalization—or rather, transnationalization—it is the primary cause of the current crisis underlying the concept of national identity" (Santaolalla 2005, 1).

These inherent complexities are reflected by the difficulty to define the very concept of (international) co-production. For many years, the only valid co-producing formula for European countries was the full contribution—financial, creative, and artistic. Due to the necessity to make more flexible co-production agreements, the European Union has permitted the figure of the strictly financial co-producer—with some particularities (Györy 1995, 3)—and even the so-called equity co-production (with Hollywood) at a corporate level (Miller et al. 2005, 195-196). These preliminary questions affect Spanish international co-productions in a very significant way, as we will see in the following pages.

Spain and the Co-Production Treaties

Right after the end of the Second World War, European governments were obliged to intervene in multiple spheres in order to recover their "national industries" and refloat their battered economies. The film industry was not an exception. For that reason, the European states created subsidy programmes and developed co-production treaties for the film industry. The American competition was high at that point, and the European film industries were obliged to produce films with higher budgets and production standards. This effort was much more affordable if shared among different countries, and by relying on the public aids granted by the respective governments. In this sense, co-production agreements started to be signed, first on a bilateral basis and later on a multilateral basis, to create rules for collaborative projects to qualify for subsidies and fulfil quota restrictions. It is interesting to note that co-production treaties in Europe, as legal frameworks for collaboration of different companies, were precedent in the European Union to other important agreements like the pool on Coal and Steel (Otero 1999, 20).

In the case of Spain, the first co-production treaties were those signed with Italy (16 March 1953) and France (31 March 1955). From then onwards, the number of co-production agreements have increased substantially. The following chart shows the currently valid co-productions agreements signed by Spain (See Chart 1).

In relation to this chart, it is important to notice that the existence of this agreement does not imply the actual existence of co-productions. In addition, Spain ratified in 1996 the European Convention on Cinematographic Co-production (Strasbourg, 1992) as well as the Ibero-American Cinema Co-production Treaty (Convenio de Integración de la Cinematografía Iberoamericana, Caracas, 11 October 1989) (Otero 1999, 20).

European countries realised the importance of co-productions and the necessity of developing common legal rules to produce motion pictures in a collaborative way. For this reason they promoted the European Convention on Cinematographic Co-production, approved at Strasbourg in 1992. The main advantages of this agreement are four: a) More flexibility in requirements, balance of contributions, and conditions of reciprocity among partners; b) Point-rating system to evaluate the different contributions (each creative or artistic talent, as well as the top crew talent are valuated in points; in order to be considered as European, 15 out of the total 19 points must be referred to European talents; c) Possibility of non-European co-producers (no more than 30%), from third countries or even the US.; d) Language must be from any of the European Union countries, therefore the English language can be also used (a very interesting issue, as we will see) (Otero 1999, 24).

In a similar move, the Latin American countries aware of the importance of cooperation in film productions also created an organism to facilitate the integration of the Latin American market. In 1988 the Conferencia de Autoridades Cinematográficas de Iberoamérica (CACI) was created—Conference for Latin American Cinematic Authorities—, who led to the establishment of the Latin American Integration Treaty. This last agreement propelled in the first few years the number of co-productions. After a brief period of impasse, the initiative was taken up again in 1997 under a new scheme named Ibermedia.

As a final thought on co-production treaties, it must be pointed out their role regarding the preservation of national identity. This idea is very well explained by Miller et al.:

> As legacies of nation-state formations under modernity, treaties measure cultural specificity by way of national borders, a demarcation that necessitates folding intra-national cultural affiliations across borders. So, although national audiovisual industries have used co-productions to stall Hollywood dominance by pooling resources to create audiovisual products with greater international appeal, co-production treaties also inscribe boundaries that distinguish a product of national cultural expression from one that is not. Such treaties institutionalise normative and static conceptions of national culture in the very process of international collaboration (Miller et al. 2005, 184).

Bridging between European and Ibero-American Co-Production Initiatives

As it has been mentioned before, European cinematographic co-productions started off in the 1950s, grew steadily throughout the 1960s and fell off sharply at the end of the 1970s to such an extent that international co-production was almost dead in some countries by the 1980s (Györy 1995, 3). Fortunately enough, the new European audiovisual policy positively affected the co-operation among the different national film industries, and co-productions rose again from the end of the 1980s onwards. In this sense, it is important to recognise the role played by several European initiatives designed to strengthen the industry and create a climate of closer co-operation: Eurimages and the MEDIA Programme in its subsequent editions.

Eurimages, created as a pan-European fund for direct investment in European multilateral co-productions, was established in 1989 within the Council of Europe in Strasbourg—in fact, it is the largest public-sector film financier. The fund comes from the subscription which member countries pay to join, according to their economic status. From the beginning, members included not only countries inside the European Union but also outside (such as Turkey, Poland, Bulgaria, the Czech Republic and Hungary).

Eurimages exists to facilitate new co-production networks, aiming in particular to bring companies from smaller film-producing countries into contact with larger producer countries in order to foster audiovisual production in small markets. Although it began with a required trilateral scheme, it has recently adopted the bilateral formula, which is more attractive to bigger producers (Wayne 2002, 13-14; Jäckel 2003, 76-80).[1]

The MEDIA Programme consists on a series of initiatives aimed to stimulate the European audio-visual sector, especially, cross-border projects. It started in 1987 and, after a three-year experimental period, has been renewed every five years. Its current edition (MEDIA Plus: 2001-2005) is equipped with a budget of 400 million euro and brings support both before and after production. It provides seed capital (co-financing) across three areas: training initiatives for audiovisual industry professionals, the development of production projects (feature films, television drama, documentaries, animation and new media), as well as the distribution and promotion of European audiovisual works (Jäckel 2003, 68-76; Wayne 2002, 13).[2]

Generally speaking, these programmes have favoured film production, distribution and exhibition in Europe at any level, although they have been also criticised for having "failed to address the structural inequalities and vested interests that have squeezed European cinema to the very margins of cultural life in Europe" (Wayne 2005, 14; see also Jäckel 2003, 88; Miller et al. 2005, 185-190).

Directly inspired in its philosophy, concept, objective, operations and terms by Eurimages and MEDIA programmes, the Conference of Iberian-American Cinematographic Authorities (CICA) approved in November 1997 a new funding scheme named Ibermedia. The first countries to sign were Spain, Mexico, Argentina, Brazil, Venezuela, Cuba, Portugal and Colombia. Its annual budget reached 3,7 millions of dollars.[3]

Spain has benefited from these programmes in different ways over the years, as Chart 2 shows. The maintenance of the current system of subsidies and pan-European and pan-Latin American training programmes will lead to a greater collaboration between producers from different countries. In this sense, due to its role as a cultural and economic 'bridge" across the Atlantic, Spain's role as a co-producing country will be reinforced (Otero 1999, 27; Chavarrías 2004, 12). Regarding the European case, it is also worthy to mention that the adoption of the euro has effectively pushed investments and co-productions even further,

---

[1] Between 1989 and 2004, Eurimages has invested 277,7 million of euros in 845 co-productions. For more information, see <http://www.coe.int/T/E/Cultural_Co-operation/Eurimages/>.

[2] The MEDIA Programme is currently in fourth installment: MEDIA Programme (1987-1990), MEDIA I (1991-1995), MEDIA II (1996-2000) and MEDIA Plus (2001-2005), finally extended to 2006. The new MEDIA Programme will start in 2007. For more information, see <http://europa.eu.int/comm/avpolicy/media/index_en.html>.

[3] Between 1998 and 2004, Ibermedia has invested in 160 co-productions. For more information see <http://www.programaibermedia.com/esp/htm/home.htm>.

reducing financial uncertainties inherent in floating exchange rates for foreign investors (Jäckel 2003, 65).

Spanish Legislation on International Co-Productions

Spain, like most European countries, has a long tradition of government intervention in the film industry. In relation to international co-productions, it is worthwhile knowing that the specific legal provisions from the recent Spanish Cinema Law (by Royal Decree 526/2002, dated 14th of June) were established in a similar way to other European countries. According to this law, films will be considered Spanish co-productions if they fulfill the following requirements: a) Be considered national in the co-producing countries, so that they can opt for the respective subsidies in each case; b) Be produced by creative staff, artistic and technical representatives of the involved countries; c) Have only one director; d) Participation will go from 20% to 80% for bilateral co-productions, and from 10% to 70% for multilateral co-productions: e) There could be at least one financial co-producer in case of a multilateral co-production, provided that the rules related to financial co-productions are respected.

As for the contributions, there will have to be considered the following criterion: 1) Technical and artistic contributions of each co-producer will have to be proportional to their own economic contribution. Cash contributions from the Spanish co-producer can not be over the 50% of the economical quantification of the contribution for work or services; 2) Each producer will have to be in charge of the expenses related to their national staff; 3) In order to assess the scriptwriter role with Spanish participation, it will have to be developed by people of this nationality, although joint script will be accepted in collaboration with scriptwriters of other nationalities; 4) The contribution of the minority Spanish co-producer regarding creative staff, artistic and technical representatives will have to consist of at least one member per each category; 5) Studio filming and post-production work will have to take place in the majority co-producing country, except self-script demand; in addition, the Spanish producer will have to be co-owner of the original negative film, although each co-producer has the right to have a film negative in his/her own version; 6) Finally, encashment and payments between residents and non-residents as a result of the co-production will be enforced by the legislation on foreign trade transactions.

Regarding financial co-productions, in the Spanish case, the following requirements are a must: a) They will have to be worth more than 1,803,036 euros; b) They will have to accept one or more minority participation of a financial sort, which the production cost of each of them will go from 10% to

25%; c) They will have to be considered national according to the legislation in the majority country; d) They will have to specify profit sharing procedures.

Finally, as for co-productions that take part in a TV network and if opting to incentives, the law states several requirements: at least 75% of the films produced by a TV network (either directly or through producing companies formed mainly by private capital TV networks, or made up of a group whose body consists of TV networks, or takes part mainly with companies linked to TV networks) have to be co-produced with an independent producing company.

In the case of TV co-productions, there are no generalised agreements between countries, but specific, depending on the sort of programme. It is more the case of greater mini-series, TV movies or cartoons. Over the last years, the number of co-production formulas continues to rise. They can be considered co-productions in its broad meaning, since, in most cases, it involves financial contribution in return for broadcasting rights.

A First Analysis of Spanish International Co-Productions

Throughout the last decade, and more specifically from 2000 to 2004, the Spanish film industry has grown substantially in terms of both production activity and new creative talent (Triana-Toribio 2003, 143-147; Everett 2005, 21). With regard to the production of Spanish films, a great capacity for innovation and the creation of original works was amply demonstrated. The growth trend of Spanish film production was constant in this period, from 56 feature-length films in 1995 to 125 in 2004 (see Chart 3). Likewise the number of international co-productions rose from 22 in 1995 to 41 in 2004, plainly indicating an expansion of the international scope of the Spanish film industry. Productions of all-Spanish films amounted to 982 while the number of co-productions was 348, for an annual average of 98 all-Spanish films and close to 35 co-productions. This represents an average percentage of 35.4% of co-production for the ten-year period (see Graph 1). In this sense, Spain is slightly under the Western European average percentage for the same period (see Chart 4).

The figures for the last five years are even more revealing of the rise of film production activity in Spain. Between 2000 and 2004, the total number of films produced accounted for were 585 while the number of co-productions was 214 (including 12 documentaries), for an annual average of 117 all-Spanish films and 43 co-productions. This means that an average 36.7% of Spanish film productions in the last five years are international co-productions, which is an indicator of the notable increase of this production strategy in this period.

As an overall picture, Chart 5 offers a first typology of international co-productions in Spain during this period—excluding documentaries—, from a triple perspective: the share of Spanish participation, the number of countries involved and the geographical origin of partners (by continents). This is the standard classification used by the public entity in charge of cinema in Spain—Instituto de la Cinematografía y Artes Audiovisuales (ICAA) in its annual report. From the first point of view, Spain participates more often as a minor partner (41.5%) than a major partner (36.1%), although there is no substantial difference between these two categories. In fact, the average share of Spanish participation for this period is as high as 41.1%, for an average budget of 3.5 million euros.

In addition, the favourite co-production strategy for Spanish co-producers is the bilateral agreement (63.0%) in contrast to the trilateral (26.7%) or multilateral (10.4%) deals. Finally, regarding the origin of partners, European countries participate in 61.8% of the total number of Spanish co-productions (46.5% wholly European partners), whereas Ibero-American countries are involved in 53.4% of Spanish co-productions (38.1% wholly Ibero-American partners). It is also interesting to point out that in 8.4% of co-productions, Spain acted as a bridge between European and Ibero-American countries.

These last observations must be completed by a detailed analysis of the most prolific co-producing countries in the case of Spain. As Chart 6 exhaustively illustrates, as many as 29 different countries have been involved in Spanish film co-productions in the last five years, which represents a significant variety of nationalities and cultures. Among them, there are 17 European countries (58.6%), 9 Latin American nations (31.0%), 2 North-American countries (6.8%) and Australia (3.4%). This same percentage is maintained at the top by the 10 most active co-producing countries (6 European and 4 Ibero-American). France and Argentina are the two main co-producing countries, participating respectively in 55 (27.0%) and 44 (21.6%) of all co-productions for this period. Whereas Argentina is our main partner in the bilateral category, France is the most active ally in trilateral and multilateral co-productions.

Some conclusions can be drawn from these first figures. Firstly, as it has been mentioned, Spanish co-producers are significantly involved in their international film productions, with an average share of more than 40%. This means that Spain is usually one of the main partners, if not the main one. Secondly, the bilateral agreement is the most frequent formula when dealing with co-productions due to its greater flexibility and its better creative and sometimes even financial advantages. In addition, Spanish co-productions reflect a tendency to work with their natural allies in Europe (especially the big five Western European countries) and Latin America (Spanish-speaking countries). It is also worth mentioning the small but interesting presence of some Eastern European countries (Hungary, Bulgaria and Romania) on a multilateral basis. On the other hand, the total absence of partners from Africa and Asia is quite significant especially given that Morocco, for instance, is one of the countries most represented in stories about immigrants, like *Said* (L. Soler 1999), *Tomándote/Tea for Two* (I. Gardela 2000) or *Poniente* (C. Gutiérrez, 2002).

Spanish International Co-Productions and European Cross-Border Films

Nevertheless, the "taxonomy" of the Spanish international co-productions would not be complete without a deeper analysis of their nature. Effectively, the previous data reflect only a sort of "formal" or external approach useful indeed for statistical purposes, but not sufficient for understanding the cultural and/or national identity issues. As Santaolalla explains with regard to the Spanish case,

> [T]he nature of co-productions varies a great deal. In some cases the degree of multinational collaboration is barely discernible in the final product; in others, the fusion of perspectives and practises is very noticeable (Santaolalla 2005, 6).

For this reason, some authors have offered an attempt to classify European international films from a broader perspective. This is the case of Mike Wayne in his book *The Politics of Contemporary European Cinema*. Discussing the relationship between national identity and international markets, Wayne offers a "model of the kinds of films which get made by a national cinema operating in an international environment" (Wayne 2002, 40), a quite convenient profile for international co-productions, as it is our case. This model is split in four categories drawn by "a mixture of economic and cultural factors" (Wayne 2002, 40): embedded films, disembedded films; cross-border films; and anti-national national films.[4]

The *embedded films* would be those which "are pitched primarily (although not exclusively) for the national market, either because of their budgets [...] or because the cultural material" (Wayne 2002, 40), i.e. the excessive "parochialism" of their plot. In other words, this category would be the typical "national cinema" mainly targeting the domestic market. Most of the Spanish films would fit into this category, from modest productions like *El Bola/Pellet* (A. Mañas, 2000) to big box-office successes like the three-installment of the *Torrente* saga (S. Segura, 1998, 2001, and 2005).

On the other hand, the *disembedded films* would be "those films which have the budget and the cultural potential to succeed in the American market"

---

[4] Wayne specifies that these are not mutually exclusively categories. In addition, he argues that although this classification is built largely around the case of the UK, it could be applied with modifications to the output of other European cinemas.

(Wayne 2002, 42). In the case of Spain, we could include in this category either some big-budgeted film productions shot in English like *Desafinado/Off Key* (M. Gómez Pereira, 2001) or *Los otros/The Others* (A. Amenábar, 2001) as well as medium-budgeted films produced by Filmax's brand Fantastic Factory, like *Darkness* (J. Balagueró, 2002).

In the third place, the *cross-border films* are defined by Wayne as "those films which travel in the international market outside America, particularly [...] the European market" (Wayne 2002, 45). According to this author, this category would include not only the art films, but also

> [...] those films which inscribe travel and a certain porosity of national identities within their narratives as a precondition of their co-productions which funded them and the broader European identities which they are exploring (Wayne 2002, 45).

Some recent examples of Spanish cross-border (art) films would be *Solas* (B. Zambrano, 2000), distributed in 13 European territories, *Lucía y el sexo/Sex and Lucia* (J. Medem, 2000), which travelled around 22 European countries, or any of the Almodovar's movies. *Hable con ella/Talk to Her* (2002), for instance, reached as much as 28 European territories.

Finally, Wayne adds a fourth category called *anti-national national films*, defined by "their critique of the myth of community which underpins national identity" (Wayne 2002, 45). Films like *Los lunes al sol/Mondays in the Sun* (F. León de Aranoa, 2002) or *Te doy mis ojos/Take My Eyes* (I. Bollaín, 2003) would be good examples.

It is also interesting to bring here the typology that Manuel Palacio specifically proposes for Spanish co-productions. In his article "Elogio postmoderno de las coproducciones" ("In Praise of Postmodern Co-Productions"), this author argues that the concept of "national cinema" or "national (film) identity" is derived not from the "official" nationality recognition of a film as by what he calls "a national look." This "national look" emerges from a unique universe, formed by a recurrent set of patterns involving characters, stories, images or any other specific cultural features (Palacio 1999, 222-223).

In this perspective, Palacio distinguishes three categories of co-productions. In the first place, the *strictly financial co-productions*, "where two or more productions companies join their financial resources to reach a better position in the international markets" (Palacio 1999, 231).[5] According to this author, no matter the mixed nationality of creative talents, cast and crew, there is a prevalent "national look" coming from the main partner. As examples, he

---

[5] From here on, all the quotes from Spanish texts are my translation.

mentions the majority of Almodóvar's films during the 1990s, structured as co-productions between El Deseo, his production company, and the French firm Ciby 2000. Secondly, Palacio points out the *international-flavour co-productions*, "which try to delete any kind of trace from the national point of view in search of an international style" (Palacio 1999, 231). As examples, he refers to some of the movies by Fernando Trueba, Vicente Aranda or Bigas Luna. Finally, this author includes the *multicultural or hybrid co-productions*, the "only" co-production in a proper sense, in his view, "not limited by an economic deal among partners, [but] reflecting the ambivalence in the construction of a collective identity [...] [as well as] breaking down the "official" stereotypes" (Palacio 1999, 232). Some of the most representative examples he comes across are two Spanish-Latin American co-productions: *Maité* (E. Olasagasti and C. Zabala, 1994), a Spanish-Cuban film, and *Martin (Hache)* (A. Aristaráin, 1997) co-produced by Spain and Argentina.

A New Typology of International Co-Productions

The two typologies described above are unquestionably useful to study the relationship between economic and cultural forces in co-productions—given that this combined perspective is the core topic when dealing with "national identity" and "cross-border" issues. Nevertheless, after analysing all the 202 Spanish international co-productions made between 2000 and 2004, I consider it necessary to re-adjust some of the categories offered by Wayne and Palacio. The advantage of this new typology is to offer a more precise image of the nature of international co-productions in the Spanish case, revealing the difficult balance between financial interests and multicultural ties.

As Chart 7 reflects, the main categories I am proposing here are: (inter)national co-productions, foreign financial co-productions, multicultural co-productions and internationally-oriented co-productions. Two prior considerations must be kept in mind. Firstly, these categories are mutually exclusive. Secondly, although the majority of the Spanish international co-productions analyzed fit well in one category or the other, I plainly admit that the criteria to classify some particular movies could be questioned.

The Spanish *(Inter)national Co-Productions* would be those films with a genuine national or local flavour (a strong taste of "Spanishness') in their story lines, characters and points of view, directed by a Spanish talent and with a significant Spanish participation (50% or higher). In addition, they are shot mainly on national soil. In this sense, these movies could be considered one-hundred percent Spanish, except for the fact that they have been formally set up as co-productions for economic reasons. This type would correspond to what Wayne calls *embedded films* and what Palacio denominates *strictly financial co-*

productions. Taking these features into account, we can identify 34 films (16.7% of co-productions) for the period of analysis. It is worthy to mention that, under this category, there is a clear unbalance in favour of European partners (25 movies) over Latin American ones (just 7 films), which reinforces the idea of economic motives, since our European neighbours are financially stronger allies.

Some significant examples of this kind of co-productions will be the following:

- *Los lunes al sol/Mondays in the Sun* (F. León de Aranoa, 2002) is set up as a trilateral co-production among Spain (80%), France (10%) and Italy (10%). With a comic-and-dramatic look, this movie tells the story of a group of unemployed people in a northern coastal city of Spain, with no ambition and facing a rootless future. Although the theme is quite universal, its approach to social criticism is based on typical Spanish references. Despite its design as an international co-production, there is no evidence of significant contributions from the other two countries, with the exception of finance and a French sound technician. The movie was entirely shot in Spain.
- *Torremolinos 73* (P. Berger, 2003), a Spanish (80%)-Danish (20%) co-production, is a dramatic comedy which narrates the love story between a door-to-door encyclopaedia salesman and his charming and faithful wife Carmen. Their ordinary lives will change when they accept an "indecent proposal": to shoot a home movie of their intimate life to be distributed in Scandinavia. This movie resembles the "españoladas" of the 1970s and it is fully Spanish in its cultural references. This movie was entirely shot in the South of Spain and its cast and crew is also Spanish.
- *El 7º día* (*The 7th Day*, C. Saura, 2004), directed by one of the best-known Spanish film directors, is a contemporary tragedy inspired by recent true events. For many years two families have been arguing over the boundaries of their properties located in the centre of the rural Spain. Much blood has already been shed over these quarrels and still revenge will be so brutal that it will leave everyone deeply shaken. Again, this one-hundred percent Spanish plot was set up as a bilateral co-production with France (80%-20% in favour of Spain), with a complete Spanish cast and crew, except for the director of photography, who was French.
- *Mar adentro/The Sea Inside* (A. Amenábar, 2004), one of the most successful Spanish films of the decade and winner of the Oscar® for Best Foreign Film, tells also a story based on real facts which had a great impact on Spanish public opinion. It is about a quadrapelegic who has spent almost thirty years lying in bed looked after by his family. The arrival of two

women changes his life: one tries to convince him that living is worthwhile, the other defends the opposite idea. At the end he will decide not to live anymore. Being a wholly Spanish story, the film was set up as a trilateral co-production among Spain (70%), France (20%) and Italy (10%). No key contributions from the last two countries appear either on the creative, artistic or technical side.

Other representative examples would be *El alquimista impaciente* (P. Ferreira, 2002), co-produced by Spain (80%) and Argentina (20%); *El embrujo de Shanghai* (F. Trueba, 2002), a trilateral adventure among Spain (70%), United Kingdom (20%) and France (10%); *Crimen ferpecto/Ferpect Crime* (A. de la Iglesia, 2004), a co-production between Spain (90%) and Italy (10%); or any of the movies produced by Morena Films, a Spanish production company specialised in crazy comedies set up as co-production with United Kingdom on a 80%-20% basis. Its most recent films are *Canícula* (A. García-Capelo, 2001), *Gente Pez* (J. Iglesias, 2001), *Peor imposible, ¿Qué puede fallar?* (J. Semprún and D. Blanco, 2002).

We could conclude that all these Spanish movies are international co-productions almost "by accident." Or as Santaolalla explains,

[...] no common denominators seem to emerge in terms of characters or storylines in [these] Spanish-European co-productions, except perhaps for the fact that a significant number of them have a wholly "Spanish" look [...]. It would appear that, in presenting essentially Spanish stories, the mere enactment of Spanishness in these films has the power of synecdochically "signifying" Europeaness [...] as opposed to, above all, Hollywood films (Santaolalla 2005, 6-7).

The *Foreign Financial Co-productions* would be exactly the opposite kind of movies to the previous ones. They are defined by being mainly "non-Spanish" films from the story, plot and character point of view as well as from the cultural background. In addition, they are directed by non-Spanish talents and have been shot in locations outside Spain. In addition to this, the Spanish participation is usually minimal (between 10 and 20% in most of the cases). Thus, other proper names for this category would be "Spanish Co-Financed Foreign Films" or "Foreign Films Partially Financed by Spain."

As it can be easily seen in Chart 7, more than 50% of international co-productions with Spanish participation, belongs in this category (105 out of 202). Being so, they do not fit in any of the classifications offered by Wayne or Palacio, which is also a significant fact. A closer look at these films would reveal that they are not properly "Spanish" from the "national identity" point of view, although some of them can resemble a certain "Spanishness" thanks to the inclusion of specific elements or references, a subplot, or one of the main or secondary characters.

In this case, there is no difference between Europe and Latin-America (48 and 47 co-productions respectively), which reflects somehow that Spain is considered by both to be a reliable financial partner.

Some significant examples of these financial European co-productions would be:

- *Mirka* (R. Benhadj, 2000), a drama co-produced by Italy (60%), France (30%) and Spain (10%), directed by an North African director, starring Karin Benhadj, Gérard Depardieu and Vanessa Redgrave. It was shot in Italy in Italian and with no involvement of Spanish talent.
- *The Old Man Who Read Love Stories* (R. De Heer, 2001) is a multilateral co-production among France (45%), Australia (25%), Spain (20%) and Netherlands (10%), directed by a Dutch director, starring Richard Dreyfuss and entirely shot in French Guiana. Despite of significant Spanish financial contribution, no Spanish key creative or artistic personnel can be found in this film.
- *Laissez-passer/Salvoconducto/Safe Conduct* (B. Tavernier, 2002), a period piece set in Paris during the Nazi occupation, is formally a French (90%)-Spanish (10%) co-production. It was entirely shot in France and has no Spanish key element whatsoever.
- *Io non ho paura* (G. Salvatores, 2003), based on the novel by Niccolò Ammanti, is a trilateral co-production among Italy (65%), Spain (20%) and United Kingdom (15%), shot in Italy and with Italian cast and crew except the Spanish actress Aitana Sánchez-Gijón in a leading role.

The same can be said from *Jet Set* (F. Onteniente, 2001), a French comedy co-produced with Spain on a 90%-10% split; *The Reckoning* (P. McGuigan, 2002), a period-piece drama set in the 14th Century England, co-produced with United Kingdom (72%) and Spain (28%); *Triple Agent* (E. Rohmer, 2004), also a period-piece multilaterally co-produced by five countries, where Spain's share is just 10%; or the last films of Ken Loach (*Bread and Roses*, 2001; *The Navigators*, 2002; *Sweet Sixteen*, 2003), Peter Greenaway (*The Tulse Luper Suitcases* trilogy, 2003-2005) and Nani Parenti (*Merry Christmas*, 2001; *Natale sul Nilo*, 2002).

Among the most representative financial Latin American co-productions we could mention:

- *Pantaleón y las visitadoras* (F. Lombardi, 2000), a Peruvian comedy co-produced with Spain (20%), tells the story of a military captain, a good man and husband, who has to deal with the sexual desire of his soldiers,

who are in the Amazonian forest. Spanish contribution is limited to the composer and director of photography.
- *El hijo de la novia* (J.J. Campanella, 2001), one of the most successful Argentinean films in Spain, was set up as a co-production between both countries on a 80%-20% basis in favour of Argentina. It tells a lovely story of family reunion during the Argentinean economic crisis of the 2000s. The movie was shot in Argentina with local talent and crew (although some actors are based in Spain). Only the composer was Spanish (Ángel Illarramendi). The same basic structure, with a bigger Spanish contribution (54%), was set for Campanella's next film *Luna de Avellaneda* (2004).
- *Kamchatka* (M. Piñeyro, 2002) keeps many similarities with the previous one. It was also a very successful film at the Spanish box-office. Set up as a Argentinean-Spanish co-production (50/50 split) directed by a Uruguayan director, it tells a family story in a very specific historical background the military dictatorship from mid 1970s onwards, when thousands of people were persecuted and kidnapped. The composer and the director of photography are the only Spanish talents involved. The movie was also shot in Argentina.
- *Whisky* (P. Stoll and J.P. Rebella, 2004), a Uruguayan social comedy co-produced with Spain (20%), tells the story of the owner of a modest hosiery factory and his wife, who is his trusted employee. Their monotone life is suddenly threatened by the visit of a relative. Halfway between absurdity and melancholy, this film tries to subtly portray how the awkwardness and small misfortunes of these three people, so different from each other, gradually come to light as they try to cover up their resentments.

Other illustrative movies from this category would be the Argentinean (78%)-Spanish (22%) co-production *Plata quemada* (M. Piñeyro, 2000); *El crimen del Padre Amaro/The Crime of Padre Amaro* (C. Carrera, 2002), co-produced with Mexico (Spanish share of 20%); the trilateral co-production *El último tren* (D. Arsuaga, 2002), among Argentina (52%), Uruguay (20%) and Spain (28%); and the comedy *Bombón, el perro* (C. Sorín, 2004), an Argentinean (80%)-Spanish (20%) co-production.

Connected to these last examples—although it could be also applied to the financial Spanish-European co-productions—, the following comment by Santaolalla is quite illustrative.

> [D]espite the frequent appeals to historic debt, Spanish-Spanish American co-productions are perhaps inevitably above all guided by economic considerations. [...] Sometimes the Spanish American element is little more than an exotic

flourish [...]. On other occasions, however, the collaboration leaves a mark on the very fabric of the film, making it a more complex, dialogical text (Santaolalla 2005, 8-9).

In the third place, the Spanish *Multicultural Co-Productions* would represent the quintessential spirit of co-productions, because they are not merely a product strictly based on financial contribution but also on a real cultural exchange. Here, the story, plot and characters reflect the hybrid nature of multiple idiosyncrasies linking together in a more natural way, as in the case of Spain, the relationship with its European neighbours or its deeper resemblance with Spanish-America. This category would coincide exactly with the one proposed by Palacio as *multicultural or hybrid co-productions* and also correspond to the *cross-border films* description offered by Wayne. Apart from that, the Spanish participation varies from 30% to 60%.

As Chart 7 reveals, as much as 25.7% of Spanish international co-productions during these last five years would fit into this category. Looking at the origin of our partners, it seems that we find it easier to develop multicultural stories with our Latin American relatives (25 films) than with our European neighbours (19 films).

- *El espinazo del diablo/The Devil's Backbone* (G. del Toro, 2001), a Spanish (54%)-Mexican (46%) co-production, directed by an internationally-known Mexican director and produced by Almodóvar, tells a fantastic story about some mysteries surrounding an orphanage during the Spanish Civil War. The movie was shot in Spain with Spanish crew and talent and the presence of a very well-known Argentinean actor, Federico Luppi. This film offers a multicultural or hybrid look, since it can be considered "clever re-writing of the quintessential 20th century Spanish historical event: the Civil War" (Santaolalla 2005, 9) from a Mexican perspective. Since Luppi's character represented Hispanic Americanness, he works as a metaphor for Mexico and its role in the Spanish War. (Santaolalla 2005, 9-10)
- *Lugares comunes/Common Places* (A. Aristaráin, 2002) was a successful and critically acclaimed Spanish (60%)-Argentinean (40%) co-production starring Federico Luppi and Mercedes Sampietro. It deals with a story about a mature couple, wonderfully in love with each other. But their calm, reflective world is deeply affected when the husband receives official notification of his compulsory early retirement without any previous warning. Apart from being shot in both countries and having a mixed cast and crew, this film shows quite clearly some cultural subplots involving Argentina and Spain, represented respectively by husband and wife.

- *Seres queridos* (T. Pelegrí and D. Harari, 2004) is a funny love story between a Jew and a Palestinian, very much in line with *Guess Who's Come to Dinner?* and *Meet the Parents*. It was designed as a multicultural co-production involving four countries: Spain (57%), United Kingdom (23%), Argentina (10%) and Portugal (10%). Directed by two filmmakers from Spain and United Kingdom, this film is a real culturally hybrid story.

Other movies we could include here are *Tinta roja* (F. Lombardi, 2001), co-produced by Spain (61%) and Peru (39%); *Nueces para el amor* (A. Lecchi, 2001), an Argentinean (54%)-Spanish (46%) initiative; *Pata negra* (L. Oliveros, 2001), a comedy co-produced by Spain (80%) and Cuba (20%); and *Roma* (A. Aristaráin, 2004), a Spanish (80%)-Argentinean (20%) co-production.

Among the multicultural co-productions with Europe, we could include some illustrative films like:

- *Yoyes* (H. Taberna, 2000), a trilateral co-production among Spain (70%), France (20%) and Italy (10%), is based on a real story of a female ETA member. The very topic of the movie—Basque terrorism—acts as a dramatic link between two neighbour countries with similar cultural roots. As a co-production, this film is quite well balanced, especially thanks to the French contribution. In addition, the movie was shot in actual Spanish and French places.
- *Una casa de locos/L'Auberge espagnole/Europudding* (C. Klapisch, 2002) could be the quintessence example of multicultural co-production, according to its English title. Designed as a French (80%)-Spanish (20%) co-production and directed by a French filmmaker, it tells the story of a young Parisian who goes to Barcelona for the last year of his university studies in Economics and shares a flat with other six exchange students, each from a different European country. The movie, with cast and crew from different countries, was shot in Barcelona. It is noteworthy that there are as many as seven different languages spoken in the film. Somehow, that small flat is a metaphor for the whole Europe.
- *El misterio Galíndez/The Galindez File* (G. Herrero, 2003), starring Harvey Keitel, Saffron Burrows and Eduard Fernández, is based on the novel done by the Spanish writer Manuel Vázquez Montalbán. The story begins when an American researcher arrives in Spain to work on her doctoral thesis about a Basque exiled in the United States after the Civil War, who was kidnapped and disappeared in strange circumstances. Her research soon leaves the academic field and goes deeper into the political and criminal sphere, and so her life is in danger. This thriller was set up as multilateral co-production involving as many as six countries, with a significant Spanish

contribution (50%). The movie is in English and Spanish and was shot in three different countries.
- *Un día sin fin/È già ieri* (G. Manfredonia, 2004) is a Spanish (50%)-Italian (28%)-British (22%) remake of the American blockbuster *Groundhog Day* (H. Ramis, 1993). In this case, a famous Italian television journalist is sent to the Canary Islands to cover how a colony of storks is settling on the summit of the Teide Volcano. A biologist from the Canary Islands is there to welcome him and help him. From that point, every day will be an exact copy of the one before. The movie was directed by an Italian, shot in the Canary Islands and spoken in both languages (Spanish and Italian).

Other examples could be *La balsa de piedra / The Stone Raft* (G. Sluizer, 2002), co-produced by Netherlands (48%), Spain (34%) and Portugal (18%); and *Imagining Argentina* (C. Hampton, 2004), a British (53%)-Spanish (47%) co-production set in Argentina.

Finally, the Spanish *Internationally-Oriented Co-Productions* would be those films primarily designed for the international marketplace. According to this aim, they are shot in the English language and involve an international cast and crew. Despite its international appeal, their "Spanish presence" is ensured by a significant contribution: either the director is a Spaniard in most of the cases, or the financial stake Spain keeps represents usually more than 50% of the share. The nature of these co-productions is more economic than cultural, so the natural partners are mainly English-speaking countries that are able to share costs and grosses (market.) Under these terms, Latin-America is not a viable option.

Among the examples of this kind of movies we could mention:

- *Sabotaje/Sabotage!* (Ibarretxe Brothers, 2000), a trilateral co-production among Spain (52%), France (28%) and United Kingdom (20%), starring David Suchet, Stephen Fry and Dominque Pinon, was shot in English in Spain, with an international cast and mixed crew. It offers a peculiar portrait of the preliminaries of Waterloo battle, where Bonaparte and Wellington are rivals not only involving military strategies but also regarding the love of Lady Edwina, a double agent and also an expert strategist. The movie had a very poor performance at the domestic box-office. Apart from Spain, it has been only released in France.
- *Desafinado/Off Key* (M. Gómez Pereira, 2001) was an expensive Spanish (70%)-British (20%)-Italian (10%) co-production, shot in Spain and France. This English-spoken film, starring Joe Mategna, Danny Aiello and George Hamilton, tells the story of a trio of opera singers reunited by a wedding ten

years after their stormy breakup. Despite its high commercial appeal, it was only released in three European countries, including Spain.
- *Sin retorno/No Turning Back* (J. Montejo and J. Nebot, 2002) was set as a Spanish (60%)-US (40%) co-production shot entirely in the US as an independent American movie. Its plot deals with the difficult situation of Hispanic immigrants in the United States. The movie was co-directed by a Spaniard and a Honduran.
- *Mi vida sin mí/My Life Without Me* (I. Coixet, 2004), co-produced by Spain (68%) by El Deseo, Almodóvar's production company, and Canada (32%), follows the usual co-producing formula of Isabel Coixet's movies, one of the internationally best-known Spanish women directors. This drama tells the story of a young mother with a sad and hopeless life. Her grey existence changes completely when she discovers she has cancer. Paradoxically, she will find out also the appetite of life. The movie was shot in British Columbia (Canada) in the English language with international cast.

Other interesting examples would be *Punto de mira/One of the Hollywood Ten* (K. Francis, 2001), a Spanish (68%)-British (32%) co-production despite its American theme; *Manjar de amor/Food of love* (V. Pons, 2002), co-produced by Spain (80%) and Germany (20%); and *Romasanta* (F. Plaza, 2004), a Spanish (78%)-British co-production starring Julian Sands and Elsa Pataky.

With this new typology in mind, there are some interesting conclusions to be drawn (see Graph 2). First of all, the vast majority of all the movies considered international co-productions in Spain (as much as 74.2%) are strictly financial co-productions, with little, if any, multicultural implications. From some perspectives, they could be defined as "false" or merely "formal" co-productions, with no creative or cultural exchange at all. Only 25.3% of Spanish international co-productions are multicultural in essence. Therefore, it must be underlined the prevalence of economic reasons over cultural motivations.

Secondly, Spain looks for co-producing partners with different criteria depending on the nature of the co-production itself. When prioritizing strictly financial issues regarding (inter)national, foreign-financed and internationally-oriented co-productions, European and North American countries are preferred to Latin American ones. Nevertheless, when it comes to multicultural exchange from the Spanish perspective, Latin America prevails over Europe. As much as half of the Spanish multicultural co-productions have been set up with Latin American countries.

Finally, Spain acts as a "bridge" between Europe and Latin America in very few cases within each category. This is especially significant in the multicultural category, where only six movies have been co-produced by Spain and countries from Europe and Latin America.

In conclusion, I would insist on the fact that this new typology reflects more exactly the inner nature of international co-productions in the Spanish case, differentiating in each category the predominance of economic or cultural interests that lie behind an agreed formula of co-operation. Of course, in my view, this proposed classification could be also applied to other national cases in Europe.

Spanish International Co-Productions at the Domestic and European Marketplaces

This study would not be complete without a comment on the commercial performance of these international co-productions. Chart 8 shows the top 25 Spanish international co-productions at the domestic box-office, including not only grosses and admissions figures, but also other variables such as countries involved, share of Spanish contribution, nature according to our proposed typology, genre, language, origin of cast and crew, and finally, country of shooting.

A careful look at this chart reveals some interesting facts. To begin with, the majority of these more successful films are (inter)national co-productions (10 out of 25), followed by multicultural (8) and foreign financial (6) co-productions. If we compare these figures to the total number of films in each category, we would also obtain very revealing percentages: 29.4% (inter)national co-productions are among the most successful, together with 15.3% of multicultural films and 4.7% of foreign co-financed movies. Curiously enough, the lower level of performance at the box-office corresponds to the most frequent type of co-production.

Another revealing fact is that, taking into account only the top foreign financial and multicultural co-productions, as much as 9 are co-produced with Latin American countries and only 5 with European partners. In other words, Spanish audiences seem to feel more enthusiastic about multicultural Spanish-Latin American co-productions, surely because of their cultural identification.

As we continue to look at the chart, we notice the performance of those same movies at the European marketplace.[6] As Chart 9 shows, the majority of these top international co-productions (16 out of 20) has been released in more than

---

[6] It is important to reiterate that this ranking does not include all the Spanish international co-productions, but only those 25 ones that were on the top at the domestic box-office. In this sense, it must be kept in mind that there are other successful co-productions with Spanish contribution at the European marketplace, like the K. Loach film *Bread and Roses* (2001), which got 653,226 admissions outside Spain and B. Tavernier's *Laissez-passer/Safeconduct* (2002), which achieved 427,560 admissions in Europe (Spain excluded).

one European territory (excluding Spain), and a small group of them (4 films) has even achieved more than 10 countries. It is difficult to establish a regular pattern out of these titles. Firstly, it is not a coincidence that 4 out of the top 10 Spanish international co-productions by number of admissions in Europe (excluding Spain) are precisely multicultural ones. Among them, two stand out among the rest: *L'Auberge espagnole/Una casa de locos/Europudding* (2002), a French-Spanish comedy, and *Los Reyes Magos/The Three Wise Men* (2003), an animated movie set up also as a Spanish-French co-production.

Secondly, it is quite paradoxical that 3 out of the 10 more successful Spanish co-productions in Europe are (inter)national titles, which mean that even very local stories and characters manage to travel and conquer audiences all over Europe, whether if they are comedies or dramas. Movies like *Mar adentro/ The Sea Inside* (2002), *Los lunes al sol/Mondays in the Sun* (2002) or *Crimen ferpecto/Ferpect Crime* (2004) are good examples of that.

This previous point can be contrasted with another apparent paradox. This ranking of the top 25 international co-productions in Spain only includes 2 films shot in English, *My Life Without Me* (2003) and *The Old Man Who Read Love Stories* (2001), neither of which was a commercial success despite their international appeal, and one with a mix of languages, *L'Auberge espagnole* (2002), which was much more successful.

Finally, it is interesting to note the five Spanish international co-productions that travelled the most in Europe (which does not mean necessarily the most viewed in all the cases). Perhaps it is not a coincidence that number one is *L'Auberge espagnole/Una casa de locos/Europudding* (2002), an example of multicultural co-production, very "European" in its plot and characters, which was released in 22 territories including Iceland, Estonia, Slovakia and Turkey, in addition to the USA and Canada. Probably it is not a surprise that a movie like *My Life Without Me* (2003) had reached 16 territories (plus Canada). Quite the contrary, as we have mentioned before, it is significant that a "local" film like *Los lunes al sol/Mondays in the Sun* (2002) was distributed also in 16 European countries. And it is a revealing fact that the other two movies able to travel widely around Europe (10 territories) are two Spanish-Latin-American co-productions, one reasonably successful commercially, *El hijo de la novia* (2001), and one with a modest performance, *El crimen del Padre Amaro* (2002). Also among the most broadly distributed movies is another Spanish-Latin American co-production, *Lista de espera* (2000), released in 9 countries but achieving higher number of viewers than the previous two. These last examples illustrate, in my view, one of the aspects of the potential role of Spain as a "bridge" between Europe and Latin America, in the sense that its participation as co-producer, even on a financial basis only, facilitates the distribution of genuinely Latin American stories through a significant number of European territories.

In sum, Chart 9 illustrates that no matter what the real nature of the international co-production (financial, multicultural or a mix of the two), the very fact of being produced through transnational partnerships facilitates the commercial exploitation of the movie in a significant number of territories.

Conclusions: More Commercial Need than Common Culture

The analysis of these Spanish international co-productions during this five-year period (2000-04), broken down into the four categories described above, exemplifies the real nature of co-productions in some European countries. As we mentioned at the very beginning, international co-productions in our continent have been often promoted as an ideal formula to achieve the difficult balance between "national identity" and "crossing-border" culture. Nevertheless, at least in the Spanish case, the more frequent motivation to set up a co-production project has been economic or financial rather than multicultural. Effectively, almost 75% of Spanish international co-productions during the last five years have been designed on a strictly financial basis, without demanding necessarily a creative or cultural exchange. Only the remaining 25% can be considered multicultural co-productions in the proper sense of the term. In addition, the average Spanish contribution accounts for more than 40%, which implies a significant presence and/or control in most of the cases. For that very reason also, the bilateral agreement is the preferred formula.

It seems that this reality can be also extrapolated to Europe. Some years ago, Ian Christie suggested that the unity to which the European film industries aspire should be a strategic one based upon "commercial need" rather than a "common culture" (qtd. in Hill 1998, 67; Jäckel 2003, 65). In light of the analysis of Spanish international co-productions in recent times, we can conclude that this is the case.

In addition, Spain has co-produced with a great number of countries, mostly from Europe and Latin America, with France and Argentina being our most prolific partners. Nevertheless, it can be useful to distinguish our favourite co-production allies based on the nature of the co-production itself. The financially-based co-productions—three of the four categories mentioned above—are supported by European and North American countries. On the contrary, Latin American nations are our natural partners when it comes to multicultural co-productions. In any case, it seems that Spain should be a more active bridge between Europe and Latin America, taking advantage of its geopolitical history and strategic position (Santaolalla 2005, 2; Chavarrías 2004, 12), and of its shared cultural traditions across both continents. In this sense, the number of

Spanish co-productions involving Latin American and European countries could proportionally increase.

Apart from statistical reasons, this variety of countries sharing cinematographic projects illustrates how the "international co-production phenomenon" has enormous potential in promoting cross-cultural references as well as in addressing questions of "national identity" and "border crossings" in films. Nevertheless, as the Spanish case reflects, if economic motivations are often more important than cultural ones, what does this fact say about the role of European cinema in the construction of a European identity? The answer is necessarily inconclusive. On one hand, the very concept of "European identity" in cinema still remains controversial and is far from consensus (Eleftheriotis 2001, 47-48; Wayne 2002, 33-45; Everett 2005, 7-14; Elsaesser 2005, 489-491). On the other, it is necessary to differentiate the point of view in using the term "cross-border film." From a multicultural perspective, the vast majority of the international co-productions analyzed could be hardly defined as "cross-border" or transnational films. Effectively, as it has been described before, we could discuss the "Frenchness" and/or "Italianness" of *Los lunes al sol/Mondays in the Sun* (a Spanish-French-Italian co-production); or about the "Spanishness" of a film like *Mirka* (a Italian-French-Spanish co-production). Nevertheless, thanks to the co-production formula, many of these films have really managed to cross national borders and travel around Europe and Latin America, achieving not only a broader market but also making at least a modest cultural impact on cinemagoers, as Chart 9 reflects.

To sum up, the Spanish case illustrates the need to redefine the concept of "international co-production." As shown, this notion nowadays has acquired a very flexible and sometimes ambiguous meaning, which cannot be reduced to a single dimension whether it is for financial or multicultural reasons. In fact, as we indicated at the beginning quoting Miller et al., co-productions are transforming the audiovisual industries from a social and geographical point of view, creating meeting points between two opposite forces: the commercial politics based on free trade (an absence of borders) and the cultural movements aimed to reaffirm national identities defining geographical borders (Miller et al. 2005, 209).

Despite some of their paradoxes, co-productions will remain an important strategy for the survival of European cinema, combining all the different possibilities. As Eleftheriotis points out,

> In the new millennium the challenge that confronts directors, writers, and producers, as well as national and transnational policy makers, is the financial survival of European cinema through the establishment and development of transnational partnerships and the production of films that can effectively cross cultural and national borders (Eleftheriotis 2005, 48-49).

The challenge, as this same author explains, is how to preserve unity while respecting and encouraging diversity (Eleftheriotis 2005, 49). Among the different categories of Spanish international co-productions proposed above, the multicultural ones succeed in approaching this challenge. Nevertheless we should not ignore the benefits of any other given formula. As we have seen in the case of Spain, even the strictly financial co-productions are helping to establish a network among European countries that will encourage future developments for a European cinema that crosses many borders.

Acknowledgements

I would like to thank Rubén Ortega and Javier Hernáez for helping me to collect and organize all the data. I must also thank Matthew Beaven for revising and correcting my written English. Finally, I am deeply grateful to Isabel Santaolalla for providing me with a copy of her unpublished essay.

Chart 1: Co-Production Treaties Signed by Spain

EUROPE		AMERICAS		AFRICA
European Union	Rest of Europe	Latin America	North America	North Africa
Germany Austria France Italy Portugal	Bulgaria Czech Republic Slovakia Russia	Argentina Brazil Cuba Chile Mexico Peru Puerto Rico Venezuela	Canada	Morocco Tunisia

Source: Ecija (2000)

SPANISH CO-PRODUCTIONS

Chart 2: Projects with Spanish Participation Funded by EURIMAGES and IBERMEDIA.

	95	96	97	98	99	00	01	02	03	04	Total
Eurimages		13	13	16	9	10	7	5	8	9	90
Ibermedia				15	15	23	26	26	30	8	143

Source: ICAA, Eurimages, Ibermedia.

Chart 3: Evolution of Film Production in Spain (1995-2004)

YEAR	95	96	97	98	99	00	01	02	03	04	Total 95-04	Total 00-04	Average 95-04	Average 00-04
Total Film Prod.	6	92	73	79	97	103	117	114	126	125	982	585	98.2	117.0
Wholly Spanish	4	66	50	52	61	69	77	57	84	84	634	371	63.4	74.2
Inter. Co-Prod.	2	26	23	27	36	34	40	57	42	41	348	214	34.8	42.8

Source: ICAA

CHAPTER FIVE

Graph 1: Percentage of International Co-Productions in Spain (1995-2004)

YEAR	95	96	97	98	99	00	01	02	03	04	Average 95-04	Average 00-04
Wholly Spanish	60.7	71.7	68.5	65.8	62.9	67.0	65.8	50.0	66.7	67.2	64.6	63.3
Inter. Co-Prod.	39.3	28.3	31.5	34.2	37.1	33.0	34.2	50.0	33.3	32.8	35.4	36.7

Source: ICAA

Chart 4: Evolution of Co-Productions in Western Europe (2000-2004)

YEAR		95	96	97	98	99	00	01	02	03	04	Total	%	Average 00-04
France	Total	97	104	125	148	181	171	204	200	212	203	1,645	100	164.5
	100% national	63	74	86	102	115	111	126	106	105	130	1,018	61.9	101.8
	Co-productions	66	57	72	78	66	60	78	94	107	73	751	45.7	75.1
UK	Total	81	127	115	91	103	90	83	84	88	75	937	100	93.7
	100% national	40	77	74	65	71	51	52	41	40	28	539	57.5	53.9

SPANISH CO-PRODUCTIONS

Germany	Co-productions	41	50	41	26	31	39	31	43	48	47	397	42.4	39.7
	Total	63	64	61	50	88	94	107	117	107	121	872	100	87.2
	100% national	37	42	47	39	44	47	57	39	54	60	466	53.4	46.6
Italy	Co-productions	26	22	14	11	44	47	50	78	53	61	406	46.6	40.6
	Total	75	99	87	92	108	103	103	130	117	138	1,052	100	105.2
	100% national	60	77	71	79	92	87	71	97	97	97	828	78.7	82.8
Spain	Co-productions	15	22	16	13	16	16	32	33	20	41	224	21.3	22.4
	Total	56	92	73	79	97	103	117	114	126	125	982	100	98.2
	100% national	34	66	50	52	61	69	77	57	84	84	634	64.6	63.4
	Co-productions	22	26	23	27	36	34	40	57	42	41	348	35.4	34.8
Big Five	Total No. Films	309	422	400	410	489	467	507	528	543	541	4,616	100	461.6
	Total No. 100% national	197	294	281	298	339	318	326	301	326	339	3,019	65.4	301.9
	Total No. Co-productions	144	155	152	144	149	149	181	227	217	202	1,720	37.3	172.0

Source: Own elaboration on EAO data. Figures from Spain has been corrected according to ICAA data.

CHAPTER FIVE

Chart 5: Typology of International Co-Productions in Spain

YEAR		00	01	02	03	04	Total	%	Average 00-04	%
	Total Number	31	39	55	40	37	202	100	40.4	100
By Percentage	Minor (<50%)	15	14	20	13	22	84	41.58	16.8	8.32
	Major (>50%)	8	18	20	14	13	73	36.14	14.6	7.23
	Balanced (all 50%)	2	1	1	0	2	6	2.97	1.2	0.59
	Financial	6	6	14	13	0	39	19.31	7.8	3.86
By No. of Partners	Bi-lateral	19	26	39	23	20	127	62.87	25.4	12.57
	Tri-lateral	10	9	14	11	10	54	26.73	10.8	5.35
	Multilateral	2	4	2	6	7	21	10.40	4.2	2.08
By Continents	With Latin America	11	17	23	13	13	77	38.12	15.4	7.62
	With Latin America & Others	13	0	1	0	0	14	6.93	2.8	1.39
	With Latin America & Europe	3	5	4	3	2	17	8.42	3.4	1.68
	With Europe	13	15	26	21	19	94	46.53	18.8	9.31

SPANISH CO-PRODUCTIONS

With Europe & Others	1	1	0	2	3	7	3.47	1.4	0.69
With Others	2	1	1	1	0	5	2.48	1.0	0.50
Total with Latin America	27	22	28	16	15	108	53.47	21.6	10.69
Total with Europe	29	20	31	24	21	125	61.88	25.0	12.38
Total with Others	16	2	2	3	3	26	12.87	5.2	2.57
Average Spanish Percentage	39.5	43.8	41.5	38.1	42.8			41.1	
Average Budget	3.82	3.45	3.35	3.28	3.51			3.48	

Source: Own elaboration on ICAA data. Documentaries excluded

Chart 6: Co-Producing Countries with Spain (2000-2004)

		Bi-	Tri-	Multi-	Total	%	Average 00-04
1	France	21	21	13	55	27.09%	11.0
2	Argentina	33	9	2	44	21.67%	8.8
3	Italy	11	21	9	41	20.20%	8.2
4	UK	10	15	7	32	15.76%	6.4
5	Mexico	16	4	1	21	10.34%	4.2
6	Portugal	6	5	6	17	8.37%	3.4
7	Cuba	10	0	6	16	7.88%	3.2
8	Chile	5	4	1	10	4.93%	2.0
9	Germany	1	7	2	10	4.93%	2.0
10	Belgium	0	4	3	7	3.45%	1.4
11	Canada	2	3	0	5	2.46%	1.0
12	USA	3	2	0	5	2.46%	1.0
13	Venezuela	2	3	0	5	2.46%	1.0
14	Netherlands	0	1	3	4	1.97%	0.8
15	Uruguay	1	2	1	4	1.97%	0.8
16	Brazil	0	1	2	3	1.48%	0.6
17	Greece	1	1	1	3	1.48%	0.6
18	Peru	2	0	1	3	1.48%	0.6
19	Switzerland	0	2	1	3	1.48%	0.6
20	Colombia	0	2	0	2	0.99%	0.4
21	Denmark	1	0	1	2	0.99%	0.4
22	Hungary	0	0	2	2	0.99%	0.4
23	Luxembourg	0	0	2	2	0.99%	0.4
24	Russia	0	0	2	2	0.99%	0.4
25	Andorra	1	0	0	1	0.49%	0.2
26	Australia	0	0	1	1	0.49%	0.2
27	Bulgaria	0	0	1	1	0.49%	0.2
28	Ireland	0	0	1	1	0.49%	0.2
29	Romania	0	0	1	1	0.49%	0.2

Source: Own elaboration on ICAA data. Documentaries excluded

Chart 7: New Typology of Spanish Co-Productions (2000-2004)

	YEAR	00	01	02	03	04	Total	%	Average 00-04	%
	Total Number	31	39	55	40	37	202	100.00%	40.4	100.00%
(Inter)National	With Europe	1	5	7	5	7	25	12.38%	5.0	2.48%
	With Ibero-America	2	0	4	1	0	7	3.47%	1.4	0.69%
	With Both	0	1	1	0	0	2	0.99%	0.5	0.25%
	Total	3	6	12	6	7	34	16.83%	6.8	3.37%
Foreign Financial	With Europe	9	4	13	11	11	48	23.76%	9.6	4.75%
	With Ibero-America	5	11	11	11	9	47	23.27%	9.4	4.65%
	With Both	1	2	1	1	1	6	2.97%	1.2	0.59%
	With Ibero-America & Others	0	0	1	0	0	1	0.50%	0.2	0.10%
	With Europe & Others	0	1	0	2	0	3	1.49%	0.6	0.30%
	Total	15	18	26	25	21	105	51.98%	21.0	10.40%
Multicultural	With Europe	5	3	4	4	3	19	9.41%	3.8	1.88%
	With Ibero-America	4	10	6	1	4	25	12.38%	5.0	2.48%
	With Both	2	2	1	0	1	6	2.97%	1.2	0.59%
	With Ibero-America & Others	1	0	0	0	0	1	0.50%	0.2	0.10%
	With Europe & Others	0	0	0	0	1	1	0.50%	0.2	0.10%
	Total	12	15	11	5	9	52	25.74%	10.4	5.15%
Internationally-Oriented	With Europe	1	2	1	1	1	6	2.97%	1.2	0.59%
	With North America	2	1	1	1	0	5	2.48%	1.0	0.50%
	Total	3	3	2	2	1	11	5.45%	2.2	1.09%

Source: Own elaboration on ICAA data

CHAPTER FIVE

Graph 2: New Typology of Spanish Co-Productions ('00-'04): Percentage by Categories

(Inter)National	16.83%
Foreign Financial	51.98%
Multicultural	25.74%
Internationally-Oriented	5.45%
Total	100.00%

Source: Own elaboration on ICAA data.

Chart 8: Top 25 Spanish International Co-Productions at the Domestic Box Office (2000-2004)

	Original Title	Director	Year	B.O.	Admissions	Countries	Spanish %	Nature
1	Mar adentro	A. Amenábar	2004	19,824,399	4,096,373	ES+FR+IT	70%	(Inter)National
2	Los lunes al sol	F. León de Aranoa	2002	9,772,064	2,103,094	ES+FR+IT	80%	(Inter)National
3	Juana la Loca	V. Aranda	2001	8,895,180	2,067,004	ES+IT+PT	70%	(Inter)National
4	El hijo de la novia	J.J. Campanella	2001	7,230,415	1,574,492	ES+ARG	20%	Financial
5	Carmen	V. Aranda	2003	6,398,307	1,380,728	ES+IT+UK	70%	Multicultural
6	Crimen ferpecto	A. de la Iglesia	2004	4,250,445	860,622	ES+IT	90%	(Inter)National
7	El espinazo del diablo	G. del Toro	2001	3,006,235	712,178	ES+MEX	54%	Multicultural
8	Kamchatka	M. Piñeyro	2002	2,983,346	628,013	ES+ARG	50%	Financial
9	Sin noticias de Dios	A. Díaz Yanes	2001	2,747,352	609,409	ES+FR+IT	70%	Multicultural
10	My Life Without Me	I. Coixet	2003	2,637,945	562,364	ES+CAN	68%	Internationally-oriented
11	Los Reyes Magos	A. Navarro	2003	2,318,961	491,737	ES+FR	50%	Multicultural
12	Gente pez	J. Iglesias	2001	2,278,425	567,956	ES+UK	80%	(Inter)National
13	Lugares comunes	A. Aristaráin	2002	1,987,053	424,756	ES+ARG	60%	Multicultural

SPANISH CO-PRODUCTIONS

14	Torremolinos 73	P. Berger	2003	1,819,410	389,307	ES+DK	80%	(Inter)National
15	La Luna de Avellaneda	J.J. Campanella	2004	1,735,176	345,609	ES+ARG	54%	Financial
16	El viaje de Carol	I. Uribe	2002	1,662,267	374,543	ES+PT	90%	(Inter)National
17	Nos miran	N. López Amado	2002	1,614,960	360,103	ES+IT	90%	(Inter)National
18	Lista de espera	J.C. Tabio	2000	1,596,208	379,999	ES+CU+FR+MEX	50%	Financial
19	L'Auberge espagnole	C. Klapisch	2002	1,438,167	308,354	FR+ES	20%	Multicultural
20	El crimen del Padre Amaro	C. Carrera	2002	1,412,424	318,834	MEX+ES	20%	Financial
21	El embrujo de Shanghai	F. Trueba	2002	1,398,874	302,780	ES+FR+UK	70%	(Inter)National
22	The Old Man Who Read Love Stories	R. de Heer	2001	1,344,253	296,912	FR+ES+AUS+NL	20%	Financial
23	Almejas y mejillones	M. Carnevale	2000	1,332,890	332,130	ES+ARG	50%	Multicultural
24	Roma	A. Aristaráin	2004	1,231,850	250,583	ES+ARG	80%	Multicultural
25	Incautos	M. Bardem	2004	1,152,059	238,362	ES+FR	75%	(Inter)National

	Genre	Language	Cast	Crew	Shot at	Production Co.	Distribution Co.
1	Drama	Spanish	Spanish	Spanish	Spain	Sociedad general de cine; Himenoptero	
2	Drama	Spanish	Spanish	Spanish	Spain	Elías Querejeta P.C.; Mediaproducción; Televisión de Galicia	
3	Period Drama	Spanish	Mixed	Spanish	Spain	Enrique Cerezo S.A; Pedro Costa S.A	Warner Sogefilms
4	Comedy	Spanish	Argentinian	Argentinian	Argentina	Tornasol Films	Alta Classics S.L Unipersonal
5	Drama	Spanish	Spanish	Spanish	Spain	Telemadrid, Star line TV Productions	
6	Comedy	Spanish	Spanish	Spanish	Spain	Sociedad Gral. De cine; Pánico films	
7	Science Fiction	Spanish	Spanish	Mixed	Spain	El Deseo	Warner Sogefilms

CHAPTER FIVE

8	Drama	Spanish	Argentinian	Argentinian	Argentina	Alquimia Cinema	Hispano Foxfilm S.A.E.
9	Thriller	Spanish	Spanish	Spanish	Spain	CARTEL, S.A.; Flamenco films; Tornasol films	Laurenfilm
10	Drama	English	Mixed	Mixed	Canada	El Deseo D.A.	
11	Animation	Spanish		Mixed		Animagic Studio, Telemadrid	United International Pictures
12	Comedy	Spanish	Spanish	Spanish	Spain	Morena Films	Hispano Foxfilms
13	Drama	Spanish	Mixed	Mixed	Mixed	Tornasol Films	Alta Classics
14	Comedy	Spanish	Mixed	Spanish	Spain	Telespan 2000, Estudios Picasso Fábrica de Ficción	
15	Comedy	Spanish	Argentinian	Argentinian	Argentina	Tornasol films; S.B Producciones	
16	Drama	Spanish	Mixed	Mixed	Mixed	SOGECINE, Aiete-Ariane Films	
17	Thriller	Spanish	Mixed	Mixed	Spain	Bocaboca Producciones	
18	Comedy	Spanish	Mixed	Mixed	Mixed	Tornasol films	Alta Films
19	Comedy	Mixed	Mixed	Mixed	Mixed	Mate Production, Castelao Productions	Sociedad General de Derechos Audiovisuales
20	Drama	Spanish	Mixed	Mexican	Mexico	Wanda Visión	
21	Drama	Spanish	Spanish	Mixed	Spain	Lola Films	
22	Adventures	English	Foreign	Foreign	Australia	Sociedad Kino Visión	Amboto Audiovisual
23	Comedy	Spanish	Mixed	Mixed	Mixed	Alma Ata international pictures	Buena vista internacional spain
24	Drama	Spanish	Mixed	Mixed	Mixed	Tesela producciones cinematográficas	
25	Thriller	Spanish	Spanish	Mixed	Spain	Alquimia cinema; Telemadrid	Hipano Foxfilm

SPANISH CO-PRODUCTIONS

Chart 9: Top 25 Spanish International Co-Productions at the European Market (2000-2004)

Original Title	Director	Yr	Genre	Language	Nature	EU Countries (*)	Admiss EU	Admiss Spain	Total EU
L'Auberge espagnole	C. Klapisch	02	Comedy	Mixed	Multicultural	22	4,428,044	308,354	4,736,398
Mar adentro	A. Amenábar	04	Drama	Spanish	(Inter)National	7	810,970	4,096,373	4,907,343
Los Reyes Magos	A. Navarro	03	Animation	Spanish	Multicultural	3	461,111	491,737	952,848
Los lunes al sol	F. León de Aranoa	02	Drama	Spanish	(Inter)National	16	453,841	2,103,094	2,556,935
My Life Without Me	I. Coixet	03	Drama	English	Internationally-oriented	16	442,611	562,364	1,004,975
Crimen ferpecto	A. de la Iglesia	04	Comedy	Spanish	(Inter)National	2	357,419	860,622	1,218,041
Lista de espera	J.C. Tabío	00	Comedy	Spanish	Financial	9	253,817	379,999	633,816
El hijo de la novia	J.J. Campanella	01	Comedy	Spanish	Financial	10	193,151	1,574,492	1,767,643
Sin noticias de Dios	A. Díaz Yanes	01	Thriller	Spanish	Multicultural	9	161,607	609,409	771,016
El espinazo del diablo	G. del Toro	01	Science Fiction	Spanish	Multicultural	3	152,439	712,178	864,617
El crimen del Padre Amaro	C. Carrera	02	Drama	Spanish	Financial	11	96,695	318,834	415,529
Juana la Loca	V. Aranda	01	Period Drama	Spanish	(Inter)National	3	76,855	2,067,004	2,143,859

Title	Director		Genre	Language	Theme	[1]			
Torremolinos 73	P. Berger	03	Comedy	Spanish	(Inter)National	6	55,228	389,307	444,535
Carmen	V. Aranda	03	Drama	Spanish	Multicultural	8	42,202	1,380,728	1,422,930
The Old Man Who Read Love Stories	R. de Heer	01	Adventure	English	Financial	6	28,523	296,912	325,435
Kamchatka	M.Piñeyro	02	Drama	Spanish	Financial	3	8,715	628,013	636,728
Lugares comunes	A. Aristaráin	02	Drama	Spanish	Multicultural	3	7,407	424,756	432,163
El embrujo de Shanghai	F. Trueba	02	Drama	Spanish	(Inter)National	1	2,053	302,780	304,833
El viaje de Carol	I. Uribe	02	Drama	Spanish	(Inter)National	1	164	374,543	374,707
Almejas y mejillones	M. Carnevale	00	Comedy	Spanish	Multicultural	0	0	332,130	332,130
Roma	A. Aristaráin	04	Drama	Spanish	Multicultural	0	0	250,583	250,583
Incautos	M. Bardem	04	Thriller	Spanish	(Inter)National	0	0	238,362	238,362
Gente pez	J. Iglesias	01	Comedy	Spanish	(Inter)National	0	0	567,956	567,956
Nos miran	N. López Amado	02	Thriller	Spanish	(Inter)National	0	0	360,103	360,103
La Luna de Avellaneda	J.J. Campanella	04	Comedy	Spanish	Financial	0	0	345,609	345,609

Source: Own elaboration on ICAA and EAO (Lumiere) data.
1 Number of European countries where the movie has been released (apart from Spain)

Works Cited

Andersen, A. 1996. *The European film production guide.* London: Media Business School-Routledge.
Chavarrías, A. 2004. La coproducción con Latinoamérica: cambiar es posible. *Academia* (Winter) 34: 12-14.
Écija Abogados. 2000. *Cómo producir, distribuir y financiar una obra audiovisual.* Madrid: Exportfilm.
Eleftheriotis, D. 2001. *Popular cinemas of Europe: Studies of texts, contexts and frameworks.* New York: Continuum.
Elsaesser, T. 2005. *European cinema: face to face with Hollywood*, Amsterdam: Amsterdam University Press.
Enrich, E. 2005. *Legal aspects of international film co-productions.* Brussels: European Audiovisual Observatory (May) <www.obs.coe.int/online_publication/expert/coproduccion_aspectos-juridicos.pdf.en> (accessed September 15, 2005).
Everett, W., ed. 2005. *European identity in cinema.* 2d ed. Bristol: Intellect Book.
Flesler, D. 2004. New racism, intercultural romance and the immigration question in contemporary Spanish cinema. *Studies in Hispanic Cinemas* 1.2: 103-118.
Forbes, J. and S. Street. 2000. *European cinema: An introduction.* New York: Palgrave.
Györy, M. 1995. *International film and television co-production contracts: legal problems and information needed.* Brussels: CERICA (February) www.obs.coe.int/online_publication/reports/00001259.html (accessed October 21, 1997).
Hill, J. 1998. The Future of european cinema: The economics and culture of pan-european strategies. In *Border Crossing: Film in Ireland, Britain and Europe.* Edited by J. Hill, M. McLoone and P. Hainsworth. 53-80. London: BFI.
Hoskins C., S. McFayden and A. Finn. 1997. *Global television and film. An introduction to the economics of the business.* Oxford: Clarendon Press.
Instituto de las Ciencias y Artes Audiovisuales (ICAA). 2003. *The Spanish film industry: trends (1996-2003).* Madrid: Ministerio de Cultura <http://www.mcu.es/cine/cvdc/ev/pdf/icaaesa.pdf> (accessed January 15, 2005).
Jäckel, A. 2003. *European film industries.* London: BFI Publishing.
Jordan, B. and R. Morgan-Tamosunas. 1998. *Contemporary Spanish cinema.* Manchester: Manchester University Press.

Miller, T., N. Govil, J. McMurria, R. Maxwell and T. Wang. 2005. *Global Hollywood 2*. 2d ed. London: British Film Institute.
Neumann, P. 2002. *The fine art of co-producing*. Madrid: Media Business School.
Otero, J.M.. May 1999. El horizonte de las coproducciones. In *Los límites de la frontera: la coproducción en el cine español. Cuadernos de la Academia* 5: 17-27.
Palacio, M. May 1999. Elogio posmoderno de las coproducciones. In *Los límites de la frontera: la coproducción en el cine español. Cuadernos de la Academia* 5: 221-235.
Rimbau, E. Winter 2003. Public money and private business (or How to survive Hollywood's imperialism): Film production in Spain (1984-2002). *Cinéaste*: 56-61.
Rix, R. 1999. Co-productions and common cause: Spain and Latin America. In *Spanish cinema: Calling the shots*. Edited by R. Rix and R. Rodríguez-Saona. 113-128. Leeds: Trinity and All Saints.
Santaolalla, I. July 2005. A case of split identity? Europe and Spanish America in recent Spanish cinema. Paper presented at *Screening identities: Reconfiguring identity politics in contemporary European cinema*, European Cinema Research Forum, 2005 Conference, University of Leeds, 1- 3 July 2005 (to be published in *Screening Identities: Contemporary European Cinema*. 2006. Special edition of *Journal of Contemporary European Studies*. Edited by P. Cooke and R. Stone.
Soriano, X. 2001. La internacionalización del cine "made in Spain.' *Academia* (Summer) 30: 169-173.
Triana-Toribio, N. 2003. *Spanish national cinema*. London: Routledge, 2003.
Wayne, M. 2002. The Politics of contemporary European cinema: Histories, borders, diasporas. Bristol: Intellect Books.

Websites

Instituto de la Cinematografía y Artes Audiovisuales (ICAA).
 <http://www.mcu.es/cine/index.jsp>
LUMIERE (European Audiovisual Observatory)
 <http://lumiere.obs.coe.int/web/search/>
Internet Movie Database
 <http://www.imdb.com>
EURIMAGES
 <http://www.coe.int/T/E/Cultural_Co-operation/Eurimages/>
MEDIA Programme
 < http://europa.eu.int/comm/avpolicy/media/index_en.html>

IBERMEDIA
<http://www.programaibermedia.com/esp/htm/home.htm>

Chapter Six

Database Cinema and the Museification of National Histories

Olivier Asselin, University of Montreal

The nation is indiscernible from the emergence of the modern state, that is, the nation-state. While certain states exist independently from the nation and certain nations remain without states, most nations are defined by their states, whether real or imagined, and most states identify themselves as nations. In modern times, states have formed nations more frequently than nations have formed states. More recently however, the disputable nature of certain political borders left over from the Cold War or colonial practices, has resuscitated nationalist aspirations towards the creation of new nation-states, as in the ex-U.S.S.R. or Africa. At the same time, economic globalization encourages the formation of large political bodies and the development of a new form of nationalism, one that is continental in nature, as with Europe or Latin America. Finally, this reconfiguration of political and economic relations has given rise to a return to religious or "civilizational" communitarianisms which, in some respects, resembles a certain kind of nationalism, as is the case with "Islam" or the "Christian West."

For the historian, however, the nation is not as concrete as the state: it is an "imagined community" (Anderson 1991), concocted by the individuals of which it is comprised and the political power by which it is represented. It requires a self-consciousness, a common awareness of forming a community and an individual awareness of being a part of that community. Despite the fact that the nation postulates the relative equality of its citizens, this imagined community is generally constructed, imposed even, *from above*, by certain elitist bodies—political, social, economic or cultural—and more notably, by the government—while being only experienced by "ordinary" people (Hobsbawm 1990). Be that as it may, the nation is founded on a fictional community, a collection of shared characteristics, of which the importance varies according to space, time and point of view: ethnicity, language, religion, culture, institutions, economy, etc. However, it also relies on the fiction of an integrated *territory*—places, landscapes, geography and, most certainly, impenetrable borders. More importantly, it relies on the fictional continuity of a story—memories and utopias, origins and projects. It is telling then, that the *map*, and more importantly, the *narrative* have always been, and remain, the preferred forms of representation for the nation.[1]

In modern times, most notably with the development of popular and mass culture, the narrative has taken on considerable importance, to the point that it has become one of the dominant cultural forms, hegemonic even, affecting all discourse and all practice. The novel has long been considered the privileged space for the formulation of narrative, however, by the beginning of the twentieth century, film had usurped this role. With its industrialization and global dissemination, narrative cinema became a dominant form, while cinema itself became the very model of narrative. In contemporary times, narrative is largely audio-visual: it is no longer presented by a narrator using words, but rather by a *monstrator* who arranges image and sound, characters, camera movements and editing. It is for this reason that cinema, like the novel before it, undoubtedly played a decisive role in the construction of history—and more importantly, national histories—despite the fact that historical discourse, that of professional historians, has long been wary of narratives, as well as of the novel and film.

So-called new media may seem to question the role of narrative within contemporary culture. With the spread of the personal computer and the expansion of the Internet in the 1990s, digital media has ceased being one among a variety of tools and has become a hegemonic technology, which mediates and radically transforms all practices. Within this movement, the various forms of the computer—its principles, operations, interfaces, both graphic and physical—influence, not only all other media—their manner of organizing information and rendering it accessible to the user—but also the general structure of experience, categories of thought and language.[2] According

---

[1] In a general manner, the narrative is simply the representation of a story. It combines two temporal sequences, which are articulated according to a specific order, duration, and with variable frequency. It generally presupposes a perspective, both spatial and temporal, and most notably, a narrator and a narratee. The narrative often has a certain unity, not necessarily a unity of action, "a single complete action" during "one revolution of the sun," as advocated Aristotle with regards to tragedy, but rather, a certain coherence in the events represented and in the representation of these events. For some, there needs to be intrigue or a plot, with a beginning, middle, and an end, and with a crux, reversal, recognition and a denouement or solution. For others, there merely needs to be some sort of transformation. If the narrative has always occupied a privileged position in the order of discourse, it is perhaps because of its apparent capacity to synthesize experience, space, time and community.

[2] On the dialogue between "new" and "old" media, see Bolter and Grusin (1999).

to Lev Manovich (2001), with such an expansion, the database, one of the many forms of data organization, has now become a dominant cultural form (214, 218-243).

The database is an "ordered collection of information." Its management system—dubbed by experts the "Database Management System"—is variable: it can be navigational, hierarchical, part of a network, relational, multidimensional, and object-oriented. Nevertheless, whatever its structure, the database always implies a collection and, above all else, random access. Apparently, this cultural form is not altogether new: the cabinet of curiosities, the museum, the library and the archive were already ordered collections, openly accessible (though not in the political sense of the term). However, the computer has radically renewed this form by digitization, automation and a greater interactivity, by new ways of archiving, researching and retrieving information. The perfect embodiment of this new cultural form is of course the Internet, which may be seen as an infinite bank of data, texts, images, and sounds, accessible from all nodes of the network and along an infinity of paths, by everyone, everywhere, at any time.

According to Lev Manovich (2001), the database is a form opposite to the narrative. "The Database represents the world as a list of items, and it refuses to order this list. In contrast, a narrative creates a cause-and-effect trajectory of seemingly unordered items (events). Therefore database and narrative are natural enemies" (225). This being said, how will the logic of the database affect the representation of national histories, which have long favored a narrative form? Two recent historical films which make central use of digital technology—*The Russian Ark* by Aleksandr Sokurov (2002) and *The Tulse Luper Suitcases: A Personal History of Uranium* by Peter Greenaway (2003-2004)—demonstrate that the logic of the database does not necessarily question the great national narratives, but rather, quite the opposite.

History as Long Take

The story is well-known. *The Russian Ark* is comprised of a single long take, lasting one hour and thirty minutes. The film was shot entirely in St. Petersburg, at the former Winter Palace of Catherine II. The palace remained the official residence of Russian Czars until the revolution of 1917. Today, the Winter Palace is the heart of the Hermitage, one of the largest museums in the world.[3] The film tells of the improbable, even anachronistic, meeting of a French Marquis of the nineteenth century—liberally inspired by the Marquis Astolphe

---

[3] The Hermitage's collection is made up of 3,000 000 works of art, of which 67, 000 are exhibited in 400 rooms. See the museum's official website (*The Hermitage Museum*).

de Custine, the author of the celebrated travelogue *La Russie de 1839*, and superbly interpreted by Sergei Dreiden—and a contemporary everyman—the director's alter-ego, who is heard, but never seen, and whose perspective is embodied by the subjective camera, and the voice-over, which consists of the director's own voice.

Together, the two men make their way through the museum—its staircases, its rooms and its nooks and crannies, the Theatre, the main galleries, several Grand Halls, the gardens, the concert hall, etc.—and witness, in a chaotic order, various scenes of Russian history—a crowd arriving for the last ball given at the Hermitage by Nicolas II, in 1913, shortly before World War I, to celebrate the 300th anniversary of the Romanov dynasty; the mistreatment of a general by Peter the Great; Catherine the Great attending a rehearsal; visitors from modern times, others, including a blind woman, from the nineteenth century; a carpenter fabricating casings during the siege of Leningrad amid the second world war; an aging Catherine crossing the Palace's garden; a solemn ceremony hosted by Nicholas I upon the arrival of a Persian ambassador; a changing of the guard at the Palace; a discussion between several directors of the museum (including the actual director playing himself) during Stalin's dictatorship; Tsar Nicholas II, his wife Alexandra and their children in an intimate familial scene in a dining room; and finally, the last great ball.

The director and the Marquis thus travel through the museum—and history. They act as our guides. They also act as angels, as they go largely unnoticed. The first of the two characters has no body, the second, whose silhouette is reminiscent of Murnau's Nosferatu, has a phantom quality. At one point, Custine asks himself, "can it be that I'm invisible?" However, the two characters converse. They speak of Russia—more specifically its relationship with the rest of Europe. The nineteenth-century French writer is largely skeptical: in his opinion, Russia is an Asiatic empire that attempts, unsuccessfully, to imitate the rest of Europe.[4] In his turn, the contemporary Russian film director defends Russia and tries to convince his interlocutor of the grandeur of the country, its leaders, its political regime and of its accomplishments. Oddly, the debate is, at times, political, but more often than not, it is aesthetic in nature. "I have never believed that a republic was suitable for a country as large as Russia" says Custine; "You Europeans are democrats who mourn the monarchy", replies the director. "In Asia, tyrants are adored" says Custine; Peter the Great "taught Russians to enjoy themselves" retorts the director; but "Peter ordered his son's execution" and "he built a European city over a swamp" replies the Marquis. Admiring the quality of an orchestra, and of a composition, Custine assumes

---

[4] As the real Custine wrote: "I don't reproach the Russians for being what they are; what I blame them for is their desire to appear what we [Europeans] are" (Kennan 1971, 81).

that the musicians are European, most likely Italian, and that the composer is, no doubt, German; "they're Russians, for God's sake!" corrects the Director. Custine believes that Russians have few original ideas and settle on mimicry: Raphael's loggias, for example, were inspired by the Vatican. "Better than the Vatican, replies the Director, this is Saint Petersburg." And so forth. At the film's conclusion, neither fellow has changed his views, but Custine seems to have a greater appreciation for Russia. Following the last great ball, as all of the guests slowly leave the premises, the two men part: the Marquis decides to remain in the museum, as in the past, while the Director leaves by a side door, heading towards an uncertain future, albeit one that seems to look favorably upon Russia. "What will we find over there?" inquires Custine. "I don't know," replies the Director. "I'm staying," states the Marquis. "Farewell, Europe," concludes the Director.

The two men's opinions are not altogether dissimilar. Moreover, the film seems to be identifying the French Revolution with the Russian Revolution, "la Terreur" with the Soviet period, as if history was not chronological, but cyclical, or even oneiric: "our Convention lasted 80 years, says the Director, a real revolution... very sad." In the final scene, the film retrospectively ascribes some of the Director's nostalgia for pre-revolutionary Russia to the nineteenth-century Marquis. With surprising conviction, the film thus adopts a political position that is wholly reactionary—nationalistic, perhaps monarchist and Catholic, even.[5]

The Russian Ark is thus a historical film. It deals with "la Grande Histoire," three hundred years of Russian history. However, paradoxically, the film does not follow a continuous narrative. While the film has a great aesthetic coherence, reinforced by the single long take, the film has no real narrative coherence. To begin, there are no main characters. Custine and the director are not actors interacting with the other characters of the film, but rather spectators, delegate spectators, who observe and comment, without being seen or heard, as if they were standing on the threshold of the story and of history itself. The other characters—whether they be "historical," like Peter the Great, Catherine II or Nicholas II, or anonymous, like the blind woman, or the carpenter—appear too rarely and too briefly to be considered the central subjects of the story. Furthermore, the film does not seem to be plot-driven. It presents a series of relatively autonomous scenes, micro-narratives, that pertain to different eras, where the protagonists, their actions are not clearly linked. Moreover, these scenes are not dramatic, but rather banal. While they often involve historical

---

[5] On this political question, see Tesson (2002); Bénédict (1991); Bouquet (2003). See also Dragan Kujundzic's excellent article "After 'After:' *The Arkive* Fever of Alexander Sokurov" (2004).

figures, they rarely portray historical events. The film even seems to avoid representing the important historical events that marked Russia's history.

The most flagrant omission is the Revolution of 1917, which is never depicted, nor named, as if its very representation was prohibited. The omission is all the more obvious in that the Revolution was one of the most important events in the history of Russia and the most notable moment of the Revolution was precisely the storming of the Winter Palace—Eisenstein had already produced a memorable cinematographic reconstruction of it in *October* (1927). While the Revolution is never depicted or mentioned directly, it is often referenced indirectly, through various figures of speech. For example, the film opens with an allegorical statement which could be interpreted as an allusion to the Soviet era: "I open my eyes and I see nothing. I only remember there was some accident. Everyone ran for safety as best they could. I just can't remember what happened to me." Similarly Alexandra, the wife of Nicholas II, informs her confidante of her "presentiment" of imminent misfortune, as if she had foreseen the execution of the Czar and his family by the Bolsheviks. Later in the film, while meditating on the passage of time, Custine also seems to envision the end of Russia's ancient regime as he utters "monarchy is not eternal." The Revolution—as with the Soviet era and indeed much of the twentieth-century—is presented here as a great catastrophe in Russian history, one that is best kept quiet and best forgotten. It is also worth noting that the film avoids any allusion to twentieth-century art, which is, today, quite well represented at the Hermitage with the integration of the Shukin and Morozov collections: the director has us visit the first floor which houses the historical masterpieces, but avoids the second floor which houses the modern art collection, with works by Monet, Rodin, Gaugin, Matisse, Picasso, Kandinsky and Malevich.[6]

This being said, the entire film, that is, each scene, is negatively marked by this catastrophe: the absence of any overall plot, the banality of the scenes and the characters' general apathy give not the impression of history in the making, but rather of the suspension of time, as if we were on the eve of, or perhaps, the day after, a catastrophe. Despite the great mobility of both the camera and the mise-en-scène, *The Russian Ark*'s temporality is similar to that of *Moloch* (1999), *Taurus* (2001) and *Sun* (2005), three films by Sokurov, which recall, both directly and indirectly, the final days of a despot (Hitler, Lenin and Hiro Hito, respectively): the characters are petrified, stuck between waiting and mourning, suspense and stupor. The overriding feeling here is melancholy. The final ball in *The Russian Ark* could be seen as the joyful conclusion of a pleasant

---

[6] Sokurov admits to being especially influenced by Russian and European literature, music and painting of the nineteenth-century. Sokurov states: "I am a conservative" (Johnson 2004, 49).

story, however, it ends on a mixed note of joy and sadness, as if it were the end of a day on the Island of Cythera—or the end of an era.

Rather than depicting the most important historical events, the film turns our attention to history's backstage, depicting the everyday lives of those in power, their courtesans and servants. These representations are more physical than psychological, just as they are more sensual than intellectual. Despite the importance of the conversation between Custine and the director's voice-over, the film is not very loquacious, it is even strangely silent at times: the characters rarely engage in dialogue, their remarks are often banal, the sentences are short, often incomplete and always punctuated by long silences. In this respect, the film concentrates less on the remarks and feelings of the characters and more on their voices, bodies and movements—Peter the Great physically mistreating a general, Catherine voicing her need to urinate, Nicholas II dining with his wife and children, actors characters acting, soldiers in formation, couples dancing—, the film concentrates less on the meaning of things and more on the sensations they yield—forms and materials, lights, lines, colours, textures and sounds, make-up, hairdos, jewelry, costumes, fabric and perfume, bodies moving, touching, breathing, etc. This dimension of the film is underlined by Custine himself, who is continuously enraptured by an architectural detail, a set of china,[7] a piece of music, a uniform, a certain scent and, obviously, in front of the masterpieces of European painting and sculpture amassed by Catherine II and her successors.

The cinematographic aesthetic obviously exacerbates the sensuality of the figures, the costumes, the works of art and the set itself. Although the director opted for a wide-angle lens (8mm), there are very few wide shots: the majority are medium shots and close-ups, bringing the viewer closer to the actors, the heart of the scene and the intimacy of history. Moreover, the great mobility of the steady cam and the single long take throw everything—characters, accessories and settings—into a dizzying whirlwind of form and colour.

The long take has long interested filmmakers, first out of necessity, and more recently as an aesthetic choice, as in the famous opening shot of *A Touch of Evil* (1958). Recently, the long take has been an object of rediscovery. Citing only a handful of examples, Bela Tarr's *Satantango* (1994), Mike Figgis' *Timecode* (2000), Gus Van Sant's *Elephant* (2003) and now Sokurov's *The Russian Ark*, have all made the long take a central aesthetic form. This aesthetic decision may express a resistance to digital technologies, and more specifically, editing, which users of new media tend to overvalue to the detriment of the shoot. However, at the same time, this choice may well depend on digital

---

[7] The real Custine would have also been sensitive to porcelain, as his family was, at one time, the proprietors of the Niderviller factory.

technologies. We must remember that the long take is one of the privileged forms of new media, most notably within the realm of video games: the navigation of a virtual space is, almost always, achieved in one long take. Furthermore, the long take is technologically encouraged by new media, as videotapes are less expensive and longer than film rolls. The single long take has been an aesthetic ideal long before the advent of video—take Hitchcock's *Rope* (1948), for example, or Warhol's *Empire* (1964). However, because film was only available in three hundred meter rolls, the takes could not be longer than ten minutes. It was not until the introduction of the video camera that this dream became a reality.

The Russian Ark's single take was carried out with a high-definition digital camera, mounted on a steady cam and directly connected to a portable hard disk drive to avoid compressing the image.[8] Only two hard disks were available, each with a limited capacity of ninety-four minutes of images, therefore the film was shot, after three false starts, in one take. The film thus required an enormous amount of pre-production work: four years in development, thirty-six hours of on-site preparation, the lighting of over thirty rooms, hundreds of actors and extras requiring costumes, hair and make-up, twenty-two assistant directors, a camera crew and another advanced crew responsible for preparing the shoot. Moreover, the actual shoot was brief, lasting only a few hours, whereas a regular shoot lasts, on average, at least thirty days. In addition, the film required virtually no editing—only a few days, while a regular film often requires several months of editing and compositing.

In the interviews granted following the release of *The Russian Ark*, Sokurov always emphasized the exigent filming conditions and the risks involved in such an enterprise: ultimately, the entire film depended on the success of one single shot—and a great number of variables; the slightest error, the slightest accident could have undermined the entire project. It is surprising then, given the high stakes and the millions of Euros invested in the project, that the producers supplied the director with only two hard disks, the equivalent of two takes. Whatever the case, the extreme filming conditions gave the shoot an element of suspense, a historical dimension, as with the great moments in history where fate is determined, or better yet, a religious dimension, as the outcome was something of a miracle. The "making of" the film emphasizes this latter dimension, as it describes how Sokurov took time to pray before the shoot, thus suggesting his prayer had been answered.

Sokurov insisted on his desire to "make a film in one breath." It was imperative not to interrupt the staging of the film and the movements of the

---

[8] For all other technical information regarding the film, see Oppenheim (2003). The film was then transferred to 35mm film for distribution.

camera, to maintain continuity of time and space and, consequently, of the spectator's experience, in order to give the impression that the *The Russian Ark* was actually filmed live or, at least, in real time. As a historical film, *The Russian Ark* is appropriating many conventions from "cinéma vérité," in addition to reality-television: the story is presented here as if it was in fact, reality. This aesthetic choice obviously demonstrates a resistance to montage (as if Sokurov had wished his approach to be diametrically opposed to that of Eisenstein). However, this does not exclude all manipulation. While the long take was not cut and the order of the scenes and the duration of the shot were not altered, the image was, nonetheless, digitally retouched, the lighting, colour and definition were corrected and embellished, dialogue was dubbed, a voice over was added, as well as sound effects, music, etc. Authenticity—an image that corresponds to reality, the reality of the shoot and the reality of history—is not really what matters here. What matters is the temporal continuity of the film, its internal coherence.

The Russian Ark is thus dialectical. The film has no great *narrative* unity, it is composed of a heterogeneous series of narrative fragments and silences; this sequence does not seem to be determined by necessity, as fate would be, but rather contingently, as if it had been left to chance—and its meaning is forever escaping. This being said, the film nonetheless maintains a great *aesthetic* unity: the long take, with its close-ups and highly mobile camera frame, assembles all of the fragments in some semblance of sensual and organic unity; it provides a unity of time and a unity of place to a story that has no unity of action.

This was, no doubt, the main function of the film. The past seldom forms a coherent story and at times, it seems to be void of any meaning—Russia's past is no exception: it is largely insignificant and irreparably fragmented, both at every moment and over time, by an infinite number of diverging interests and disparate events of various importance, with unpredictable and chaotic effects: changes in regime, social conflicts, revolutions, disasters, war, etc. History is but "sound and fury." However, by virtue of the long take, *The Russian Ark* has endeavored to construct a coherent story, the fiction of a national history that is both unified and pacified. The film presents a sensual synthesis in order to mask the impossibility of making a rational synthesis, as if aesthetics could succeed where politics failed and the beauty of art could conjure up the chaos of history in order to reconstruct a community that is, at the very least, sentimental. For the director, aesthetics and ethics are, and must remain, separate: "I'm not a judge. I'm presenting a feature film dealing with emotional collisions, says Sokurov (…). It's not the role of art to judge. History and God put everyone in their place."[9]

---

[9] Sokurov, as cited in McNab (2002, 20). See also Christie (2004).

In this respect, *The Russian Ark* is dream-like, as the characters of the film continuously acknowledge. "I open my eyes and I see nothing" murmurs the narrator at the beginning of the film, even before the first images appear. "Is this a dream?" asks Custine, shortly thereafter. However, the film remains ambivalent. It endeavors to forget history as it happened, by dreaming of another story, one that is both monarchist and nationalistic. But *a contrario*, this mad dream may well bear witness to the ruins of our present historical landscape, more eloquently than can any "objective" history. What returns here is neither the repressed, in the form of symptoms (as with neurosis), nor the foreclosed in the form of hallucinations (as with psychosis), but rather the denied, in the form of the fetish (as with perversion). The long take is the ambivalent sign of a lack that is both denied and acknowledged.

It is not surprising then, that *The Russian Ark* presents the museum as the ideal representation of history. The museum amasses not texts, but things, objects and images, gathering them in a single hermetic space, preserving them for eternity. While the works are often arranged chronologically or by national schools, territories or periods, the principal function of this organization is not to create a unified narrative, but rather, to form a collection. In this regard, it is symptomatic that in *The Russian Ark*, the directors of the Hermitage become characters within the great political and social history of Russia. In an important scene, the current director of the museum (Boris Piotrovsky, who plays himself) and his two predecessors (Boris Piotrovsky Senior and Orbeli, portrayed by actors) are discussing, with hushed voices, the political situation and the historical role of the museum: "Everyone can see the future but no one remembers the past," says one of them; "We managed to preserve all this through the catastrophes," continues another. The title of the film also presents the museum as a salvaging force, by comparing it to the biblical ark which saved humanity and all other life forms from the flood. "Look, the sea is all around," says the film-maker as he leaves the museum. "We are destined to sail forever. To live forever."

The Russian Ark presents the museum as an allegorical model for the cinema. However, at the same time, it presents cinema as the ideal museum in that it could, more efficiently than the museum itself, "museify" the ruins of the past and unify them in a coherent national history. It is likely then, that the *Russian Ark* cited in the title, refers, not to the museum, but to the film itself, with the film director as a new Noah.

History as Network

The Tulse Luper Suitcases: A Personal History of Uranium is, without a doubt, Peter Greenaway's most ambitious project, not only because of the scope of the story, but more significantly, because of the forms it takes. The project is not a film, but rather, a seemingly infinite collection of works, produced in a variety of media and at various sites, mainly a trilogy of films, an exhibition of installation work and a website, to be followed by ninety-two DVDs, a television series, an on-line game, etc. According to the official release, "*The Tulse Luper Suitcases* reconstructs the life of Tulse Henry Purcell Luper, a professional writer and project-maker, caught up in a life of prisons. He was born in 1911 in Newport, South Wales, England and presumably last heard of in 1989. His life is reconstructed from the evidence of 92 suitcases found around the world—92 being the atomic number of the element Uranium." Tulse Luper is, of course, an imaginary figure, and Greenaway's project is a fictional biography.

Tulse Luper thus travels across the world and through the twentieth century. He crosses the paths of many characters and many destinies, he witnesses the great moments of twentieth-century history and, on several occasions, the history of uranium, from its scientific discovery to the fall of the Berlin Wall, through the detonation of the first atomic bomb and the Cold War. And then we lose all trace of him.[10] However, whatever his activities, or his location, Luper always ends up being imprisoned for one reason or another. His life is thus a series of tragicomic sojourns in various prisons around the world, sixteen to be exact: the coalhouse in the backyard of the Luper house in Newport, a jailhouse in Moab, Utah, a bathroom in the Antwerp station, etc. However, "Luper learns to use his prison time, writing on the prison's walls, inventing projects in literature, theatre, film and painting, and engaging with his jailers in all manner of plots, schemes and adventures" (*The Kasanderfilm Company*). One of such

---

[10] Luper was born in Newport, Wales, in 1911 (the same year that Marie Curie received the Nobel Prize for Chemistry). During the 1920s, Luper studied archaeology in Dublin. From 1930 to 1934, he makes an expedition to Moab, Utah (at the same time that Fermi, without knowing it, succeeds in creating the first nuclear fission). From 1934 to 1938, as a correspondent for two prominent British newspapers, Luper sojourns in Antwerp, at the height of fascism (during which time, nuclear fission is demonstrated). From 1938 to 1940, Luper resides in Vaux; from 1940 to 1941 he resides in Strasburg, in 1943 he remains in Turin and in 1943-44, he stays in Rome where he witnesses the arrival of the Americans. From 1944 to 1950, he travels throughout Eastern Europe, including Budapest (the year of the the bombing of Hiroshima), and Moscow (Luper lands in Moscow shortly after the Rosenbergs are condemned to death for sharing secret atomic information with the Soviets). From 1950 to 1959, Luper spends his time in Germany, traveling between East and West Germany (in the midst of the Cold War). In 1960-62, Luper stays in Hong Kong, and during the next six years, travels to various other locations. In 1989 he witnesses the fall of the Berlin Wall (which marks the official end of the Cold War). For a summary of Tulse Luper's life-story as told through his train trips, see "Suitcase_49 – Trains" (*The Tulse Luper Journey*).

activities consists of packing various suitcases which are then abandoned throughout the world.[11]

The project begins with Tulse Luper's disappearance: he is most likely dead. His life is thus *reconstructed*, several times over. Luper's life is first told in a trilogy of films, which remains the most visible component of the project. Each film focuses on three episodes from his life and each episode corresponds to a particular place and, more specifically, to a particular prison: *Part I: The Moab Story* (2003), *Part II: Vaux to the Sea* (2004) and *Part III: From Sark to the Finish* (2003). These films recount Luper's life-story in a fragmented way. Following an aesthetic that was sketched out in *Prospero's Books* (1991) and further developed in *The Pillow Book* (1996), Greenaway not only presents Luper's life in a linear fashion, through temporal montage and in the succession of shots which together form a narrative: he displays Luper's life on the surface and in the depth of the film, through spatial montage and in the juxtaposition and superimposition of images, texts and sound, thus forming elaborate visual figures. While this aesthetic approach seems to derive from the twentieth-century avant-garde, who radicalized collage, photomontage and superimposition, it also derives, and more notably so, from digital technologies.

---

[11] The contents of the suitcases are organized thematically. In general, each suitcase houses a category of objects: both natural and artificial elements (lumps of coal, alcohol, perfume, honey, light bulbs, candles, water, rainbows, shower heads, 92 atomic elements, broken glass, light, ice), vegetable (cherries, dead roses, green apples, flower bulbs, green figs), animals, which are, for the most part, dead (fish, frogs, dog bones, crab claws, feathers and eggs, dog, fossils), human beings, which are, for the most part, alive (a sleeper, children, body parts), games (toys, trains, china dogs, tennis balls, wheels, board games, dolls), works of art (Vatican pornography, Anna Karenina novels, erotic prints, 55 men on horseback, Ingres' paintings, obelisks), codes and representations (numbers and letters, dollars, coins, place names, ideas of America, code, maps, the phrenological book), tools, both artistic and otherwise (pencils, cleaning fluids, dental tools, locks and keys, radio equipment, clean linen, needles, brushes, musical instruments, yellow paint, sauce pans, violin splinters, ink, measuring tools, a typewriter), images of, and by, Luper (Luper's photographs, Luper's lost films, Luper's uniforms, prison movie film clips, the manuscript for the baby of Strasbourg, drawings of Luper, Luper 1001 story manuscripts). It is important to note that the majority of these suitcases contain relics, that is to say, objects that belonged to someone at one time or another, and which came into physical contact with someone, thus testifying to a past life (love letters, passports, bloodied wallpaper, men's clothes, women's clothes, holes, Moab photographs, food drops, boots and shoes, Holocaust gold, smoked cigars, Moitessier gowns, bottle messages, spent matches, restaurant menus, Roman postcards, holy earth, mortuary notes). Each suitcase is a reliquary and the museum that exhibits them thus becomes a sanctified space. However, a number of the suitcases contain a critical dimension which reflects on the very idea of collecting, like the suitcase which houses 92 objects, the "zoo animals ark" or yet, "the fabrication of Luper's life."

These technologies impose a logic of selection and compositing, collage and layering, not only in each image, through 2D and 3D compositing and animation software, but also in each page, with graphic design or website design software, and on each screen, with the graphic interfaces of various operating systems, like Windows, which permit the opening of several windows at once. The three films are thus structured like digital photomontages, websites, and computer screens—without interactivity.

Tulse Luper's life story is also recounted in the space of the museum, notably in an exhibition that took place at the Compton Verney Art Gallery in Warwickshire in 2004.[12] Greenaway is no stranger to the museum, he was often asked to create installations and curate exhibitions for both art galleries and museums: he thus produced *Le bruit des nuages (Flying Out of this World)* for the Louvre in Paris in 1992, *The Physical Self* at the Boymans van Beuningen Museum in Rotterdam in 1992, *100 Objects to represent the World* at the Hofburg Palace in Vienna in 1993, and *Watching Water* at the Palazzo Fortuni in Venice in 1993, among others. Today, the distinction between artistic production and curatorial work is tenuous at best, and is often put to the test by concerned artists who are keen to control the reception of their works and by curators who have become veritable *auteurs*.[13] Greenaway's museum interventions straddle the border between the two practices: they not only include the fabrication of new images and new objects, but also the selection and installation of previously made images and objects (including historical artifacts and works of art) in the gallery space and throughout the entire museum.[14] In the eight rooms allotted to him at Compton Verney, Greenaway presented Tulse Luper's ninety-two suitcases, displayed on tables or on plinths, in glass cases, affixed to the walls or ceilings, some closed and the others open, thus revealing their precious contents.[15]

Lastly, the story of Tulse Luper is also recounted on-line through a website designed specifically for this project (*The Tulse Luper Suitcases*). The website consists of three large sections. The first, an "introduction," briefly presents, in three pages, "Tulse Luper's life, the historical background and the network."

---

[12] The exhibition, organized by John Leslie, marked the opening of the museum: the exhibition ran from March 27th to October 31st, 2004. For more details, see Leslie and Ward (2004).

[13] On this subject, see Heinich and Pollack (1996).

[14] Regarding these questions, see Pascoe (1997).

[15] For an analysis of the exhibition— and of the suitcase motif in Greenaway's work—, see Elliot and Purdy's excellent article, "Man in a Suitcase: Tulse Luper at Compton Verney," in Gary Kochhar-Lindgren (2005). Rightly so, the two authors approach Greenaway's project through the lens of Marcel Duchamp's *Boite-en-valise*, an artist who indeed figures prominently in the filmmaker's artistic formation.

The second section, entitled "Stills," includes a collection of "2 x 92 images of the reconstruction of Tulse Luper's life," consisting of a grid of one hundred squares, ninety-two of which contained static images that could be enlarged with a click of the mouse. The majority of the images are stills from the first film of the trilogy, *The Moab Story*.[16] When one clicks on the word "Vaux" which appears in one of the squares, not far from the center, the entire grid is replaced by another grid of ninety-two stills from the second film of the trilogy, *Vaux to the Sea*.[17]

The third section of the website, entitled "Archives," is by far the most important, given the amount of information it does, and could, contain. This section has six sub-sections. The sub-section "timeline" presents "a chronological reconstruction of the Tulse Luper Suitcases set against a personal history of the 20th century."[18] The dates on the time-line are linked to other pages on the Greenaway website, as well as to other Internet sites presenting varied information.[19] The sub-section "location" presents "an overview of all locations and exterior information spanning some 60 years of 20th century history." The first page consists of a large map that the user can navigate and from which other pages, which describe the many places Luper has visited, can be accessed.[20] The sub-section "category" mainly presents Luper's life thematically according to twenty-three categories, "from the 92 suitcases, the 16 prisons, maps, a Tulse Luper Cookbook, to the Atomic Table, etc." and including "the Characters," "the Experts," and "the Historians."[21] The sub-

---

[16] Several images are found material: geographical maps, postcards, frames from old films, period photographs: German armies, Hitler in Paris, a view of Strasbourg, ruins from a bombed-out city, the atomic bomb explosion in Hiroshima, anonymous photographs, Dreyer's Joan of Arc, Judy Garland in *The Wizard of Oz*, Ingres' portrait of Madame de Moitessier, etc.

[17] The third film in the series, *From Sark to the Finish*, is not mentioned, as if the site was still under construction—a work in progress or definitely unfinished.

[18] In fact, only the first part of Luper's life (1911-1946) is described in any detail.

[19] The links offer us a sub-chronology of Luper's or the lives of those that came into contact with him, information regarding the cities to which he traveled (for example, there is a link to a site for the city of Newport), a link regarding the scientific discovery of uranium (i.e. the Niels Bohr Archive), historical context, etc.

[20] By following the hyperlinks, we gather general information regarding each city and the historical events that took place within each city, a summary of a particular period of Luper's life, descriptions of the specific location in which it took place, of each person that plays a role in this episode (physical description, milieu, relationship) and, finally, a description of the contents of the suitcases and the circumstances surrounding their discovery years later.

[21] Surprisingly, the section contains only a few hyperlinks. From a list of twenty-three categories, only six are actually active and include a sub-list of elements, and, from the

section "characteristics" is described as "92 x 92 descriptions that somehow relate to the Tulse Luper Suitcases," providing ninety-two narrative characteristics—a list of actions, often trivial, but historical nevertheless—to each of the ninety-two characters, for a total of 8464 narrative items, creating just as many narrative possibilities.[22] And finally, the sub-section "manual" is "a weblog for news and updates for the Tulse Luper Network from the archivists; you can post your own comments here," however this section is "temporarily closed."

Thus, *The Tulse Luper Suitcases* project tells both the life-story of an imaginary character and a history of the twentieth-century; this double story is retold several times and in differing ways in the various works that make up this project—the film trilogy, the art exhibition, and the website. The narrative, which is the most commonly used form of representing history, is here multiplied and fragmented into an infinite number of narratives, micro-narratives, scenes, images, as if in a kaleidoscope. In this respect, the project seems to undermine, through various means, traditional narrative structure and time itself—the temporality of the story, the narrative and the user's experience.

In this regard, the project is constantly spatializing the narrative. For example, a chronological and narrative order is imposed on each film through the staging of each shot, the editing of the entire film, and then, by the mode of presentation, whether through theatrical or DVD release. However, the story is continuously disrupted by the overlaying of a numerical order onto the narrative order (the ninety-two suitcases that punctuate Luper's life), and by an accumulation of information in the diegetic space, by the juxtaposition of scenes, characters, accessories and sets, as well as in the depth and on the surface of the image, by the overlaying and juxtaposition of images—and sound.

---

six sub-lists, there are only a few elements that contain active hyperlinks: only twenty-one suitcases that present an image and textual description of their contents, and the theses of three experts, which are presented in essay format and which resemble Borges' pastiche of scholarly papers: "Etymologic-onomastic Attempts on the Name 'Tulse Luper'," "The Influence of Water in the Late Work of Tulse Luper" and "the World Regarded as Theater—Possibilities in the Present." This last work proposes a reflection on interactive narratives beginning with an episode from Luper's life (his imprisonment at the Château de Vaux-le-Vicomte in 1945). However, the user is only given one choice, which is to select a character and a costume (among the three options) and to insert them within a given location (among the five options).

[22] In fact, only ten characteristics are posted, each one containing one underlined word, with a link to a single image. The sub-section "stories" was supposed to gather "the Tulse Luper Suitcases Stories, a contemporary rewriting and retelling of the Sheherazade stories," a collection of ninety-two short stories written by Luper. However, only three stories actually appear on the site. Additional stories written by Tulse Luper appear on another site (Peter Greenaway).

Here, as is often the case in Greenaway's work, the script is rather conventional in form, with a clear story-line that is both chronologically and dramatically well-structured, and pointed dialogue. However, the theatrical *mise-en-scène*, the camera work, with both static shots, slow mechanical movements and a generally frontal point of view, and, above all, the editing, compositing and mixing which multiply the visual and sound effects, all work together to scramble the story to such a point that it is difficult for the viewer to identify with the characters, immerse his/herself in the diegetic space and even understand the narrative. It is as if the director, through some defense mechanism, had wanted to undermine his own text through image and sound and to break off all communication with the spectator.

Greenaway's exhibition at Compton Verney features a similar spatialization, and thus deconstruction, of the story. The suitcases are displayed in various rooms of the museum, Tulse Luper's life unfolds within an architectural structure: while the museum always favours a particular trajectory for visiting an exhibition, it nonetheless opens up an infinite number of alternatives. This is also the case with the website: in the "Stills" section, the images are presented chronologically on a grid and are to be read left to right, and top to bottom, as in traditional reading or writing, however, they are accessible in any order and following other trajectories. In the "Archives" section, Tulse Luper's life-story is presented chronologically, on a "timeline", and geographically, according to "locations" on a map, however, neither representation requires an ordered reading of history or the world.

The story is thus called into question, not only because of the spatialization of information, but also because of its transformation into a museum, an archive—a database. As the website states, this is clearly a crucial part of the programme: "Our ambition in the next 3 years is to build and extensive, online Archive of [Luper's] adventures, the places he visited, the characters he met, his prisons, the projects he made, the objects that were found in the 92 suitcases and some events in 20th century history." In this respect, the website is, perhaps, more than the film trilogy or the exhibition, the most important part of *Tulse Luper's Suitcases* in that it may be the fragment that best represents the whole: the project is indeed structured like a database, as is, without a doubt, Greenaway's entire oeuvre.[23]

The Tulse Luper Suitcases resembles a database both on the whole and in each of its parts. It forms a collection, not only as a result of *what* it represents—an entire life, an entire century—, but also in *how* it represents through materials and forms, through an assemblage of quotes, references,

---

[23] This judicious hypothesis is put forth by Lev Manovich (237-239). See also Benjamin Noys' article "Tulse Luper Database: Peter Greenaway, the New Media Object and the Art of Exhaustion," in Kochhar-Lindgren (2005).

allusions, imitations, pastiche, and many other intertextual and hypertextual practices. Together, the mise-en-scène, images and sounds represent an ensemble of characters, accessories, sets, actions and stories, while at the same time, they make reference to a variety of other texts, images and sounds.[24] *The Tulse Luper Suitcases* accumulates data and forms a collection that represents itself as *a collection*. It is, of course, not accidental that the project's central motif is a suitcase and that its general structure is a collection of suitcases. A suitcase is already a collection of sorts, and in this case, it becomes a metaphorical representation of the museum, the archive or the database, as well as a metonymic representation of the entire project—and of the entire universe. The project thus establishes a *mise en abyme*, which perpetuates an infinite meditation on the infinitely great and the infinitesimal, as if the collection mirrored both the general form of the universe and the basic structure of matter. This *mise en abyme* is nowhere better expressed than in suitcase 42 which contains "92 objects to represent the world" and, above all, in suitcase 92 which contains "the fabrication of Luper's life," that is to say, the entire *Tulse Luper Suitcases* project.

Moreover, *The Tulse Luper Suitcases* resembles a database in that its collections seem eminently partial, arbitrary and incomplete, as it they were only one possible selection among many others, from a vast and perhaps infinite ensemble. Each part of the project—the exhibition, the website and the films—remains largely incomprehensible without the other parts. Likewise, the entire project remains incomprehensible if it is kept separate from the immense cultural reserve it continuously draws from. All of Greenaways' works resemble a museum, a library, an archive or a database, of which we perceive but an infinitesimal part: a few gallery rooms or a few shelves from a larger collection stored in the vaults, a few screens from memory stored on a hard-disk, a server or an entire network. These works emphasize the selection process and its arbitrariness: the selection is nothing but a choice among an infinite number of possible choices. It is, most notably, in this manner that the narrative is called into question: not only through the fragmenting or multiplying of the storyline, but also in constantly demonstrating that the narrative is but one mode of data organization among an infinity of others.

However, in spite of what has been said, the database is not necessarily opposed to the narrative. In the narrative form, information is ordered on a temporal axis that is oriented and irreversible, like a series of cause and effect, with an origin and an end. In the case of the database, information is also ordered, but the order is not hierarchical, it is fundamentally egalitarian: in

---

[24] In regard to quotes and, more generally, repetition in the work of Peter Greenaway, see Karine Bouchy, "Let's make a renewal. Répétition, multiplicité, bifurcations: les stratégies de Peter Greenaway," in Kochhar-Lindgren (2005).

principle, all of the information is equal, equally present, equally close and thus equally accessible, from anywhere at anytime. However, by accessing the database through a physical interface, a graphical user interface and software, the user organizes information, both spatially and temporally, inscribing the information within a frame or in a series and possibly a narrative. In this respect, the database may well be the condition of possibility of the narrative. The database contains, at least potentially so, an infinite number of possible links, juxtapositions and successions, which can be both random or organized, poetic or logical, chronological or geometrical, historical or geographical, etc. The narrative is only one of an infinite number of possible interfaces within the database, as it was merely one of the many ways of representing the world.

By imposing the logic of the database onto the representation of a person's life and of the twentieth-century, *The Tulse Luper Suitcases* may well offer a new conception of history. By insisting on the collection and random selection, it neither represents the past as a disorderly series of "sound and fury," nor as a great linear narrative, that is both determined and teleological: it is presented as an open and complex system where a multitude of avenues are possible, at all times. This project could ascribe an indeterminist logic to history, like that which Werner Heisenberg discovered at the core of matter, at the subatomic level. It also acknowledges the decisive role played by the historian's retrospective view in the configuration of history. In a very Nietzschean proposition, both the film and website proclaim: "There is no such thing as history, there are only historians."

This being said, this application of database logic to the rendering of history can be understood in another way. First of all, it is important to point out that *The Tulse Luper Suitcases* database is not highly interactive. While the project's website is indeed interactive, in the most technical sense of the term, it is only superficially so: the user may change the order of presentation of data, but not the data itself, he/she is invited to discover a predetermined story—that of Tulse Luper and the twentieth-century—in the order that he/she chooses, but he/she cannot invent, nor even alter the story itself. The website has a classical arborescent structure and is little developed: the paths are clearly hierarchical and there are very few of them (in its most complex section, the site has about ten levels) (Ryan 2006). It is certainly possible to consider that, while the project is not terribly interactive in the technical sense of the term, it may be interactive on another level: by exposing its highly selective mode of writing, it is perhaps, in turn, encouraging a selective mode of reading—free-floating attention and free association—which may be the psychological equivalent to random access. However, while the order of the narrative may seem open, the story itself is entirely predetermined.[25] Narrative responsibility is not really shared: the user may access the story in any he/she wishes, but the author retains all authority.

Furthermore, *The Tulse Luper Suitcases* database is, in fact, finite. The exhibition, while ephemeral, was immutable—the objects were chosen, assembled and installed in a particular order and remained unchanged throughout the duration of the exhibition. Likewise, the films are finished works—images and sound were selected and edited once and for all. The website seems variable and expandable—it contains links to other sites, and the users are invited to leave comments—, however, this openness is limited—the related sites are very few in number and are, likewise, stable, the weblog remains a peripheral component, and is already "temporarily closed". It is fair to say that from the beginning, the duration of the project was clearly defined—it was to take over three years.

According to *The Tulse Luper Suitcases* project description, the proposed database was to be both interactive and infinite. However, as we have seen, its interactivity and expandability are rather limited. The project is not an open system but a closed one and doubly so. Its model is perhaps less of a network than the *Gesamtkunstwerk*, and its purpose may be less about communication and more about conservation.[26] *The Tulse Luper Suitcases*, like all of Greenaway's cinema, is led by a totalizing ambition. It manifests an absolute desire, certainly insatiable, to both represent and conserve everything—a man's life story, the entire twentieth-century and perhaps, even, the history of the world. Of course, the project seems to allow for an infinite proliferation of representations—stories, chronologies, maps, lists, and the like—however, it remains inevitably finite. The suitcase itself is an enclosed space, the number of suitcases is limited to ninety-two, the story takes place within a fixed amount of time: 1911-1989, the world is limited to a small number of cities, eleven to be exact, and so on. Evidently, these lists are often incomplete like Borges' famous map which is as vast as the land it represents, incoherent like his list of classes of animals, and "mises en abyme," like the book of books in the library of Babel. In this respect, these lists retain an ironic, even parodying, dimension: they demonstrate the vacuity of lists, the complexity and insurmountable heterogeneity of the world and of history. However, being essentially mimetic,

---

[25] In that sense, the website presents a purely "exploratory" interactivity: the user may alter the narrative discourse but not the story itself (Ryan 2006, 107-122). In the on-line game that was recently developed around Greenaway's projet, the user has more "ontological" impact on the story itself, but the overall architecture of the game remains a flowchart (*The Tulse Luper Journey*).

[26] Regarding the question of the *Gesamtkunstwerk* as it relates to intermediality, see Oosterling (2003).

parody takes part in whatever it criticizes. And irony changes nothing: *The Tulse Luper Suitcases* remains obsessed by the desire to preserve everything.

It is not surprising then, that food, digestion—and cruelty—play such a prominent role in Greenaway's oeuvre. *The Cook, the Thief and her Lover* is a perfect example of these preoccupations: the entire film takes place in the kitchen, dining room and restroom of a restaurant. Greenaway's cinema is certainly tormented by bulimia—as was noted by Pauline Kael[27]—and retention. Psychoanalysis has demonstrated a clear link between the anal sadistic stage and the desire for order, parsimony and obstinacy, all traits that remain central within the practices of collection and conservation. It has also established the importance of power relations, control and domination during this stage. In this regard, *The Belly of an Architect* is, without a doubt, one of Greenaway's most lucid films, as it associates constipation with the museum and neoclassicism. It is worth noting that neoclassicism is already an imminently museological art form, as it involves both historical appropriation and an appreciation for ideal and monumental forms.

Whatever the case may be, the story that is being preserved throughout *The Tulse Luper Suitcases* is not the whole story. Luper is a cosmopolitan and well-traveled character, however the world that he traverses is mostly an occidental one. Upon first glance, the map featured in the "Location" section of the "Archives" is a world map, but upon closer inspection, it appears to centralise the Western world. When one accesses this section, the map automatically focuses on the North Atlantic. And while all of the countries and continents are marked, only Europe and North America, consisting of merely nine European and two American cities, contain hypertext links. Similarly, the chronology featured in the "Timeline" section, focuses predominantly on Western historical events. In the rare instance that world events are mentioned, they are described from an occidental, and more specifically European, point of view. Furthermore, the Western history that is presented is rather conventional: it focuses on individuals, events and, at times, progress: it is the canonical history of science—the great names and the great discoveries: Curie and radium, Einstein and relativity, Bohr and quantum mechanics, etc.—, and the official history of the twentieth-century—the great men who governed, the great political and military events: World War II, the Cold War, the fall of the Berlin Wall, etc. This account of history does not acknowledge the many epistemological transformations experienced by twentieth century historical discourse, most notably, with the "École des Annales" and social history.

---

[27] "Greenaway is a cultural omnivore who eats with his mouth open." As cited on Peter Greenaway's website (*Peter Greenaway*).

The Tulse Luper Suitcases appears to question official histories. The project underscores and problematizes the close relationships between science, politics and the military, between knowledge and power. Moreover, it diverts official history to focus on the life-story of an anonymous character. Finally, it intimately mixes fact and fiction, history and literature, as if to demonstrate that history itself is largely a construction. However, in so doing, the *Suitcases* is always at risk of fictionalizing history and presenting it as a simple backdrop or, worse yet, as a reservoir of forms, motifs and narratives from which one can liberally draw, with a clear disregard for chronology, and the real conditions and causes of history. Furthermore, in creating this interplay between anecdote and history, the individual and the collective, the private and the public, fact and fiction, *The Tulse Luper Suitcases* resembles those traditional historical novels and films which only further confirm the official version of history—that of textbooks—and the common views regarding historical causality—that which attributes change to individual freedom or to some divine intervention.

The Tulse Luper Suitcases also seems to offer a critical reading of the artist's situation within modernity. Tulse Luper is indeed a marginalized individual in the society in which he lives, in twentieth-century history: he is often misunderstood as he spends much of his time imprisoned. The prison is not only a metaphor for the human condition, it is also a metaphor for the artist's studio or the writer's study, and as such, it provided an image of the artist's fate within totalitarian regimes or capitalist societies. Evidently, Tulse Luper is also Peter Greenaway's alter ego. The character was already present in several of Greenaway's earliest films, such as *A Walk Through H* (1978), *Vertical Features Remake* (1978) and *The Falls* (1980). Like Peter Greenaway, Tulse Luper, was born in Newport, Wales, and is an artist and writer, or, more precisely, a "project-maker." Some of Greenaway's actual works are even attributed retrospectively to Tulse Luper, such as his *92 Objects to Represent the World*.[28] At times, the imaginary biography of Tulse Luper reads like an autofiction, through which the author takes pleasure in anticipating the posthumous consideration of his life and work by future historians, all the while inscribing himself in the annals of history. While the work may have a fragmented structure, it nevertheless remains centripetal: all fragments refer back to the same absent, but structuring center: the figure of Tulse Luper, his body, his name—that of Peter Greenaway. The project thus revisits the literary and filmic genre of the lives of artists, with its hagiographic tendencies, as well as the individual art museum, with its preoccupation with relics—and all of this to the author's credit.

---

[28] Greenaway's project—an exhibition presented in Vienna in 1992—was entitled *100 Objects to Represent the World*.

With regards to the intertextual and hypertextual level, *The Tulse Luper Suitcases* is concerned with the preservation of a very particular history. As with the majority of Greenaway's oeuvre, most of the quotes, references, allusions, imitations and pastiches that make up this project, make reference to high Western culture—to the great names and masterpieces of Western history: Dante, Shakespeare, Rembrandt, Vermeer, Boullée, Ingres, Manet, Borges, and so on—but rarely to popular culture, mass culture or non-Western cultures. Moreover, despite appearances, Greenaway's project seems to favor textual culture over visual culture, literature over painting, words over images, speech over the body. It is possible to consider this reference to the past as ironic or, at the very least, ludic, as was collage and assemblage in modern art, or pastiche and parody in certain postmodern practices. However, it is likely a more serious appropriation, akin to classical and neoclassical imitation. In this instance, tradition is not ironically imitated for the purpose of criticism and consequently emancipation, but rather, seriously, for the purpose of confirmation and reinforcement—with maybe a desire to insert oneself in this long history. Through the relentless citation of historical works, Greenaway's works constitute and reconstitute the Western Canon, as if this collection was not only historical, but also eternal, not relative, but universal—beyond space and time.[29] In this case, the database assumes the form of a library, a European Library, or that of a museum of fine arts with a finite collection.

Through their use of digital technologies, the *Russian Ark* and *The Tulse Luper Suitcases* may well manifest a similar fetishistic fantasy—that of museification. While Sokurov's film relies on the long take, and Greenaway's project on a more arborescent structure, they are both taken with the dream of historical continuity and cultural totality. This fantasy is defensive and perhaps reactionary: these works demonstrate a similar concern for the fate of high culture in the age of mechanical reproduction and mass culture, for the fate of nations, Europe and the Western world in the age of global capitalism. Paradoxically, they also testify, and maybe more eloquently than any other contemporary work, to the ruins of history.

Archive Fever

In his inaugural text on the "lieux de mémoire," Pierre Nora (1996) discusses the present proliferation of commemorations—ceremonies,

---

[29] It is not my intention here to criticize the lacunas within Greenaway's oeuvre—all collections are selective—, but to simply underline the canonical coherence of his cultural references. Among the abundance of literature regarding the question of the canon, see most notably Gates (1992); Bloom (1994); Pollock (1999).

monuments, museums, libraries, archives—and databases. For the historian, this wave is but a symptom of the acceleration of time[30] and, more notably, of a radical transformation of our relation to history. The present is no longer thought of as a continuation of a living past, but rather as a rupture with a past that is definitely lost. There was a time when the past was experienced through *memory*, spontaneous memory, both personal and collective; it was acquired through experience, preserved and transmitted across generations by traditional institutions such as family, church, school and State. Today, the past is not experienced through living memories, but rather, reconstituted by history, by an artificial, voluntary, critical and essentially individual history. "Memory is constantly on our lips because it no longer exists," states Nora (1). "What we call memory today is therefore not memory but already history. The so-called rekindling of memory is actually its final flicker as it is consumed by history's flames" (8).

For Nora, memory is today, essentially archival, it collects and it records: it favours traces, monuments, documents, recordings. It is both material and sensual: it prefers objects, images and sound. It cultivates the presence of the past or its painstaking reconstitution, as demonstrated by the revival of orality, the return of narrative and, to be sure, the importance of the image, most notably the indexical image, as with photography or film. Memory is now led by an "archival obsession," which seems to aim at the integral preservation of the entire past—and the entire present—as if everything already had, or could eventually have, some historical significance, and thus deserves to be immediately archived and forever protected against the passing of time.[31] In the

---

[30] This idea is most likely borrowed from Halévy (2001). See also Jeanneney (2001).

[31] Nora's final judgment regarding the archive (as well as his judgment on the novel, images and technology) appear corporatist and even, conservative. However, his analysis is convincing. Since then, numerous historians have come back to that question and have arrived at similar conclusions, notably David Lowenthal (1985; 1996) and François Hartog (2003). Working with Reinhart Koselleck's reflections on the experience of historical time, Hartog attempts to define the contemporary regime of historicity. While the old regime was characterized by a certain "passeism"—which uses the past as a model and which presupposes an asymmetry between our experiences of the past and our expectations for the future—and modernity by a certain "futurism"—which believes in progress and presupposes an inverted asymmetry between the past and the future—, our contemporary world is marked by a certain "presentism"—a maximum distance between the field of experience and our horizon of expectation, a suspension of historical time in an omnipresent present (with regards to these ideas, see also Laïdi [2000]; Augé [2003]). "La lumière projetée depuis le futur baisse, l'imprévisibilité de l'avenir augmente, le présent devient la catégorie prépondérante, tandis que le passé récent—celui dont on s'étonne qu'il "ne passe pas" ou dont on s'inquiète qu'il "passe"—exige d'être incessamment et compulsivement visité et revisité" (Hartog 2001, 153). In fact, for

context of generalized preservation, the nation has also changed. The idea of the nation has already been problematized by historiography: history today is more social than national. Within public discourse, the nation is no longer thought of as a living subject, fully developed or in formation, playing a role within the great national narrative, with its mythic origins and its utopian ends, but as an historical object, whose past has to be preserved and commemorated. Today, the nation is a place of memory, and the nation's history is its heritage. Even the occasional resurgence of the nation and nationalism within historiography and in public discourse seems to participate in this "memorialization": the nation is no longer prospective, but retrospective, it is not teleological, but rather, nostalgic.

This memorial passion has a variety of causes. However, it is, no doubt, related to the extension of capitalism and its particular temporality. The acceleration of trade, production and consumption affects traditional continuities—experience is thus fragmented, family is weakened, communities are multiplied, society is atomized—thus causing a variety of identity crises, on both the individual and social levels. From this point of view, this obsession for preservation could well be a defense mechanism against the acceleration of time and of history, a reassuring refuge against general disaffiliation.[32]

Works Cited

Anderson, B. 1991. *Imagined communities: Reflections on the origin and spread of nationalism*. Revised Edition. London and New York: Verso Books.
Augé, M. 2003. *Le Temps en ruines*. Paris: Gallimard.
Bénédict, S. 2003. Insomnie. *Cahiers du cinéma* 577: 82-83.

Hartog, the contemporary proliferation of memorials does not contradict "presentism," but rather the contrary: it is a response to this new regime of historicity—of which it is a symptom (206). And just as Nora considers this obsession with archives to be an exemplary trait of this new historical memory, Hartog sees this concern for memorialization ("patrimonialisation") as being at the heart of contemporary presentism. In fact, in contemporary times, the past is constantly "presented", as if it was necessary to provide an experience of the past by any and all available means: the past, the sensual past, prevails over history, "la présence du passé, l'évocation et l'émotion l'emportent sur la prise de distance et la médiation" (199, 206). Inversely, the present is immediately historicized, as if everything was already historic or would very soon become historic: events are already include their "autocommemoration", and objects call for their instant museification (138, 156, 201). With regards to the question of the archive, see also Derrida (1995).

[32] I would like to thank Mikaela Bobiy for her generous help with the translation of this article and to Claude Chamberlan for having given me access to precious documentation on *The Tulse Luper Suitcases*.

Bloom, H. 1994. *The Western canon: The books and school of the ages.* New York: Harcourt Brace.
Bolter, J. D., and R. Grusin. 1999. *Remediation: Understanding new media.* Cambridge, Mass.: The MIT Press.
Bouchy, K. 2005. "Let's make a renewal. Répétition, multiplicité, bifurcations: les stratégies de Peter Greenaway." In *Opening Peter Greenaway's Tulse Luper Suitcases.* Edited by G. Kochhar-Lindgren. Spec. issue of Image [&] Narrative 12 (15 June 2006).
<http://www.imageandnarrative.be/tulseluper/tulse_luper.htm>
Bouquet, S. 2003. Des films et des gestes. *Cahiers du cinéma* 578: 52-53.
Christie, I. 2004. The civilising Russian. *Sight and Sound* 14.4:10-15, 52-53.
Derrida, J. 1995. *Mal d'archive. Une impression freudienne.* Paris: Galilée.
Elliot, B. and A. Purdy. 2005. Man in a suitcase: Tulse Luper at Compton Verney. In *Opening Peter Greenaway's Tulse Luper Suitcases.* Edited by G. Kochhar-Lindgren. Spec. issue of *Image [&] Narrative* 12 (15 June 2006) <http://www.imageandnarrative.be/tulseluper/tulse_luper.htm>
Gates, H. L. 1992. *Loose canons: notes on the culture wars.* Oxford: Oxford University Press.
Halévy, D. 2001. *Essai sur l'accélération de l'histoire.* 2nd ed. Paris: Fallois.
Hartog, F. 2003. *Régimes d'historicité. Présentisme et expériences du temps.* Paris: Seuil.
Heinich, N. and M. Pollack. 1989. Du conservateur de musée à l'auteur d'expositions. L'exécution d'une position singulière. *Sociologie du travail* 31: 29-49. Translated 1996. From Museum Curator to Exhibition Auteur. In *Thinking about exhibitions.* Edited by R. Greenberg, B. Ferguson and S. Nairne. 231-247. London: Routledge.
Hobsbawm, E. 1990. *Nations and nationalism since 1780.* Cambridge: Cambridge University Press.
Jeanneney, J-N. 2001. *L'histoire va- t-elle plus vite? Variations sur un vertige.* Paris: Gallimard.
Johnson, W. 2004. Russian Ark. *Film Quarterly* 57.2: 48-51.
Kennan, G. F. 1971. *The Marquis de Custine and his Russia in 1839.* Princeton, Princeton University Press.
Kochhar-Lindgren, G., ed. 2005. Opening Peter Greenaway's Tulse Luper suitcases. Spec. issue of *Image [&] Narrative* 12 (15 June 2006) <http://www.imageandnarrative.be/tulseluper/tulse_luper.htm>
Koselleck, R. 1990. *Futures past: On the semantics of historical time.* Translated by K. Tribe. 2nd ed. Cambridge MA: The M.I.T. Press.
Kujundzic, D. 2004. After 'After:' The arkive fever of Alexander Sokurov. *Quarterly Review of Film and Video* 21: 219-239.
Laïdi, Z. 2000. *Le Sacre du présent.* Paris: Flammarion.

Leslie, J. and A.Ward. 2004. *Peter Greenaway: Luper at Compton Verney.* Compton Verney: Compton Verney House Trust.
Lowenthal, David. 1985. *The Past is a foreign country.* Cambridge: Cambridge University Press.
—. 1996. *Possessed by the Past: The heritage crusade and the spoils of history.* New York and London: The Free Press.
Manovich, L. 2001. *The Language of new media.* Cambridge, Mass.: The MIT Press.
McNab, G. 2002. Palace in Wonderland. *Sight and Sound* 12.8 (2002): 20.
Nora, P. 1984/1997. Entre mémoire et histoire. La problématique des lieux. In *Les lieux de mémoire.* Edited by P. Nora. Vol. 1. 23-43. Paris: Gallimard. Translated as "Between memory and history." 1996. In *Realms of memory: Rethinking the French past.* Vol.1. 1-20. New York: Columbia University Press.
Noys, B. 2005. Tulse Luper database: Peter Greenaway, the new media object and the art of exhaustion. In *Opening Peter Greenaway's Tulse Luper suitcases.* Edited by G. Kochhar-Lindgren. Spec. issue of *Image [&] Narrative* 12 (15 June 2006).
<http://www.imageandnarrative.be/tulseluper/tulse_luper.htm>
Oosterling, H. 2003. Sens(a)ble intermediality and interesse: Toward an ontology of the in-between. *Intermedialities* 1: 29-46.
Oppenheim, J. 2003. Tour de force. *American Cinematographer* 84. 1: 85-95.
Pascoe, D. 1997. *Peter Greenaway: museums and moving images.* London: Reaktion Books.
Pollock, G. 1999. *Differencing the canon: feminist desire and the writing of art's histories.* London and New York: Routledge.
Ryan, M-L. 2006. Toward an interactive narratology. In *Avatars of story.* Minneapolis and London: University of Minnesota Press. 97-125, 237-240.
Tesson, C. 2002. Restauration. *Cahiers du cinéma* 569: 48-49.

Websites

The Hermitage Museum (14 September 2006)
<http://www.hermitagemuseum.org>
The Tulse Luper Suitcases: A Personal History of Uranium (11 September 2006) <http://www.tulselupernetwork.com>
The Tulse Luper Journey (14 September 2006)
<http://www.tulseluperjourney.com>
The Tulse Luper Journey. Moccu (14 September 2006)
<http://www.moccu.com/ci/show/ensptl>
The Tulse Luper Suitcase (14 September 2006) <http://www.tulseluper.net>

Peter Greenaway (14 September 2006) <http://petergreenaway.co.uk>
The Kasander Film Company (14 September 2006)
 <http://www.kasanderfilm.nl>.

PART III:

EUROPEAN FILM AND ITS OTHER BORDERS: CROSS-CULTURAL, NATIONAL, AND TRANSNATIONAL PERSPECTIVES

CHAPTER SEVEN

IMMIGRATION IN THE POST-INDUSTRIAL AGE

CLAUDIO MAZZOLA,
UNIVERSITY OF WASHINGTON

Some of the most typical characteristics of a modern nation may include a common language, well-defined geographical borders, and a strong reliable central government. From the official political unification in 1861, it took Italy almost a century before some of these characteristics materialized on its own territory, finally allowing Italy to be internationally recognized as a unified country. Until the end of World War II, Italy struggled to cement a gamut of regional and local realities, while unable to defeat many groups' interests, often left over from the 15th and 16th centuries city-states. Not even the Fascist dictatorship, that strongly stressed a Roman ideal of power and greatness to resuscitate a dormant patriotism, was able to erase the divisions that prevented actual unification. Ironically it was just the effort to fight Fascism that succeeded in promoting the unification. The common Fascist enemy pushed together people from all regions of Italy, mixing different languages and cultures and erasing any social class difference. The various governments that took over the leadership of the country, after the transition from Monarchy to Republic in June 1946, understood the importance of cultivating this newly discovered national identity by providing strong social structures, like a unified school system where standard Italian was taught, and a political system based on the needs of a nation and not reflecting personal interests. After centuries of separation, Italians needed to see themselves as part of a well-organized system that would allow them to develop a sense of belonging. The end of twenty years of Fascist dictatorship provided the perfect political and psychological moment to overcome the problems that had hindered unification in 1861. Slowly, Italians developed what had already been for almost two hundred years common to all the modern western European countries: a sense of unity. The political chaos of the Renaissance was due to the existence of a myriad of local laws that constantly fluctuated according to the changing needs of the ruling family. It was a hierarchy where most of the people were at the bottom of a pyramid and only a few were at the top, and where there was no possibility of an exchange because there were no rights given to those at the bottom. With the formation of the modern state, the pyramid still existed but it was more stratified, with clearly marked boundaries of social and political activities; the Constitution gave specific rights and duties to every citizen. The situation that effectively took shape in Italy after World War II helped develop a way of thinking that was based on binary oppositions in all major areas of social life (politics, economy or culture). The Communists were constantly juxtaposed to the Christian Democrats, the upper class to the proletariat, high culture to entertainment or popular culture. No matter which side of the barrier one was on, one always ended up developing his/her strategies around specific dichotomies.

At the end of World War II, cinema followed the development of Italian society very closely. The Italian cinema of that period, defined by many critics with the label of Neorealism, was characterized by a strong socio-political commitment. Many of the movies made between 1945 and 1955 presented either a political theme (the fight against Fascism) or a social one (the right for everybody to have a job and a home). It is enough to remember the almost didactic presentation of historical facts in Roberto Rossellini's *Paisà* (1946) and the cartoonish representation of the Nazi in *Open City* (1945) to understand how Neorealism dealt with World War II. While technically these movies redefined the representation of reality in commercial cinema and established techniques that influenced the filmmaking of directors like Antonioni and Fellini, the plot often counted on a rather simplified juxtaposition between two opposite sides (very often a plain "good" versus "evil" game). The situation did not change in the 60s and 70s, a period in which political movies, although in decline, still based their structures on a strong juxtaposition of forces. Movies that criticized the status quo and the leading government party (the Christian Democrats) or that exposed the criminal activities of the Mafia often employed simplified stereotypes to make their point.

Up to this point we can clearly say that Italian society was characterized by clearly distinct social classes, within a very rigidly structured economic and political system. All this was radically shaken by the international events of the mid-late 80s. The socio-political situation started to change dramatically with the collapse of Communism and the fall of the Berlin Wall. The opening up of the Soviet block borders signaled the beginning of the strongest phase of the globalization of the continent: new markets, new working opportunities, and new political environments. This contributed to the redefinition of two elements that have been the base of modern industrial societies since the beginning of the last century: the concept of *time* and *space*. While space remained invariable and time could be changed or altered, nobody could really foresee that we had almost reached instantaneity. As Zygmut Bauman (2000) says:

> "Solid" modernity was an era of mutual engagement. "Fluid" modernity is the epoch of disengagement, elusiveness, facile escape and hopeless chase. In "liquid" modernity, it is the most elusive, those free to move without notice, who rule (120).

The political system and the economy were literally swept away by the new developments and, at first, the individual was just an amazed and shocked spectator. Then, when the waves of change were not just part of a virtual reality seen on television, but concrete facts that were altering everyday life, individuals realized that they had to make some much-needed adjustments. For example, economically speaking, globalization introduced stiffer competition in markets once dominated by local products and not at all used to war prices. It shook up an economic system that, in some countries like Italy, never had to deal with the concept of productivity as the main aspect defining the individual worker. After all, the Italian working environment rarely made the worker feel directly responsible for the well-being of the company. Jobs, especially in a market dominated by small companies and big nationalized industries, were primarily perceived as a right for everyone to earn a living in order to support a family. One's job was a lifelong contract with an employer in a place where one was born, got married and most likely was going to die. The demands of international competition and the privatization of major companies drastically changed all this. A sense of precariousness was introduced into the job market. The place of work changed (no longer the typical modern location i.e. the office and the factory); the hours spent on the job also changed (no longer rigidly confined to the standard eight-hour day). The typical Fordist division of work was disappearing, which also meant that the definition of responsibilities and opportunities was also being altered. In a modern society like Italy, with a strong feudal history system in its background, the individual was always identified by the particular position that he/she occupied in a hierarchy of values that were well-defined spatially and temporally: one always knew where he/she was standing and where he/she wanted to go. Although mobility within the social scale was somewhat limited, the social state provided a kind of safety net that gave even to those at the bottom of the hierarchy (the proletariat) a minimum sense of security. Now that globalization has erased all this, individuals cannot clearly see themselves in a social context as they had before. The drawing line has disappeared, anything is possible, but the risk is incommensurably higher. More freedom means also more confusion, while there seems to be no one available anymore to provide comfort or support, and everyone is talking only about doing better than before, and better than the person next to them. All this while the family, which in the past provided the biggest psychological and physical cushion for Italians, has gone through serious changes, as it takes on a different role. In any manifestation of everyday living, the individual cannot rely on the ability to see himself/herself clearly positioned for the future. The transition from a society dominated by a vertical hierarchy and what Lawrence Friedman (1999) calls a "horizontal society" is in action. But this development brings more confusion to the individual:

> In a horizontal society, identity becomes, perhaps for the first time, problematic. It becomes, in short, a matter of (apparent) choice.... We have, in short, a certain degree of control over identity: over which identity to put on top of the pile. Or, to be more accurate, we either have this control, or, what comes to the same thing socially, we think we do (9).

We believe that we have this freedom but we are not really sure how to use it. In fact, because institutions have not kept up with these changes, most Italians seem to be counting on the old structures, and the government is simply encouraging that. It is in fact very revealing that still in 2006 Silvio Berlusconi, the Italian Prime Minister, leader of a coalition not characterized by a particular ideology, based his political campaign for national election on his opposition to Communism. Besides the actual validity of such a claim, it is interesting because it indicates how Berlusconi understood the need to try to draw a line between "us" and "them" and, in times where this division is ideologically non-existent, he recuperated a cold war term so that Italians could orient themselves in the chaotic world of the politics of today.

While the new international social order started to influence the structures of Italian society from the early 90s, in the same period another major social change, strictly connected to international changes, was taking place domestically: the arrival of a constantly increasing number of immigrants from North Africa, Central America and the Far East. This immigration exposed the inadequacy of social structures in the face of the new international situation. For almost a century Italy was mainly a nation of emigrants; it was a nation that dealt with problems of racism and discrimination from the victim's position. Suddenly the country found itself dealing with opposite problems: Italians were accused of being racists and of discriminating against immigrants. The Italian institutions reacted very slowly to this phenomenon, delaying any prompt intervention, while spreading fear and diffidence toward the newcomers with the tendency to see Italy barricaded behind strong values. For many Italians it was extremely difficult to interpret what was really happening because immigration was overlapping all the changes brought about by globalization. In their essay on the global self, Chiara Giaccardi and Mauro Magatti (2003) point out very clearly the difficulty of interpreting a fast changing reality:

CHAPTER SEVEN

> ... economia, politica e cultura non sono più contenute – nè contenibili – entro i confini dello Stato. Con la globalizzazione, questi tre ambiti tendono a organizzarsi in modo autonomo e su spazi che sono sempre meno coincidenti con quello della società nazionale. ... La perdita della complanarità spaziale delle tre dimensioni della vita sociale mette in moto tutta una serie di fenomeni che fatichiamo a interpretare, dato che la loro logica non può essere fatta rientrare negli schemi interpretativi del passato. La debolezza delle nostre interpretazioni è testimoniata dalla coesistenza di una pluralità di posizioni antitetiche che troviamo confusamente intrecciate nel dibattito contemporaneo (35).[1]

In modern society, and since the 18th century Colonialist period, the distinction between "us" and "them" has always been clearly marked by the juxtaposition of religion, culture, and language. In the past, immigrants were looking at their new country in search for some kind of stability (mainly financial and political), often in exchange for the unconscious partial loss of some aspects of their cultural identity. Stories of repression, misery, and abuses were taking place in an environment where the host country stood behind its social and political order. Immigrants, although often critical of their host country, were ready to absorb the new political and economical structures and pay a price for integration. In contemporary Italy—where the people's dissatisfaction with the State is at a peak, and the major structures of society are under pressure for reforms that the government is not inclined or able to grant—there is not much that the country can offer as far as models for a successful integration of immigrants. A superficial display of wealth apparently easily available to anyone, in combination with more relaxed immigration laws (if compared with other European countries), is constantly attracting people from all over the world. In these conditions the new immigrants are less interested in absorbing the local culture, except for some superficial traits, because there are no models provided to them by Italian society.

Historically, Italian cinema has dealt only marginally and mostly through documentaries with the emigration towards the US and South America. Much more attention was given to the internal emigration of the 60s from the South toward the industrialized North. Although some directors had a serious approach to the topic, making intelligent and provocative movies—like Luchino

---

[1] "... economics, politics and culture are no longer contained, nor containable, within the boundaries of the State. With globalization these three components tend to become autonomous and get organized around spaces that less and less coincide with those of national identity. ... The loss of the contemporary existence of these three dimensions of social life generates a series of events (phenomena) that we are unable to interpret since their logic cannot be related to interpretative structures of the past. The weakness of our interpretations is proven by the existence of many antithetical opinions that we find chaotically interwoven in contemporary discussions" (my translation).

Visconti's *Rocco and His Brothers* (1960)—, the prevailing mood within the film industry was to take advantage of the most trite stereotypes about Northern and Southern Italians to develop a comic formula that would be employed in comic movies. In fact, between the mid-sixties and the mid-seventies, there were a number of very popular movies dealing with domestic emigration that did very well at the box office (the most famous is probably Lina Wertmuller's *The Seduction of Mimi* [1972]). The choice of turning domestic emigration into a comic act is indicative of the fact that this was not a problem that was deeply shaking the structures of Italian society. The differences in language, habits, moral standards, etc., were taking place within a similar substratum which was slowly absorbing all differences.

Instead, international immigration to Italy directly threatened the roots of Italian society (the school system, the family, the job market); the first movies to deal with this issue (appearing in the early 90s) were more concerned with exposing the inadequacy of Italian society rather than looking at the problem of integration. Movies like *Vesna va veloce* by Carlo Mazzacurati (1995) and *Un'anima divisa in due* by Silvio Soldini (1994) are stories of loss and confusion where the Italians are as much at loss as the foreigners. Probably the strongest and the most original statement of the early wave of movies concerned with immigration (1993-1997) is *Lamerica* by Gianni Amelio (1993), a movie that from the very title connects the recent phenomenon to the emigration of Italians toward the United States at the beginning of last century. Amelio explores how difficult it is in today's society to understand someone else's position, to accept "otherness," especially when this implies operating within different cultures, but also, as Friedman stated earlier, the choices that one has in dealing with his/her own identity. Amelio's two protagonists (Fiore, the older, and Luigi, the younger) are the perfect representatives of the old status quo. The two men arrive in Albania to set up a new shoe factory, just at the moment when a lot of Albanians are trying to enter the Italian embassy in an attempt to leave their country after the fall of Communism. The Italians are supposed to be the new entrepreneurs who understand the mechanics of the global market and are ready to bring their expertise abroad. In reality, Fiore and Luigi are more like old-fashioned Capitalists, or swindlers who are trying to take advantage of the Albanians in order to get all they can for themselves. The shoe factory is in fact a mockery: they are trying to collect money from the Italian government that is awarding large sums of money to entrepreneurs who set up businesses in developing countries. In order to do this they bribe the Albanian authorities exactly like they would bribe their countrymen. Their mentality is that of the colonialists of the 18th century; they base their actions constantly on a sense of superiority and a rejection of any attempt to understand the local culture. While traveling in their jeep with a local translator, they harshly criticize the Albanians for being unable to cultivate their land and to turn a profit. This is taking place while they are leaving Valona, the port of arrival from Italy. The camera shows the Italians driving their jeep on a very long straight country road; they are the only ones going toward the mountains, while everyone else is going toward the sea in trying to embark to Italy. Fiore and Luigi are deeper into the heart of a country that will soon disappear, at least in the way they perceive it. While Albanians can only use their feet or their animals to get to Valona, Luigi and Fiore rely on the typical modern means of transportation: the car. Their jeep is the most obvious symbol of how modernity handled the harmonious relation between time and space; their traveling fulfills their need for adventure while giving them the feeling of being in total control. On their part, there is almost a physical need to possess the land they come to use for their business. Luigi and Fiore are still living the classic modern experience of the conquerors. They have not realized that among the many things that globalization has brought about there is the idea that there is no more land to conquer; our world has become smaller, no more places to hide, to seek refuge or to impose one's superiority.

Actually, with the fall of the Soviet Union, there is not even the fear of the existence of boundaries from which a political threat might come. Terrorism, the major threat of the new century, does not have a fixed geographical home. We cannot identify boundaries that can be either the fulfillment of our dreams or the realization of our fears. Luigi and Fiore are ignoring all this; they are exporting their modern view of the world in a land that appears "backward" to them and that soon will be ruled by a typical post-industrial economy where the service industry will dominate the job market. There is an episode in the movie that stresses this point. When asked for extra help by Luigi, the local translator says that he cannot help him because he has a previous engagement with a German businessman. Luigi seems surprised that others may be interested in Albania, except that, unlike the Italians, the others are for real. The Germans are in Albania not to cheat their own government or the Albanians, but to build a resort hotel. They perfectly understand how to take advantage of the new opportunity, while the Italians have a myopic view of the situation and think only of the short-term profit of the illegal business they are setting up. Only a major trauma can force Luigi to realize that their way of thinking is totally out of sync with reality. The first event that wakes him up from his dream world is the disappearance of the wheels of his jeep. While riding with an old man who is going to pose as the chairman of the non-existing shoe factory, he takes a break and, after having parked the car, goes to look for food. At this point, with no cellular phone and no support from the more experienced Fiore, who has returned to Rome, the jeep is the only element that connects him with his world. There couldn't be a more symbolic place than the no-man's land for the robbery to occur. In a large unpaved square, there is a squalid, one-story building and a lot of debris, probably from artillery fire. The place is full of idle Albanians, mostly men; some are sitting while others are standing, and they all curiously observe Luigi's actions. When he exits the building, he finds out that somebody has stolen the wheels of his jeep. At this point Luigi loses his temper, accuses all of them of being thieves, threatens to call the police and, in the end, says he will take the law into his own hands. The camera underlines the absurdity of all his claims by juxtaposing his hysterical behavior with the desperate calm of the Albanians. The plea to law and order made by Luigi sounds ridiculous when contrasted with the sense of destruction and precariousness of the Albanians' lives. While Luigi shouts and screams, the camera moves around him, so that at the end of the sequence we have a 360-degree panoramic view of the location. The sequence ends with Luigi abandoning any rational claim and shouting: "You damned Albanians!" This is the beginning of the end for Luigi, or rather the beginning of a new beginning. Now that he has lost the most tangible sign of his alleged superiority, his car, Luigi begins a long journey back to Valona in what is like a *Bildungsroman*, a realization of his "otherness" through a search of his own identity. Step by step, Luigi learns to understand the Albanians' point of view; he learns to reason as a human being with human beings, and forgoes basing his interactions on stereotypes. His inner transformation is symbolically matched by his external one. Slowly, he loses all the traits that made him physically different from the Albanians. By the end of the movie, he is dressed like them, he looks like them and he has the same desperate look on his face. In fact, the last phase of this transformation shows him returning to the place where everything started and he is arrested. The authorities are not really after him but after the Albanian official who was bribed by Fiore and Luigi. Still, Luigi will be stripped of the last mark that distinguishes him from the Albanians: his anagraphical identity. The police officer who perfectly knows the kind of person Luigi is, starts the interrogation by praising Italy for its natural beauty, espresso and all the other stereotypes that actually made Luigi feel superior. Luigi seems totally comforted by the policemen's speech and believes he can easily get out of this situation. Suddenly the policeman changes tone and takes Luigi by surprise. He tells him that he is free to go, provided that he hands over his passport to the Albanian police. When Luigi complains, the policeman tells him that he does not need a passport, that no Albanian has one. While throughout the entire movie Luigi tried to shout in the face of every Albanian he met that he was Italian, now he realizes that his stupidity and his arrogance have put him in that situation, and that the only way to be free is, ironically, to be an Albanian. The only thing he can now do is try his luck as an illegal alien. Not even the language can grant him a free safe ride to Italy since most of the Albanians he met, including the police officer, spoke Italian very well. By stripping him of all the superficial traits that made him different from the Albanians, Amelio shows how Luigi must now prove that he can make choices on his own, that he can be someone without hiding behind Fiore, the jeep, and his language. In the last sequence of the movie, we see the big boat full of clandestine immigrants sailing toward Italy. The boat is so old that the images could recall the boat full of Italian immigrants going to the US in the last century. Luigi, who always scorned the Albanians for imagining a life of luxuries in Italy, is now there with them; he has certainly understood how those illusions are necessary, even when one knows that they are just illusions, to carry on, to survive. In this last sequence Gianni Amelio shows the Albanians on the boat juxtaposing a series of long shots and close-ups. There is a strange feeling of uniformity that emerges from each shot. As individuals, they obviously show personal physical traits that make them different from one another, and yet there is something similar in each single close up. It is as if the common inner struggle is somehow transforming their individual physical traits. They all look different and yet they all look alike. As such, the long shots show the boat as a black spot of human hopes like an island surrounded by the calm waters of the sea. That is how the Italians are going to see it when it will land and they will obviously apply all the stereotypes that Luigi and Fiore themselves used when they arrived in Albania. But now Luigi is one of them; he has learned how easy it is to cross that boundary that separates you from clandestinity, from poverty, from crime.

A more flexible perception of his identity is what characterizes Sandro, the protagonist of Marco Tullio Giordana's *Quando sei nato non ti puoi piu' nascondere* (2005). Giordana, who made this movie more than ten years after *Lamerica*, uses Amelio's same idea of an Italian returning home with a group of illegal aliens, although the "educating" process takes a few different twists because of the age of the protagonist. Sandro is a teenager from the Northern industrial town of Brescia, in the heart of a very wealthy region that employs a great deal of foreign workers and where xenophobic sentiment runs very high. Sandro's father, who could be Luigi a few years later, belongs to the old guard: humanly open to the immigrants but deep down racist. He has the typical paternalistic attitude toward every major social issue and shows a good dose of machismo in educating his son. In his factory he employs immigrants, where he seems to be treating them fairly well, although it is obvious that he does that more from a sense of guilt. He is mainly concerned with his well-being and his factory's productivity. Sandro is struggling between the well-established middle class sense of security that his family gives him and his natural curiosity to explore and understand what is going on around him. In the opening sequence of the movie we see him through the gray and empty streets of Brescia running into a man who is trying to make a telephone call from a booth. The man, who speaks a foreign language that sounds like an African language, does not understand that the phone does not work. Sandro wants to help him so he tries to explain what the problem is. The man gets out from the booth and starts speaking to Sandro; he repeats the same sentence with words that although meaningless to him will vividly stick in his mind (what the man says is the actual title of the movie: when you are born you cannot hide any longer). Sandro's curiosity is leading him to places and exposing him to situations that the adults would easily reject. In a world that reduces the possibility of socializing with a foreigner to a minimum, it is obvious that the encounter with a foreigner is also perceived as something to avoid. The streets of Brescia are symbolically empty and we have the feeling that Sandro's parents do anything they can to avoid encounters that would embarrass him and be perceived as threats to their son. At the end of the opening sequence, while Sandro is still elaborating what is happening, some policemen come to take the foreigner away. The turning point of the movie is when, during a vacation with his father off the coast of Greece, Sandro falls off the sailing boat and is later rescued by a boat of illegal aliens on their way towards Italy. The boat is overcrowded with people from many different countries. Unlike Luigi, who always clung to his identity to make clear that he was not "one of them," Sandro learns very quickly that being Italian does not mean being better. In fact, when he wakes up after being rescued, the first thing he sees and hears are the two Italians who are leading the boat. The Italians are "scafisti" and common criminals who take advantage of the immigrants by taking them by boat from Northern Africa or the Southern Adriatic to Italy, and then abandoning the immigrants and the boat a few miles off the coast. Sandro hears them discussing his rescue because he looks like a wealthy kid and they see the possibility of asking for a ransom. When interrogated by the two men, Sandro decides to keep his nationality hidden; to confuse them he pronounces the same words he heard from the man in the telephone booth. Symbolically this phrase becomes the representation of his new life and at the same time indicates how the line that separates "us" from "them" does not really exist. Any pre-existing notion of what is "good" and "evil" is slowly erased during the part of the movie in which Sandro observes the hard life of the immigrants on the boat. The strongest learning experience is probably when he sees one of the two young Romanians that he befriended selling her body to one of the Italians in order to get some water. The girl painfully accepts the man's advances when suddenly Sandro interrupts the encounter. He is rigidly applying his concept of "good" and he does not understand the girl's behavior. He is very surprised when both his friends tell him that he is wrong, that the girl's sacrifice would have meant getting some water for the three of them. While Luigi was constantly exposed to the Albanian's reality and never for a second tried or thought about considering their point of view, Sandro reflects on what he has just learned and is able to find a balance between direct experience and mediated experience. In fact, he slowly learns how to become more and more skeptical about any pre-conceived notion related to the people around him. When he gets to Italy and meets his parents at the immigrant recovery center, he finds their attitude unacceptable because they treat the two Romanian friends paternalistically. Once Sandro has completely deleted the barrier between him and his friends, he cannot see things the way his parents do. In an interview that Marco Tullio Giordana ("Giordana," 2005) gave when the movie was released, he explains why he chose the boy's point of view to present the movie:

> Il film è come se fosse una soggettiva, come se la mdp fosse il bambino. La mia scelta è di seguire solo lui. Non racconto la ricerca affannosa dei genitori, la guardia costiera, gli elicotteri. Non racconto il rientro in Italia, la curiosità morbosa dei media, le interviste. Non racconto tutto questo intanto perchè il mio protagonista, Sandro, non se lo può immaginare nè vorrà pensarci, impegnato come è nella propria sopravvivenza. E' il partito preso di un film che assume come punto di vista quello del suo protagonista che non vuole e non può conoscere quello che avviene fuori dalla portata del suo sguardo (20).[2]

The movie avoids presenting the director's point of view with the usual melodrama of the "lost-child-reunion" story. The actual meeting with his parents after his disappearance at sea takes place in a rather anticlimactic atmosphere. There is no tension about their meeting; it actually feels like it takes a long time to reach him because the movie is focusing on his protagonist's discovery that there is a bigger truth hidden below the superficial aspect of the events. Giordana avoids the most mundane aspect of the whole story. Sandro has become the talk of the nation; everybody knows about him but the director does not want to rely on this aspect and actually makes a point of letting the spectator know that this is not what interests him. On a couple of occasions, Sandro is recognized on the streets as the boy who went through the terrible ordeal with the immigrants. Sandro always answers in a rather annoyed way, rejecting both people's superficial understanding of his adventure and their commiseration. The director rejects what we can call "the mediated-mediatic" experience. Unlike Luigi, who was unable to process the two realities he confronted, Sandro is in the position of seeing all the possibilities and of

---

[2] "It is as if the movie were presented through a subjective point of view. It is as if the camera were the boy. My choice is to follow him exclusively. I am not describing the painful search of the parents, the coast guard, and the helicopter. I am not describing the return to Italy, the morbid curiosity of the media, the interviews. I am not describing all of this first of all because the protagonist, Sandro, cannot even imagine it, nor does he want to think about if because he is busy trying to survive. It is the specific choice of a movie that takes as the main point of view that of his protagonist who does not want and cannot know what is happening outside his field of vision" (my translation).

choosing one, even if he cannot always comprehend all the consequences of his actions. Sandro's development is exemplified by the most challenging moment in the movie. After running away from the refugee center, the two Romanians find shelter at Sandro's parents' house. Rejected by Sandro's father because with their escaping they have become officially illegal aliens, Radu and Alina steal what they can and run away. Giordana saves the film from the paternalistic and safe ending that seemed to take over the story once Sandro left the immigrant center and returned home. In fact, Giordana shifts the movie back to the boy's point of view at the moment when he could have chosen a politically correct perspective. The theft seems to re-establish the line that divides good from bad: illegal aliens are indeed bad, after all, no matter what you do and how much you trust them, they end up stealing from you. These are some of the statements that bounce back and forth in the boy's mind and this is what ultimately his father tells him. But Sandro has grown beyond these meaningless statements. He remembers the case of Alina prostituting herself for water and his misjudging the situation. At first Sandro is confused and lost but, interestingly enough, he does not ask for help from either of his parents. He goes first to the foreign classmate and then to the immigrant worker in his father's factory; in both cases he wants to find out more about immigration from the perspective of those directly experiencing it. Although surrounded by subtle forms of racism, Sandro's simple soul knows that he can obtain more satisfying answers from the immigrants than from his parents. The man answers Sandro's question by confirming that once he was illegal and that he was also forced to steal to survive, but that does not mean that he is a thief. While his father was able to accept Alina and Radu as long as they played by the rules of Italian society and Sandro could not help them once they escaped from the refugee center, Sandro understands that there are many other ways to interpret their actions. He learns that it is wrong to judge according to his society's standards. Without telling anybody, he goes by train to Milan, where he thinks he can find Alina and Radu. Here, in the middle of an old dismantled factory, among debris, barracks, and a world apart from the wealthy big city, he finds Alina. Her make-up, her flashy clothes clash with the memory of innocence that Sandro had in mind when they were on the boat. Here Sandro is faced with another mystery of life: sex. Alina is forced into prostitution and Sandro wonders if Radu is really her brother. But at this point, he has already jumped the fence; he has already stepped beyond the line that his father did not dare to cross and that Luigi in *Lamerica* did not even know existed. The point of view through which this last sequence is presented is again that of the young man. Very few words are exchanged between the two teenagers. Explanations are avoided because they would be out of place, they would be words that the director placed in the young protagonist's mouth imposing his own view of the facts. Alina and Sandro do not say much also because neither of them knows how to explain what is happening to them. In the last shot of the film, Alina and Sandro are sitting on a sidewalk in the outskirts of the city. It is night, it is cold and the long shot shows them completely lost in this foreign environment. Alina and Sandro are facing a reality much bigger than them, and have very few answers, but they understand that they are living in a horizontal society. They possess what Zygmut Bauman (2000) calls a sense of civility:

> The main point about civility is—let me repeat—the ability to interact with strangers without holding their strangeness against them and without pressing them to surrender it or to renounce some or all the traits that have made them strangers in the first place (104).

When in the early 90's the first movies dealing with the recent immigration started to appear nationwide, their main characteristic was the representation of a situation that to the vast majority of Italians was above all disorienting and unexplainable. From the very beginning of the movie it is obvious that Luigi and Fiore can neither understand nor actually conceive of the concept of diversity. The situation gets even worse when these words become embodied in real life experience imposed upon them by the development of their own situation in Albania. The two Italians are part of a transitional generation, too removed from the period when Italians were themselves victims of oppression, and too unconscious of what is happening to their country to realize that things will never be the same. In fact, many Italians totally misjudged the repercussions of a phenomenon (immigration) that they believed to be temporary, to be as seasonal as the arrival of tourists in summertime. Fiore and Luigi speak as if the problems in Albania are going to disappear soon and the flux of people toward Italy is only a transitory event. They cannot fully comprehend the mechanism until they became part of it. *Lamerica*, even by its title, proves this point: it represents the illusion that all Italians had when they searched for a better life in America and the illusion that the Albanians have presently. Ridiculing their hopes is like ridiculing themselves; but Luigi learns it only at the end of the movie and he is left with the big question looming over him regarding the kind of Italy he will find once he lands with all the illegal immigrants. Giordana's movie, on the other hand, focuses on the generation that grew up with the changes brought about by immigration. Sandro (clearly born in the early 90s when the old order was already disappearing) has the curiosity and the desire to see things differently. His struggle with his parents and the authorities indicate how he is unable to conform to a form of political correctness that emerged in the absence of a real acceptance by Italian society. It will probably take another generation before the country shows its ability to adapt to the horizontal society. But these structures will be in a state of flux because in this fluid modernity, as

Bauman says, "duration" is "a liability and not an asset" and it needs people like Sandro, always ready to adapt and change.

Works Cited

Amelio, G. 1993. *Lamerica*. Italy: Cecchi-Gori.
Bauman, Z. 2000. *Liquid modernity*. Cambridge: Polity Press.
Friedman, L. 1999. *The horizontal society*. New Haven and London: Yale University.
Giaccardi, C. and M. Magatti. 2003. *L'io globale*. Bari: Laterza.
Giordana, T. M. 2005. *Quando sei nato non ti puoi più nascondere*. Italy: Rai Cinema.
—. 2005. Giordana non si nasconde. Interview edited by F. Pedroni. *Duellanti* 17 (June): 20-21.

CHAPTER EIGHT

CHANGING DIRECTION: IRISH CINEMA REVISITS ITS BORDERS

RUTH BARTON, UNIVERSITY COLLEGE DUBLIN

> Irish culture rediscovers its best self, not self-consciously, not self-regardingly, but in its encounter with other cultures—continental, British, American, etc. For as long as Irish people think of themselves as Celtic Crusoes on a sequestered island, they ignore not only their diaspora but the basic cultural truth that cultural creation comes from hybridization not purity, contamination not immunity, polyphony not monologue. By reminding us of the many migrant minds which make up its heritage, Irish culture reveals that the island of Ireland is without frontiers, that the surrounding seas are waterways connecting it with "foreigners," that the *navigatio* towards the other presents the best possibility of coming home to itself (Kearney 1997, 101).

Preamble

As Richard Kearney suggests in the quotation above, it behooves us to think of our physical boundaries, the seas that make us an island community, as a link rather than a barrier. Irish culture has long been defined by migration, outwards for a long part of its history, and more recently inwards, as our growing economy starts to require borrowed labour and our living conditions make the country an attractive place for economic and other refugees. As a consequence, our own narratives, how we explain ourselves to ourselves and to others, are also undergoing rapid change. In this essay, I want to look at how the motif of the journey has radically altered in recent filmmaking, complicating as it does notions of native and stranger, self and other, home, and exile. I will be asking why Irish cinema has for so long failed to imagine the encounter with the other as one between Ireland and Continental Europe; and would like to conclude by suggesting that the growth of a new Irish immigrant underclass has been appropriated by filmmakers to readdress issues of social exclusion and alienation.

The Journey Home

As I mentioned above, the motif of travelling is one that has a long history in Irish cinema; whether in films made in or about Ireland, the narrative focus has often been on a lone individual who makes a journey into, from or within Ireland. From its inception, Irish-American cinema created tales of impoverished immigrants coming to America and flourishing both professionally and personally. The most famous of these productions, John Ford's *The Quiet Man* (USA, 1952), reversed that journey to take its protagonist, Sean Thornton (John Wayne), back "home," to a land painted in Technicolor and signalled, as so many critics have discussed, as a fantasy, the dream of a returned immigrant (Gibbons 1988, 2002; McLoone 2000, 52-59). Local scholarship tends to read such films as specific to the Irish experience of immigration, yet undoubtedly they spoke equally to the many other ethnic and cultural groups that had themselves undergone similar geographical shifts and who shared a common dream of return to an idealised homeland. This, amongst other tropes, according to Hamid Naficy (2001), is a defining feature of films made by and for exilic and diasporic communities in what he defines as an "accented cinema":

> journeys, real or imaginary, form a major thematic thread in the accented films. Journeys have motivation, direction, and duration, each of which impacts the travel and the traveller (33).

Three types of journey are defined by Naficy here: "outward journeys of escape, home seeking, and home founding; journeys of quest, homelessness, and lostness; and inward, homecoming journeys." Naficy's categories correspond closely to those defined in *Travellers Tales* as the migrant's tale, the exile's tale and the nomad's tale (Robertson et al. 1994, 3).

Until recently, Irish travel narratives have been concerned with two journeys in particular, to and from America and to and from Britain and correspond most closely to Naficy's first and third categories. Lately, however, the idea of homelessness or lostness has increasingly come to the fore; in particular, as I will be discussing, in terms of being homeless at home. A third, internal journey takes place between the city and the country, usually between Dublin and the West of Ireland, from modernity to tradition. If the first can be read primarily as an allegory of emigration, its counterpart speaks more directly to the relationship engendered by colonisation. In this context, Brian McIlroy has suggested that where the British journey is conventionally represented as traumatic, the journey to America is more often celebrated as the realisation of a dream (McIlroy 2004, 69-77). The journey, whether from America or Britain, into Ireland is seldom as painful, and its dynamic, although overtly that of the return home, is also closely connected to the discourse of tourism, with its overtones of utopianism and its simultaneous movement in time and space: "The journey and its destinations are often described as a passage through symbolic time, forwards towards a resolution of conflict and backwards towards a lost aspect of the past" (Curtis and Pajaczkowska 1994, 199). Conversely, the journey to America and to Britain has been one from backwardness to modernity, with the attendant consequences for the local Irish (time) traveller.

The motif of the British (usually English) traveller to Ireland has a long representational history; most commonly such narratives describe the arrival in Ireland of an Englishman, his encounter with an apparently lawless Irish culture, his love affair with a spirited young Irish woman and his eventual integration into Irish society. Such was the template established by Sydney Owenson's (Lady Morgan) *The Wild Irish Girl* (1806), to be elaborated on with increasingly comic effect in literary fictions from those of the nineteenth century dramatist, Dion Boucicault, to the Anglo-Irish pairing of Edith Somerville and Violet Martin, particularly in their Irish R.M. novels (1899 onwards), subsequently a popular television series (in the 1980s). *The Wild Irish Girl* was published in the wake of the Act of Union and is widely seen as providing the literary consummation of that union (Corbett 2000, 22-54; Gibbons 1988, 204-210; Leerssen 1996, 54). The potential for reconciliation between the two countries via the National Romance underpinned much of this writing, and continued to do so well into the twentieth century (Butler-Cullingford 2001, 13-78). This trope also provided indigenous Irish writers and filmmakers with a device to scrutinise their own society as we can see in the Abbey Films of the late 1950s: *The Big Birthday* (George Pollock, Ireland, 1959), *Home is the Hero* (Fielder Cook, Ireland, 1959) and *This Other Eden* (Muriel Box, Ireland, 1959). Based on plays from the Abbey repertoire and featuring Abbey actors in the secondary roles, "each one establishes in its plot an 'outsider' character through whose point of view images of national identity and historical narratives are seen" (Monahan, "A frayed collaboration", 2004, 58).

Tourism and the redemptive discourse of homecoming are even more closely intertwined in the Irish-American journey (back) to Ireland. In the celebrated opening sequence of *The Quiet Man*, the locals initially assume that Thornton has come to the West of Ireland for a spot of trout fishing and part of the performative aspect of the film references the native predilection for acting Irishness for the benefit of the outsider. In any culture that is regularly exposed to the intrusions of tourism, however economically beneficial that might be, such a strategy allows for the placing of an invisible barrier between self and other, between the curious gaze of the outsider and the privacy of the native inhabitant. This masquerade of identity similarly establishes an insider dialogue with local viewers, who understand the performance for the charade it is. As the West of Ireland "characters" understand it, identity is a commodity.

The "journey" film thus symbolically fulfils a multiplicity of functions, allowing a filmmaker to address issues of emigration, colonialism, national identity/identities and the dynamics of tourism, key concerns for twentieth-century Irish viewers, locally and within the diaspora. Further, it has rendered Irish films intelligible to a global audience familiar with the dynamics of travel and emigration. With some consistency, films such as those listed above, and others, offered the viewer a double point of diegetic identification, with the stranger and with the community, permitting them to be simultaneously outsiders and insiders. From a pragmatic perspective, the stranger figure in such films allowed for the casting of a recognisable and thus bankable Hollywood or British star, with the (less-recognisable) indigenous Irish actors being relegated to support parts.

The Traumatic Journey

The ubiquity of the journey motif in traditional Irish narratives provided the new filmmakers of the revitalised Irish film industry (of the late eighties onwards) with a narrative model that they could re-shape according to their changing concerns. As I have discussed elsewhere, we can see the transformation of this paradigm in auteur/director Jim Sheridan's 1990 film, *The Field* (Barton 2002). Here, as in *The Quiet Man*, a returned Irish-American arrives in a West of Ireland community, planning to buy the eponymous field and settle down. Instead of meeting the welcome he has expected, the Yank (Tom Berenger) finds himself ostracised by the locals who distrust his motives and his disruption of their traditions, seen here as small-minded and regressive. Irish rural society of the 1930s, in Sheridan's imagination, is a place of stunted emotions that find their release in drink and violence. This vision of Ireland's past as the locus of personal trauma has informed any number of Irish films made since the early 1990s and this, more than economic necessity, has been used to explain the journey outward, most commonly to the United States. Sheridan's young couple in *In America* (Ireland/USA, 2003) have relocated to New York to leave behind them an Ireland associated with the death of their child and more nebulously the death of the self.

Other recent films, too, have represented the journey to America as one of escape—in *2by4* (Jimmy Smallhorne, USA, 1997), it is from old memories of child abuse; in *The Nephew* (Eugene Brady, Ireland, 1998), a prohibited love affair, and the same again in *This is My Father* (Paul Quinn, Ireland/Canada, 1998).Writing in 2000, Martin McLoone observed that:

just as Ireland begins to mould its political destiny more in line with Europe, its 'special relationship' to America seems to assume greater importance. The more European Ireland gets politically, in other words, the closer its imaginative axis is drawn to America, the culture most influenced by its emigrant population (McLoone 2000, 6).

McLoone, further, has questioned the extent to which Americanisation has been beneficial to local film culture. Although he concedes its potential to liberate Ireland from its old ways and mores, he concludes that most contemporary young Irish filmmakers are too immersed in American culture to be considered anything other than formally (or by extension thematically) conservative, nor has "the exploration of Irish-European identity... as yet, produced a truly memorable film" (199).

It is very certainly true that the dominant cultural influence in Ireland is American. In the short space of time since the publication of McLoone's book, this process has accelerated to the extent that it now seems that Irish filmic characters no longer need to travel to America to discover a cathartic modernity, they only have to look around them to find much of the iconography and many of the values of that society. Perhaps it is because of this, or perhaps because of other factors, including the downturn in emigration from Ireland, but the last five years have only seen one significant representation of the filmic voyage to America, the aforementioned *In America*, a project that, in any case, had its genesis in a much earlier script. The waning of the effects of colonisation have seen an equivalent abandonment of the "Englishman in Ireland" narrative, its only interesting re-working being Neil Jordan's *The Crying Game* (GB, 1992), in which the travelling Englishman, the soldier Jody (Forrest Whittaker) is black and, himself, the representative of a colonised culture.

As Monahan commented (above) in relation to the Abbey Films, one function of the outsider-figure was to provide a perspective on the indigenous culture. Elsewhere, Monahan has discussed recent Irish cinema's search for a sense of the "cinematic self," one that has so often been achieved by appeal to its "other" (Monahan, "Keeping it imaginary," 2004). Even those films that have not included a "foreign" other have consistently, Monahan argues, placed a character in the spectator position, watching and framing the action.

The Journey to Europe

Before looking at the shifting dynamics of the relationship between the travelling other and the indigenous self in recent Irish cinema, I want briefly to use this formulation to question Irish cinematic culture's failure to imagine an Irish-European identity. Crucially, for a medium so reliant on stereotypes and archetypes, Irish film has been unable to create an image of the continental

European. Outside of the British, European characters in Irish cinema are few and far between. When they do appear, they are most commonly invoked to represent some form of sexual liberation/transgression. To take one relatively recent example, in a scene at the end of the "comedy of the sexes" urban drama, *Snakes and Ladders* (Trish McAdam, Ireland/Germany/UK, 1996), a group of swimmers is diving into the water at a fictional Dublin swimming spot, the Thirty-Foot, where they are joined by the lesbian Scandinavian partner of one of the film's main characters. Stripping off briskly, she responds to queries as to the need for nudity with a pragmatic, "This way I can get in much faster." Then again, in *With or Without You* (Michael Winterbottom, GB, 1999), the young Northern Irish couple's relationship with each other is thrown into crisis by the arrival of the wife, Rosie's (Dervla Kirwan) former penpal, Frenchman, Benoit (Yvan Attal), who represents sex as pleasure rather than for procreation.

A few recent Irish films have made the reverse journey, from Ireland to continental Europe; one such, Pat Murphy's *Nora* (Ireland/Germany/Italy/GB, 2000), opens in Ireland, with Nora (Susan Lynch) leaving her Galway home and coming to Dublin. There she meets the young James Joyce (Ewan McGregor) and they fall in love. It is only when the couple travel to Italy that they begin to explore what is, for Irish cinema, a remarkably mature sexual relationship, and one that exists outside of the imperatives of child-bearing and child-rearing, leaving the couple's son and daughter, particularly Lucia, as on-lookers to their parents' relationship. This relationship is later fuelled by Joyce's observation that Prezioso (Roberto Citran) is in love with Nora; but also enabled by their escape from the restrictions of Irish culture. *Nora* is a film of interiors, with little in it to remind the viewer of the cinematic view of Italy in which films such as *A Room With A View* (James Ivory, GB, 1985) luxuriate. The latter is driven by the tourist fantasy of the holiday romance, of achieving intimacy with the locals; Nora and Joyce achieve intimacy with each other, inhabiting rather than posing against the spaces offered by Trieste. Visually, through the film's palette of deep blues, goldens and ochres, Murphy's film recalls a European practice of representation dating to the Renaissance.

Another quite different film, this time with a contemporary setting, that involves a journey to Italy, is John Lynch's *Night Train* (Ireland, 1998). The story concerns the encounter between a minor English conman, Michael Poole (John Hurt) and an unmarried Dublin woman, Alice (Brenda Blethyn), whose one brush with love was in Paris, in 1969, with a young French student. They talked through the night, she remembers to Poole, about Sartre and Simone de Beauvoir and then, nothing happened: "I came home to this." *Night Train* explores the tentativeness and hesitancy of mid-life romance; Poole collects model trains and has constructed a miniature Europe in his bedroom for them to run on. His Europe is indebted to a kind of *Heidi* meets the *Sound of Music* vision of the continent, a pâpier maché replica of a landscape of snowy mountains and romantic castles. "It's better to imagine places, I think," he tells Alice. When the couple finally do flee Alice's suburban Dublin home and her pathetic, demanding mother (Pauline Flanagan), and travel on the Orient Express to Venice, they are now, at last, free to make love. Yet they have been pursued by Poole's shady past in the shape of the gangster's hitman, Blake (Paul Roe) and in Venice Alice leaves Poole and flies home. That night, Poole walks on his own through Venice, and encounters a group of late night revellers, masked and dressed in Carnival costumes. Returning to his hotel where he must decide whether to accede to Alice's ultimatum, to hand the money back to the gang, or split with her, a montage of images is invoked to express his dilemma. As he sees alternately: Alice walking towards him, the abattoir in which he worked, a gang member doused in petrol burning alive, the Carnival party and a vaporetto passing under a bridge, so the viewer is invited to remember the cinematic Venice of *Death in Venice* (Luchino Visconti, Italy, 1971) and, more specifically, *Don't Look Now* (Nicolas Roeg, GB/Italy, 1973). Eventually Poole will return the money and go back to Dublin and Alice. Although Lynch's film was shot with a second unit on location in Venice, the point is that Poole's vision of the city is mediated via a history of images borrowed from European cinema. In fact, what this film and *Nora* have in common is that continental Europe, Italy, is represented more by spaces than people. Murphy's film draws on the tradition of the classic European art film to combine rich visuals with an intense exploration of sexuality; it is place that defines Joyce and Nora's journey not the encounter with the indigenous other. Lynch's film too forges a sharp visual contrast between Alice's home in suburbia, in which everything is cramped and petty bourgeois, and a baroque, imperialist Venice. As Myrto Konstantarakos (2000) has argued in her introduction to *Spaces in European Cinema*, the visualisation of space(s) in European film is crucial to meaning-creation:

> European Cinema is articulated around spatial oppositions [...] the recurrent theme is that of centrality and marginality and, more precisely, of exclusion and inclusion–a leitmotif one does not find in the film making of other cultures with quite the same obsession (4).

The layering of space and time, articulated by Bakhtin in his definition of the chronotope (the materialisation of time in space) is employed here by Konstantarakos as a distinctive motif of European cinema and one that is particularly evident in *Nora*.

The significance of space as a point of differentiation in these encounters between Irish characters and continental Europe is again crucial to another film that takes its Irish characters on an existential journey out of Ireland, *The*

Disappearance of Finbar (Sue Clayton, Ireland/GB/Sweden/France, 1996). Dermot Bolger's adaptation of a novel, *The Disappearance of Rory Brophy* by Carl Lombard, opens in a disadvantaged area of Dublin, a location familiar to viewers from the Roddy Doyle adaptations, *The Commitments* (Alan Parker, US, 1991) and *Family* (BBC, 1994), and other films such as *Into the West* (Mike Newell, Ireland, 1992). An early establishing shot identifies the estate in which the two boys at the heart of the narrative, Danny Quinn (Luke Griffin) and Finbar Flynn (Jonathan Rhys Meyers) live as Aachen Close. An unfinished flyover complements this visual irony, suggesting rather obviously a broken link to the film's European other. *Finbar* starts with Flynn going to Switzerland for a trial with a football team, the AC Grasshoppers. He is soon back home, unable to take the pressure. Restless and bored in Dublin, he hangs out with Danny and quarrels with his family and schoolteachers. One night he climbs over the flyover and disappears. Despite a mammoth effort to find him, all that is achieved is a revitalisation of the community spirit. Then, one night, Finbar leaves a message on Danny's answering machine and the latter sets off to Stockholm to locate his friend. At this point, the film makes an abrupt shift in visual register. Abandoning the realist, television-style shooting that it uses to depict its Dublin environment, it suddenly develops into an apparent pastiche of an Aki Kaurismäki or Jim Jarmusch film, complete with wide, little-inhabited spaces and a collection of quirky, maudlin Swedish characters. Finbar Flynn has become something of a local hero, it seems in Sweden, being the subject of a local hit, the rearranged disco version of "The Ballad of Finbar Flynn." Danny eventually catches up with Finbar in the far North, close to the Arctic Circle, where he has become an electricity farmer. There Danny falls for Flynn's girlfriend, Abbi (Fanny Risberg) who lives in a remote homestead with her grandmother, Johanna (Sif Ruud), and Finbar once more moves on.

Finbar enjoyed a brief theatrical release and reviews that appreciated it more for what it attempted to do than what it actually achieved. For those in tune with its ambitions: "In the 'new' Europe of the film, where borders can be more invisible than overtly political, the universality of cultural experience is always manifest yet becomes irrelevant in the individual's search for belonging" (Hayden 1997, 36). These common cultural links—specifically articulated through music and the composition of the ballad (in Ireland) that becomes the disco number (in Lapland)—suggest a view of Ireland and continental Europe's commonality that contrasts with that articulated by Murphy and Lynch in their films. Where their Europe is visualised through a high culture tradition that has its roots in the Renaissance, Clayton and Bolger's derives from an embrace of kitsch and folk culture that they further associate with the aesthetics of recent Scandinavian filmmaking. I have discussed elsewhere Irish cinema's expression of a local cultural identity via an aesthetic of kitsch (Barton 2000), and certainly there are common connections to be made here with other European cultures. Where *Finbar* loses its focus is in its failure to conceive of continental Europe outside of a given set of inherited cinematic images. The characters Danny encounters emerge as little other than stereotypes, more pastiche than organic; as the critic from *Sight and Sound* wrote, the film lacked a sense of place rather than location (White 1998, 47).

The Absent European

Just why the majority of contemporary Irish filmmakers have so signally avoided conceptualising the encounter with Continental Europe is a matter of speculation. The pragmatic explanation is that their low budgets have militated against location shooting. There is, I think, more to it than that, however. Irish literature from the same period is equally bereft of equivalent narratives and it is more the case that the primary conduit for cultural exchange has until recently been provided by the dialogue with America. Naficy's voyages of exile and return are still potent material while, at the same time, the dissemination of images of American popular culture has been generously facilitated by their ubiquity on Irish television. The brief mushrooming of hacienda-type bungalows in the Irish countryside during a similar period was, after all, as their names testify, inspired less by trips to Spain than by watching *Dallas* on television. Is there perhaps too a sense that European high culture is far removed from the Irish experience and that an encounter with it will leave the travelling Irish looking ignorant? Culturally, continental Europe has been under-represented in Ireland; European films play in the hallowed spaces of the arthouse cinema circuit; European television makes an annual appearance with the broadcasting of the Eurovision song contest; American popular culture in all its accessibility is, by contrast, everywhere. Without the benefit of a representational history, the continental European remains unknown and unknowable.

The three films just discussed belong to a period of filmmaking whose product was regularly critiqued for its co-production structure, one that, it was felt, led to a film type best known as the "Europudding." In order to attract continental European funding, the argument went, films from national cinemas would be obliged to incorporate elements from their co-funders' film cultures—be it materially, in terms of actors and locations, or thematically, via storylines that would appeal to viewers from those cultures. As I hope to have demonstrated here, although co-financing with European partners did on more than one occasion lead to the gratuitous introduction of Continental characters into Irish film narratives, the opportunities afforded by combining technical and creative resources also allowed filmmakers to open up their representations beyond the physical borders of Ireland and to explore new cinematic spaces, a voyage in which the other is defined via culture rather than the individual.

New Medium, New Migrants

All three of the above films are also representative of the type of mid-budget cinema that is associated with the resurgence of indigenous filmmaking in the wake of the restructuring of the Irish Film Board in the early 1990s (Barton 2004, 104-112). As I will be discussing in this final section of my essay, the new medium of digital filmmaking opened up opportunities for a younger generation of emerging practitioners to respond with greater immediacy to social and political issues, in particular those arising out of what is commonly termed the Celtic Tiger, or the swiftly expanding domestic Irish economy. This newly buoyant Irish economy, as I mentioned above, redefined Ireland for the first time as an immigrant economy. The most visible of these new immigrants have been from China, Nigeria and the accession states of the enlarged European Union. The in turn has seen a reconfiguration of the travel narrative, one that corresponds most closely Naficy's category of "journeys of quest, homeless, and lostness." Increasingly filmmakers have turned to these migrant figures to provide a new perspective on Irish society and to question the Irish reputation for hospitality and "Céad Míle Fáilte" (One Hundred Thousand Welcomes).

It would be misleading to suggest that this latest phase in Irish filmmaking's fortunes represents a return to the "golden age" of the independent productions of 1970s and early 1980s Irish cinema—those much lauded works by Joe Comerford, Pat Murphy, Thaddeus O'Sullivan, Bob Quinn and others—that saw low-budget films confront an array of social issues; indeed many of the recent films amount to little more than "boys with guns" thriller/comedies. As I have discussed previously, for many emerging Irish filmmakers, it has been important to distance themselves from the intense exploration of identity politics evident in that earlier cinema (Barton 2004, 104-112). At the same time, the Celtic Tiger phenomenon has not been short of its critics, with many pointing to the social consequences of a rapidly growing economy and the government's failure to address the evident inequalities of Irish society (Allen 2000; Kirby, Gibbons and Cronin 2002).

One of the earliest films to rework the voyage inwards was a short Irish-language production, *Yu Ming is Ainm Dom* (*Yu Ming is My Name*) (Daniel O'Hara, Ireland, 2003). The winner of prizes at, amongst others, the Celtic Film and Television Festival, the Montreal Film Festival, the New York Film Fleadh and the 2004 IFTA awards, *Yu Ming* was highly acclaimed critically and enjoyed a theatrical release in Irish cinemas alongside *In America*. Running to thirteen minutes, the film opens with a young Chinese man, Yu Ming (Daniel

Wu) disconsolately working in a Chinese grocer's. Fed up with the customers and his boss, he goes to his local library and, spinning a globe, randomly picks Ireland as an alternative location in which to work. A further perusal of the encyclopaedia reveals Irish to be its official language and he duly learns to speak this. He practices in front of the mirror, rehearsing in Irish the "You looking at me?" speech from *Taxi Driver* (Martin Scorsese, USA, 1976) as he shaves. On arrival Yu Ming goes to a youth hostel where a jovial Australian welcomes him. Assuming that Yu Ming is asking for a bed in Chinese, the Aussie hails an Asian who is helping in the hostel. The latter reminds him that since he is Mongolian, he does not speak Chinese. Feeling increasingly isolated Yu Ming tries to eat with a knife and fork but ends up turning them around and using the handles as chopsticks. The next day we see him walking along the canal where he stops beside the statue of Patrick Kavanagh and asks of him, "An bhfuil tusa ag labhair liomsa?" ("Are you talking to me?"). From there he goes into a pub to ask for work. The barman presumes he is ordering a drink and offers him a Stella Artois (mispronounced). Finally he is rescued by another customer, Paddy (Frank Kelly) who is amazed by his fluency in Irish and explains to him that in Ireland, English not Irish is spoken. The astounded Yu Ming observes that the signposts are in Irish; Paddy replies that only in the Gaeltacht is the language actually spoken. "Here, did you know that our Paddy could speak Chinese?" the barman calls to his friend in admiration. In the final scene of the film, a mini-bus arrives in Connemara's Gaeltacht, a tourist steps out and walks into a pub to be greeted in Irish by Yu Ming, now established behind the bar and pulling a pint of Guinness.

Yu Ming is a cool exercise in postmodern filmmaking that revels in its ironies. For one, it was made for a television station established to promote the national language but happily asserts that, outside of those in the Gaeltacht, no one in Ireland actually speaks Irish. Then there is the referencing of *Taxi Driver*, a film made by a Hollywood director influenced by European cinema, now re-played by a Chinese actor in an Irish-language film. A second set of references is more locally specific—Patrick Kavanagh followed Joyce and Beckett to Europe but, unable to fit in there, returned to Ireland, remaining an outsider in his own society. O'Hara films Dublin from Yu Ming's point of view, bathing the city in a blue light that renders it cold and unfriendly, its landmarks reimagined from the perspective of the outsider. Only when he relocates to the Gaeltacht does the point of view change so that the final shot in the pub is filmed from the perspective of the tourist, with Yu Ming now the insider, welcoming the traveller from behind the counter. Now too, O'Hara drops his system of colour washes (China was yellow and green), revealing a gleaming, brilliantly coloured West of Ireland.

A conscious reversal of the journey to Ireland narrative, *Yu Ming* replaces the traditional Englishman or Irish-American with a young Chinese man, today's economic migrant. Instead of travelling back in time to a pre-lapsarian Ireland, Yu Ming is met with a society that is alienatingly modern. Only by making a second, internal journey, to the West of Ireland, does he achieve the traveller's quest of becoming at home abroad. Now employment rather than marriage permits integration and the film manages to embrace both an essentialist and an anti-essentialist position—essentialist in its definition of the Gaeltacht and its deployment of the common trope of the journey to the West, and anti-essentialist in suggesting that anyone, be they Australian, Mongolian or Chinese, can become an insider in today's cosmopolitan Ireland. A commonly voiced exhortation in liberal Celtic Tiger Ireland is to remember the millions of Irish who migrated to America and Britain when we consider how we treat the new migrants who come to Ireland looking for work. It is this aspiration that underpins *Yu Ming*.

Strangers in Their Own Land

Homelessness and lostness are the defining motifs of what has become one of the most critically acclaimed films of the new digital era, Lenny Abrahamson's *Adam and Paul* (Ireland, 2004). Following two junkies, the eponymous Adam (Mark O' Halloran) and Paul (Tom Murphy) on their odyssey around Dublin in search of a fix, the film bears out Thomas Elsaesser's definition of a new cinema of abjection, that concerns: "human beings that have, for one reason or another, lost the ability to enter into any kind of exchange, sometimes not even one where they can trade their bodies" (Elsaesser 2005, 125). With its latter-day incarnations of Vladimir and Estragon, *Adam and Paul*'s debt to Beckett is pointed, without being laboured. These two are at the bottom of the social heap in an uncaring city, their morals (unspeakably, they mug a special-needs teenager) eroded by their addiction, ostracised by friends and strangers alike. "Here, if we were black, you wouldn't be throwing us out," their mate, Karl (Ian Cregg) admonishes the shop manager as he hurls them onto the pavement. In one of the film's black comic sequences, the two share a bench with a Bulgarian immigrant (played by Ion Caramitru). Having exchanged heated views on whether or not he is a "fuckin' Romanian," they then fall out further over whether Bulgaria or Dublin is a "shit-hole" "Bulgaria is not a shit-hole," the immigrant expostulates, "beautiful, it is beautiful. And now, Dublin, it is the shit-hole, full of liars, and fucking maniacs ... and fucking Romanians." "Well," Adam comes back, "Why are you here so?" "Why am I here? Did you ever ask yourselves the same question," he turns to them, "why are you here? Why the fuck are you here?"

Adam and Paul are indeed in a state of Kristevan abjection; living amongst the detritus of a city, a "shit-hole," that carelessly dumps the signifiers of family life—Adam sleeps on a mattress abandoned on waste ground—they count for so little that we in fact never discover which one is Adam and which Paul; only by being familiar with the two actors can the viewer find the answer to this in the closing credits. As they criss-cross the internal and invisible boundaries between the homes of their estranged friends and the streets they share with Dublin's derelict underclass, they are as effectively exiled from the mainstream of Irish culture as if they had left the country. Travestying the redemptive possibilities of the internal voyage Yu Ming makes, the twosome finally wind up at the seaside, on Dublin's shoreline. In a vista dominated by the landmark industrial chimneys of the Pigeon House, they settle down to rest. When Paul awakes he finds that Adam has died in the night. Briefly contemplating his companion's body, he reaches into his pocket and removes the small packet of heroin Adam had stashed there before stumbling off, his own death an inevitability.

The difference between *Yu Ming* and *Adam and Paul* is that where the short film bears witness to the transformative potential of travel, a belief that has underpinned this paradigm to date, the latter envisages the voyage as circular and futile. The encounter with the European other in Abrahamson's film serves simply to articulate its theme. Have Adam and Paul ever thought what they are doing "here"? What do they learn from their meeting with the Bulgarian/Romanian? Nothing, evidently.

What has also changed are the dynamics of this exchange; where Thomas Elsaesser's "significant other" (Elsaesser 2005, 41) was once the representative of either the former colonial power or the dominant world power, now this figure is beginning to take on quite a different identity. Very certainly, this is only the start of a new process of revisiting the paradigms of self/other within Irish culture, and one that is predicated on new power shifts within global identity politics.

That the Irish may themselves be the most alienated people in a society structured upon layers of alienation is the subject of my final filmic example from the new digital film era, Perry Ogden's *Pavee Lackeen* (*The Traveller Girl*, Ireland, 2005). The language of the title is that of Traveller culture and the film marks one of a number of recent attempts to capture this marginalised community on film. Travellers are the most discriminated against members of Irish society; living often on roadsides, their children playing in the dirt outside their caravans, or on official halting sites, they have remained firmly outside of Celtic Tiger modernisation. Ogden is himself English; like Alen MacWeeny, who was responsible for the documentary *Traveller* (Alen MacWeeney/John T.Davis, Ireland, 2001), he is an established photographer whose first encounter with Travellers was through taking their photographs and who subsequently returned to make a film about them. Unlike MacWeeny, Ogden chose to mix documentary and fictional re-creation in order to depict episodes from the life of the eponymous Traveller girl, 10-year old Winnie Maughan. We see Winnie being thrown out of school, socialising with her mother and other family members in their caravan, which they keep parked on an abandoned site owned by Dublin Corporation, fetching water in a bucket from a tap across from the caravan, doing herself up for a trip to the chip van with one of her sisters and being hauled out of a recycling bin where she was picking out clothing for herself and the other children. In an extended sequence, Winnie, now living without the structure of a school day and aimlessly filling up her time, wanders in and out of the city's shops. Each of these is staffed by the country's new immigrants, a Russian video shop manager, an African hairdresser, Asian arcade workers. They treat the girl without prejudice, explaining in the case of the first, for instance, that she will not understand the video she is examining because it is in Russian. The point that Ogden appears to be making is that in the new Dublin, the marginalised Traveller child and the new migrants have more in common with each other than with the older Irish (represented here by social workers and educational authorities).

In all the above films, Dublin has become a transient space, populated by characters defined by their liminality. Where Irish film culture of the pre-digital era unambiguously divided the world into "home" and "away," and created a set of fictional and geographic boundaries that marked this distinction, in the new Ireland represented by these more recent films, the dividing lines have shifted. Now you can be in exile at home, or an exile who is at home, away. This new discourse on identity and belonging liberates concepts of Irishness from their narrowly defined geographic roots and reconfigures the journey film accordingly. Just who is an outsider in Irish culture, and who an insider is no longer a certainty, a shift that, in a sense, relocates Irish cinema to within a European film movement that defines its metropolitan spaces as Dublin is defined here, as a meeting place for multiple ethnicities. Coming to Ireland is no longer inevitably a journey home, just as the opportunity to leave Ireland as a means of exorcising an old trauma in not an option for these most marginalised of individuals. They are instead defined by a state of internal exile, their best hope, as Winnie demonstrates, being to find common cause with the new immigrant culture.

As I hope to have demonstrated here, travel and boundary-crossing remain potent tropes within the new Irish cinema. With its increasing interest in the figures of the immigrant, the Traveller and the social exile, there is an indication that Irish cinema is moving formally towards a trend within European filmmaking culture that deterritorialises national identities. Within this discourse, Ireland's "significant others" are not the old Europeans but the new:

the migrant Chinese, the Bulgarians and the Russians. Defined less by their difference than by degrees of commonality, they join with the dispossessed Irish to form a new and potentially subversive energy within Irish film culture. No longer "Celtic Crusoes on a sequestered island," the Irish are now being invited to contemplate the consequences of their isolation finally being breached.

Works Cited

Allen, K. 2000. *The Celtic tiger: The myth of social partnership in Ireland.* Manchester: Manchester University Press.
Barton, R. 2000. Kitsch as authenticity. *Irish Studies Review* 9.2: 193-202.
—. 2002. *Jim Sheridan: Framing the nation.* Dublin: The Liffey Press.
—. 2004. *Irish national cinema.* London and New York: Routledge.
Butler-Cullingford, E. 2001. *Ireland's others.* Cork: Cork University Press.
Corbett, M. J. 2000. *Allegories of union in Irish and English writing, 1790-1870.* Cambridge: Cambridge University Press.
Curtis, B. and C. Pajaczkowska. 1994. "Getting there": travel, time and narrative. In Robertson et al: 199-215.
Elsaesser, T. 2005. *European cinema, face to face with Hollywood.* Amsterdam: Amsterdam University Press.
Gibbons, L. 1988. Romanticism, realism and Irish cinema. In K. Rockett, L. Gibbons and J. Hill, *Cinema and Ireland*, 194-257. London and New York: Routledge.
—. 2002. *The Quiet Man.* Cork: Cork University Press.
Hayden, J. 1997. From Tallaght to Lapland. *Film West* 29: 36-7.
Kearney, R. 1997. *Post nationalist Ireland: Politics, literature, philosophy.* London and New York: Routledge.
Kirby, P., L. Gibbons and M. Cronin, eds. 2002. *Reinventing Ireland.* London, Sterling Virginia: Pluto Press.
Konstantarakos, M., ed. 2000. *Spaces in European cinema.* Exeter and Portland, Oregon: Intellect Books.
Leerssen, J. 1996. *Remembrance and imagination.* Cork: Cork University Press.
McIlroy, B. 2004. Exodus, arrival and return: The generic discourse of Irish diasporic and exilic narrative films. In *Keeping it real: Irish film and television.* Edited by R. Barton and H. O'Brien. 69-77. London and New York: Wallflower Press.
McLoone, M. 2000. *Irish film: The emergence of a contemporary cinema.* London: British Film Institute.
Monahan, B. 2004. A frayed collaboration: Emmet Dalton and the Abbey theatre adaptations at Ardmore Studios. In *National cinema and beyond.* Edited by K. Rockett and J. Hill, 52-60. Dublin: Four Courts Press.

—. 2004. Keeping it imaginary, cultivating the symbolic. In *Keeping it real: Irish film and television*. Edited by R. Barton and H. O'Brien. 185-96. London and New York: Wallflower Press.
Naficy, H. 2001. *An accented cinema*. Princeton and Oxford: Princeton University Press.
Robertson, G., M. Mash, L. Tickner, J. Bird, B. Curtis, T. Putnam, eds. 1994. *Travellers' tales*. London and New York: Routledge.
White, R. 1998. The disappearance of Finbar. Review. *Sight and Sound* 8.11: 46-47.

CHAPTER NINE

GNOME IS WHERE THE HEART IS: THE NEW
EUROPE IN GERMAN–LANGUAGE–CINEMA

JOHN E. DAVIDSON, THE OHIO STATE UNIVERSITY

"Der echte deutsche Gartenzwerg ist kult—Denn nur die Harten kommen in den Garten."[1]

"The verse is in English! La lingua pura!" Sir Leigh Teabing (Brown 2003).

In assessing the contributions of German-language films to the idea of a broader European identity today, this essay is interested in whether the contradictory institutional and aesthetic demands in the current production climate bring forth nods to the German *and* the European that foster a hybrid identity to be valorized or an artificially compounded one that is at once both and neither. Although the influence of both local and pan-national funding constraints must be counted as prominent in that climate, my modest proposal here will be that those films seemingly most focused on specific Germans, or on the specifically German, may in some cases contribute largely to some sense of positive intercultural contact. Such contact can be usefully understood as the shadow of a "Europeanization" that is all too often conceived solely in terms of "polities, politics, and public policies."[2] Hidden in that shadow are two self-contradictory cultural interconnections that support Europeanization: to the U.S. as "America" and to language as a carrier of a cultural memory that facilitates

---

[1] "The real German Garden Gnome rules, because only the hard ones get in the gardens" (Slogan for <ZwergPower.com>).
[2] For example, "Europeanization denotes a complex interactive 'top-down' and 'bottom-up' process in which domestic polities, politics and public policies are shaped by European integration and in which domestic actors use European integration to shape the domestic arena. It may produce either continuity or change and potentially variable and contingent outcomes" (Dyson and Goetz 2003).

functioning in the everyday world.

In the contemporary climate of media saturation in Europe, national identity (as well as any "European" counterpart) is an abstraction supported by tropes extrapolated from localized stories especially to be found in film and television.[3] Such localism is inherently involved in the cultural construction of particularities like the "German" as well as the "European." Various models have emerged from disciplines ranging from political science to European studies that seek to untangle the way in which "Europeanization" is taking place that recognize and try to account for this; however, these disciplines tend to privilege conventional political structures and straightforward empirical data in analyses that are not always sensitive to the complexities of cultural components that the studies nonetheless gesture to as vital. A fine example of this disciplinary quandary is evinced by Katrin Voltmer and Christine Eilders (2003), who begin by noting that

> successful European integration requires more than the implementation of efficient institutions and the harmonization of national and European policy-making. It also involves processes of cultural integration and the emergence of a communicative sphere that allows citizens to get involved in public discourse about European politics (173).

These authors rightly foreground the importance of the media in such processes, but then propose the "Europeanization of the national public sphere" as a means of understanding the movement in that process so far, given that there is not, and is not likely to be a "European media" (178). The problems that enter the article at that juncture are both conceptual and methodological, the most important of which in this context is the reduction of the public sphere to newspaper editorials and of "cultural integration" to forthright political debate. Thus, it misses both the blogs of the internet and, more to the point here, that fact that "localization and globalization are inextricably bound together in the current phase" of uneven development, not just in the economy but also in the thickets of identificatory politics.[4] On the other hand, an approach to those

---

[3] This holds in the US as well, of course, as is exemplified by the repeated singling out of individuals in the audience (accompanied by highly orchestrated cutaways) whose stories stand for "us" at televised rituals of national construction such as the annual State of the Union address. For a discussion of the visual politics of such "PRolicy" (public relations as policy) in the US context in anticipation of the introduction of the notion of "Kitsch" below, see Lugg (1999).

[4] Mike Featherstone (1996) describes "localism" in terms that, at least initially, are strikingly reminiscent of *Heimat* discourse to the Germanist's ear: "It can be argued that the difficulty of handling increasing levels of cultural complexity, and the doubts and anxieties they often engender, are reasons why 'localism,' or the desire to return home,

issues based in the analysis of cultural texts is free to enter those thickets at different points. Thus, the topics around which I will structure my discussion of the German as a means to broader cultural contact are ones which traditionally have been seen as particular cites of identification: questions of local identity, language, and place as deployed in the cinema. If not set in stone, then the intertwining of the local and the European, and the slippage in and out of national discourse that accompanies it will at least be cast in plaster for us in that silent cultural icon that speaks such volumes—the garden gnome.

Champions of the "Gartenzwerg" point out that they form a marvelous symbol of the positive German traditions. Yet, the bent and bearded figure has long been associated by many with the most laughable kitsch in German culture: in some cases it stands in for German culture *as* kitsch (Venske 1983;Van Helsing 2003). These associations have been used in recent films by Germans (and other central Europeans) to make points about Germanic insularity and self-centeredness. Paul Poet's *Ausländer 'Raus–Schlingensiefs Container* (Foreigners Out! [2002]) documents Christian Schlingensief's spoof of Austrian immigration policies using a reality-show format that allows pedestrians to vote foreigners out of the country. In it a garden gnome ironically raises a warning finger behind the German cultural philosopher Burkhardt Schmidt as he expounds upon the situation. Another example: the most banally fanatical figure in *Die Mitte* (The Center [2004]), Polish director Stanislaw Mucha's investigation of sites that lay claim to being Europe's epicenter, is an elderly German man in Cölbe, who insists fervently but with no evidence whatsoever that his *Zwerg*-studded garden is that very spot. According to popularized etymology, they are modeled after noble and wise creatures: "The word 'gnome' is said to derive from the New Latin *gnomus* and ultimately from the Greek *gnosis*, meaning knowledge. According to myth, gnomes hoarded secret knowledge just as they hoarded treasure." In the case of *Die Mitte*, the secret knowledge of the gnomes seems to be that the shape of Europe is largely in the mind of the beholder: gnome is where the heart is.

Despite the long tradition of seeing the *Gartenzwerg* as something essentially Germanic, we would do well to remember that these figurines have meaning far beyond those borders as well.[5] There has been an exponential

---

becomes an important theme–regardless of whether the home is real or imaginary, temporal, syncretized, or simulated, or whether it is manifest in a fascination with the sense of belonging, affiliation, and community attributed to the home of others" (47).

[5] The first "garden" gnome appeared when a British aristocrat, Sir Charles Isham, brought twenty-one terracotta *Zwerge* back to Northamptonshire from a trip to Bavaria in 1847 and put them out in his grounds. They have spread ever since and become so enmeshed in a particular sense of British life that *Wallace and Gromit*'s "Anti-Pesto" service can hide its rodent detectors in the figurines that dot every garden from the

increase in visibility for the garden gnome across Europe in recent decades, including the international cinematic celebrity brought them with Jean-Pierre Jeunet's Oscar-winning *Le Fabuleux destin d'Amélie Poulain* (*Amélie* [2001]).[6] Less famous than the role of his cousin in *Amélie*, but perhaps more germane for the consideration of the erasure of class both through fetishized identity and its cynical rejection that follows, would be the appearance of the garden gnome on the US-American TV-series *King of the Hill*. This animated show skewers the petty mindedness of the small-town American family, especially the Texas variety. In one episode the mother, Peggy Hill, puts a gnome in the yard to give it "her special touch" for all to see, but her husband, Hank, is mortified because it represents effeminate strangeness. After much back and forth, the figurine is removed from the front yard only to come to rest on the bureau overlooking their bed. Though slightly unnerved by the vigilance of the gnarled little man, Hank accepts this arrangement because it saves the family from the public humiliation he would have caused them were he to have remained outside. The gnome thus comes to indicate that notions of propriety for those who have lower-class means and middle-class aspirations must themselves necessarily be the stuff of kitsch: the beauty of Hank's unadorned, chemically produced lawn outside (the envy of his neighbors) is merely the reflection of the gnome inside.

Although seeming to have its potential for a critique of class, the humor of *King of the Hill* might more accurately be described as being based in an eighteenth-century notion of "taste." The show's Arlen, TX, is a place where nobody has taste, and the assumption is that if you don't have it you can never get it.[7] The use of the gnome here, as in the other snippets mentioned above, recalls elements of what Vilashini Cooppan (2003) calls a familiar colonial narrative in which an elite artifact is appropriated through the market by the hoi polloi and then rejected as a national symbol, "only to find an ironic afterlife in the domain of popular culture and in the diasporic abroad."[8] The questions of

---

manner to the mudhole (2005), and Devonshire is host now to a real-life Gnome Reserve and Museum. Indeed, "one of [Isham's] original batch of gnomes survives: *Lampy* as he is known, is on display at Lamport Hall, and is insured for one million pounds." This quotation, as well as the previous etymology, can be found at <http://en.wikipedia.org/wiki/Gnome>.

[6] Jeunet turns this "German" figurine into an emblem of the phobic rootedness that attends French petit-bourgeois life, which is highlighted and finally shaken off by sending the gnome on a world tour. Photos of the beloved clay dwarf in famous tourist destinations around the globe becomes a running gag within the film, and has since been picked up as the commercial hook for a web-based travel service.

[7] See Gronow (1997) for an excellent discussion of the historical roots of this sentiment.

[8] This is the description of the development of nineteenth-century Indian calendar art generated by a review of feminist studies of this art (Cooppan 2003). While not suggesting that Germany's history is parallel to that of nineteenth-century India, I do find

authenticity and taste that are always at stake in any discussion of a kitsch artifact, while seeming to stand on opposites sides of the object of contestation, are united in their tendency to erase class specificities that are both local and global. I want to suggest, borrowing from Cooppan's work on the image of "kitsch-India," that the *Gartenzwerg* can attain the "paradoxical status of 'authentic' [German] kitsch" (269) which, because of the very porous nature of meaning attached to the garden gnome at home in Germany and abroad, has the potential both to center and dislodge such mutually reinforcing oppositions in the German-language cinema within the new Europe.

One issue that proves to be problematic from the outset, of course, is that of "German-language" cinema. Take, for instance, the recent winner of both the Berlinale's Golden Bear and the European Cinema prize, Fatih Akin's *Gegen die Wand* (*Head-On* [2004]), which comes from Germany but features Turkish as the predominant spoken language. Even more interesting, it is English rather than German that arises to both complicate and facilitate the most direct expression regarding identity made by the male lead, Cahit. Earlier in the film, Cahit married Sibel to allow her freedom from the strictures of her conventional Turkish family and culture. They roomed and partied together in Hamburg's seedy Altona district, but over time and contrary to his intentions he developed genuine feelings for her, leading to a violent outburst against one of her lovers. After sitting out a jail sentence of some years for this, Cahit goes to Istanbul to reunite himself with Sibel and tries to explain his need to do so to her cousin. He slips from Turkish to English and back again with no recognizable pattern as he struggles to express emotions that he has long hidden behind his adopted personae of a German-speaking "Penner" (bums) who wants nothing to do with "Kanaken" (pejorative [especially] for Turks—Cahit's terms). While the use of English in that scene is motivated in the narrative by the poor state of Cahit's Turkish (previously established) and the likelihood that the hotel manager is more familiar with English as the international business language than with German, it is a unique moment in the film and draws attention to the role that English has played in German cinema since the fall of the wall.

Prior to that time the New German Cinema was well known, among other things, for its need to negotiate American influences, and the strategic use of the English language as one tool in that process. Prominent directors, such as Rainer Werner Fassbinder or Wim Wenders before 1990, often used English-language

---

the relationship of the *Gartenzwerg* to the first modern German nation intriguing in this regard. Initially a hand-crafted item, the *Gartenzwerg* first went into serialized production in late 1872, that is, within the two short years of economic expansion that followed the declaration of the German Empire at Versailles in 1871, and almost immediately became a contested symbol of Germany once available on the commercial market.

pop culture as a point of identification for their characters, while at the same time employing spoken English to reflect alienation or enact a distanciation. At the end of the 80s, Michael Verhoeven's protagonist in *Das schreckliche Mädchen* (*The Nasty Girl* [1989]) signaled a different approach to English as a mediator for European youths prior to the fall of the Iron Curtain. Sonja recalls that, after she had won an essay contest and joined the winners of other nationalities in Paris, trying to explain the difference between the two Germanys so that everyone would understand them was difficult:

Sonja (voiceover in German): Everyone had to tell something about their homeland. In my case that wasn't so easy.
Student 1: So Pfilzing is in Germany?
Young Sonja: Yes, in the Federal Republic, not in the GDR: the "so-called" GDR.
Student 2: Pfilzing is in the GDR?
Young Sonja: No, no, not German–Democratic–Republic... Bavaria!
Student 1: Bavaria not democratic?
Young Sonja: No, uh yes, but, um, Christian. Christian Socialistic Uni...
Student 3: Socialistic!?!? ...

Judging by moments like this, or pieces such as Monika Treut's irreverent *My Father is Coming*, by 1990 English had become a vehicle of cultural expression available to everyone across Western Europe, but in which Germans could not be quite at home, a status that had become as funny as it was existentially fraught.

Since then it has been rare to see English surface as an unproblematic means of communication, although in works like Wenders' films of the '90s it serves as a sort of postnational "European" tongue.[9] But, what seems to have remained most constant in German film is the continued association of English with some notion of cultural inauthenticity linked to conceptions that may still be roughly termed "Americanization." Even in phrases, English tends to serve as a pointer toward this problematic. Another recent European Cinema prize recipient, Wolfgang Becker's *Good-bye Lenin!* (2003), is an apt example. That phrase never appears in the film, yet from the opening credits it gestures to the Western victory in the cold war which brings the Americanization of (East) Germany in its wake. If one excludes the brand names "Burger King" and "Coca-Cola" (the latter, at least, long since germanified), only two words of English appear—or rather one word spoken twice: two West Germans moving into the protagonist's building both greet his mother with "Hi" as she takes her fateful walk away from her sickbed and out into the Berlin she does not know has been unified.

---

[9] As I have argued elsewhere, this lasts for Wenders until he returns to the West coast of the US to reconnect with the American themes of his early career (Davidson 2004).

Assessing *Good-bye Lenin!* we might well surmise that, in the new millennium, English can be used as one of the many indicators of the difficulty of genuine identity or the presence of an inauthentic one in German film, the employment of which may be quite poignant or funny. What makes this film distinct from, say, *Gegen die Wand*, is that in Akin's film, the specifically Turkish identity struggled after concerns itself openly with European identity only to the extent that the Federal Republic is already seen as embodying the new Europe. Indeed, what seems to separate *Gegen die Wand* from Akin's earlier *Kurz und schmerzlos* (*Short, Sharp Shock* [1997]) is that Istanbul has now been painted into the image of the new Europe as well, representing qualities that the protagonist Cahit abandons in the end by boarding a bus to return to the village he left so long ago.[10] The (post-East) German voice in *Good-bye, Lenin*, on the other hand, is more accepting of the new situation at the end, but still equates the new Germany with American commercial and cultural expansion.

In order to lace together my two concerns about language and icons of national identity, I want to step back in time just a bit to discuss *Deckname Dennis* (Codename Dennis), Thomas Frickel's viscious 1997 satire of German foibles. Frickel reverses the trope of the "American" as an inauthentic and corrupting influence that is signaled in language: here a German actor plays an American secret agent, whose assignment is to pose as a documentary filmmaker in an effort to explore what the Germans "are really up to" these days. Dennis speaks a German so stereotypically Americanized that the viewer wonders that it does not draw attention to itself. The voiceover ruminations on his preliminary findings from roughly half-way through the film provide an excellent example of these *gemischte pickles* (here the reader will have to supply an immensely noticeable American twang). Over shots of his plaid-shirted frame and close-ups of the newspaper clippings he has amassed in his research, Dennis thinks about what he has learned of Germany:

> Hier ist nichts selbstverständlich. Hier fährt man nicht mit dem Auto, um irgendwo hinzukommen, sondern man fährt mit dem Auto um für die Freie [sic] und Menschenrechte zu demonstrieren. Hier fährt man mit dem Fahrrad, um gegen die Autos und das Benzin zu demonstrieren und für die Bäume. Hier isst man nicht, um satt zu werden, sondern die Deutschen essen um zu ziegen, dass

---

[10] Cahit's trauma stems from an undefined event that took his first wife from him and is associated with this village. By contrast, the lead figure in *Kurz und schmerzlos* finally decides that he has been led astray in contemporary, multi-cultural Berlin and, after rediscovering Islamic prayer with his father, embarks for Istanbul as a means of remedying it. It is not until the later film that the Turkish metropolis, too, is associated with (post) modern decadence.

sie etwas vom richtigen Essen verstehen…[11]

Even alone in his room, the voice-over maintains the attitude of naiveté that makes Dennis so successful in conversation with Germans. One might think that the combination of his accent and errors in grammar and structure with an immense, instantly accessible vocabulary would raise an eyebrow during the Michael-Moore-like interviews that he conducts. To the contrary, this language not only arouses no suspicion, but the perception of this hayseed as a sympathetic American listener is generated by meeting and exceeding the stereotype, which in turn elicits bare-faced honesty from the furthest reaches of German society. The following exchange is taken from the very next scene, in which Dennis visits the first German garden gnome museum:

> *Director*: Guten Tag. Herzlich willkommen! Ich bin Günter Griebel, Direktor des ersten deutschen Gartenzwerg Museums…Hier ist Ihre Eintrittskarte, die ist übigrens eine Mütze. Wir müssen jetzt Ihre absetzen.
> *Dennis*: Eine Mütze! Muss man sie aufsetzen? Das ist ein typisch deutscher Gruss?
> *Director*: Genau, das ist eine typische "Zipfelauf" Mütze. Augenblick, Knick muss 'rein, das ist ganz wichtig beim deutschen Gartenzwerg. So, jetzt sind Sie, ummm, haben Sie das richtige Outfit.
> *Dennis*: Und wie, wie, was machen Sie hier? Sind Sie ein Huter [sic] von Gartenzwergen?
> *Director*: Ja, ein Hüter eines deutschen Kulturobjekts. Weil etwas typisch deutscheres kann ich mir gar nicht vorstellen. Er repräsentiert alles, was im Deutschen verborgen ist, im Guten und im Schlechten. Natürlich viel spiessiges, aber auch, würde ich sagen, viel bodenständiges, ehrliches, zuverlässiges: im Grunde die Züge, die uns ausmachen, wir Deutschen.
> *Dennis*: Aber die Leute haben eine gespaltene Meinung über Gartenzwerge…
> *Director*: Ja sicher, deswegen ist es auch typisch, na? Jeder hat so seine Meinung dazu. Aber in der Regel überwiegen die Gartenzwerg-Freunde: die Gartenzwerg-Hasser werden immer weniger.
> *Dennis*: Und die Gartenzwerg-Hasser…ist das, umm, ist das vielleicht, umm, ein Gruner [sic] oder eine politische Ansicht?
> *Director*: Nein, ich würde sagen, die Grünen neigen eher auch zum Gartenzwerg. Der Gartenzwerg war ja der erste Grüner überhaupt im Deutschland. Der Streit geht eher darum, das er etwas spiessig ist, dass der Gartenzwerg ungute Eigenschaften repräsentiert. Aber das möchte ich gerade

---

[11] "Nothing is self-evident here. One doesn't drive a car to get somewhere; rather one drives a car to demonstrate for free[dom] and human rights. Here one rides a bicycle to demonstrate against the cars and gasoline and for the trees. Here one doesn't eat to get full, the Germans eat in order to show that they understands something about proper eating…"

verneinen.[12]

After a preliminary shot of the museum's sign and a shot tracking along the wall of the entrance, this scene is initially depicted in a two-shot with a counter separating the two discussants. At the first mention of "typically German" we cut to a slightly low-angle frontal shot of the dumpy Dennis (now in his gnome "outfit"), and then to a similar shot of Günter Griebel. During the mention of the "Garden-gnome haters" the film pans from a high angle across a gnome in a mouse trap to one with a knife in the back, and then cuts back to the initial two-shot for the final statements about the gnome representing good German qualities. The museum keeper here is a mild example of pro-German attitudes in the film, while many others, all "normal" citizens, express views on film to Dennis that are in many ways beyond the pale.

Though it envisions it differently, *Deckname Dennis* joins with *Gegen die Wand* in rejecting what it sees as the core of contemporary Germany, but it does so because Germany seems to have remained intensely parochial rather than opening itself up to the new Europe. Indeed, all the demons of "German"

---

[12] Although the film does not make mention of it, the director's name is a link to the history of the *Gartenzwerg* as well: Peter Griebel began the first mass production of the items in 1872. Translation:
Director: Hello and welcome!. I am Günther Kriebel, Director of the first German Garden-Gnome Museum...Here is your ticket, which by the way is a cap. We have to put yours aside now.
Dennis: A cap! Do you have to put it on? Is that a typical German greeting?
Director: Exactly, this is a typical "heads up" [*Zipfelauf*] pointed cap. Just a minute, it's got to be bent, that's very important for a German garden gnome. There, now you are, um, you have the right outfit.
Dennis: And how, how, what do you do here? Are you a guardian [mispronounced] of garden gnomes?
Director: Yes, a guardian of a German cultural object. Because I can't imagine anything more typically German. It represents everything that is within the German, the good and the bad. Naturally some cheesiness (Spiessiges), but I would also say a lot that is grounded, honest, reliable: basically the characteristics that define us Germans.
Dennis: But people have divided opinions about garden gnomes...
Director: Of course, that's why it's so typical, see? Everyone has an opinion about it. But in general the friends of the garden gnome are winning out: the garden-gnome haters are growing fewer.
Dennis: and the garden-gnome hater... ist that, um, maybe a Green or a political point of view?
Director: No, I'd say, the Greens tend to like the garden gnome. The garden gnome was the first Green in Germany anyway. The argument is more about the cheesiness, whether the garden gnome represents undesireable traits. But that's precisely what I want to argue against.

identity are on display in this film; yet, the film's take on Günter Griebel's depiction of the garden gnome as something typically German touches on the paradox of reactions to "authentic German kitsch." Its affirmation relies on identification that remains rooted in the "Volk" while its rejection relies on assumptions of taste that ultimately have the propensity to essentialize class as well. The image inserted of Dennis-the-American as a living garden gnome in the museum reminds us that, in the contemporary world qualified by a blurring of cultural boundaries, even something manifesting the "essentially German" is not safely ensconced within borders. While the cynicism embodied in Frickel's satire could only heap ridicule upon such superficial transnational commonality, a different approach can read the international erasures legible in that surface. And, just as the transatlantic military alliance survives the cold war because it began not just to oppose the USSR but to shore up the underbelly of dreams of a united Europe,[13] so too does the contradictory cultural connection to America embodied by Dennis remain a vital part of that notion.

 An interesting counterpoint to *Deckname Dennis* is Michael Schorr's *Schultze Gets the Blues* (2003), which, like *Good-bye Lenin*, bears an English title and focuses on an Eastern German's inadequate identity. It opens with a stark, Tarkovsky-like construction showing a flat desolation marked only by a huge wind turbine towering above screen right, and a tiny mountain in the background at its base. After several seconds this austere view is humorously interrupted and made softer when a large man bicycles across the screen. In this manner we are unwittingly introduced to our main character, Schultze, who along with two friends has his last day of work in the local mine at the film's outset. He enjoys fishing and drinking beer with these friends, but most of his time is spent playing the accordion and tending his *Schrebergarten* populated with garden gnomes. His early, forced retirement proceeds quietly, until chance has him hear a zydeco tune late one sleepless night, after which he finds it impossible to return to the traditional polkas favored by his music club. He works odd jobs in order to be able to travel to Louisiana, the home of this music, but the introduction of the Euro foils his plan. The monetary unification of Europe brings with it hidden price hikes and dashes the German's American dream. Schultze's outburst at discovering this marks the only point in the film at which he shows any agitation at all. He rues this lost opportunity all the more as he watches TV-news images of garden gnomes being bulldozed into mass

---

[13] Dana H. Allin (2001) points out that the Atlantic Alliance has outlived the cold war because its initial purpose was not simply to be a counter weight to Soviet power, but to provide "a necessary complement to the dream of European unity" shared by so many who had opposed Hitler. The same can be said for the complex cultural relationship to the US in those years and beyond.

graves, which must seem a further assault on what he holds dear.[14] Though the members do not approve his new style of playing, to honor his birthday the music club chooses Schultze to be the guest-musician at the German-Festival hosted by their American sister-city in Texas. Once there he decides not to perform, but instead acquires a boat and moves ever-deeper into bayou country, where he makes a few acquaintances and then quietly dies on the roof of a houseboat on a backwater under the stars.

In Schultze's character and surroundings we recognize the way institutional imperatives accompanying localized funding find their way into the fabric of films. In this case support from Berlin-Brandenburg and Sachsen-Anhalt makes itself felt, as Schulze is not just a beer-drinking, garden-gnome-collecting, Schreber-garden-tending German, but an "Anhalter" as well. The playful banter between his friends, Manfred his fellow Anhalter and Jürgen the Prussian, often recalls traditional regional prejudices and occasionally touches a raw nerve. Specific Germans, but not unified Germany, are referred to here—reunification only exists through the oblique reference to the conditions requiring that these friends be retired early. Similarly, membership in the new Europe only arises with the introduction of the Euro. Thematically, the local groundedness of these characters is paramount, but the viewer is not required to have a thorough knowledge of German regionalisms in order to understand this film, for the local is most importantly embedded in the visual aesthetic of the film.

Schorr's landscapes and people shot lovingly, but then often set against each in contradictory images that are often both humorous (like the montage-within-the-frame of the opening shot) and full of bite. For example, early in the film a long take of a glorious sunset photographed across the flat landscape occupies the screen, evoking wistful beauty and serenity, only to be followed by a quick series of confined shots showing Schulze's weather-beaten front door and cramped, stultifying "living room." This type of juxtaposition is also used in reverse, as when the group celebrating Schultze's birthday gathers at his garden house. Filmed from inside the garden the revellers look happy, and their communing occupies the entire screen. A jump cut to a long shot of the pitiful building, its grounds filled with little people dwarfed by both a mountain of slag and the vast flat expanses beyond, gives a savage twist to the previous image of their fulfillment. The *Spiessigkeit* of the German working class—perhaps more accurately the integration of the mindset of the working class with that of the *Kleinbürgertum* (the petit-bourgeois average citizen)—and the quiet desperation it should engender seem overly easy targets here; and yet, without realizing it consciously, Schultze instinctively moves through and beyond it to show this

---

[14] For this viewer there is a disturbing parallel to documentary images of concentration camp victims raised by the screen direction, motion, angles, and editing of these TV shots here, although Schultze clearly does not seem aware of it.

world of little people in a differentiated light.

The first thing we notice is that there are two attitudes in this lifeworld, closed- and open-mindedness, which are both on display at the music festival put on by Schulze's *Musikverein* "Harmonie." The camera faces the stage flanked by two long dining tables. The symmetrical nature of this composition seems to separate the groups neatly, but the two attitudes are not so evenly divided, as is shown in the reaction to Schultze's performance. Roughly three-quarters of the audience insists on its accustomed kitschy fare (polkas and marches), so Schulze's last minute change from the traditional to the new song does not suit them. Only a few hands clap at one corner of one table; from the other someone yells "Scheiss Negermusik" into the silence that follows the limited applause. A few tense moments ensue and then a toast is offered by the approving minority to defuse and incorporate that description: "Auf die Negermusik" and then, "Auf Schultze."[15] Because of their true affection for Schultze, a handful of the people at his table are able to get beyond themselves and at least hear something different, showing that the intimate can become the gateway to the new and strange.

As can be seen in the humorous presentation of Manfred's love for anything American, the director does not want to privilege just *any* affinity for the foreign, but openness to the foreign always holds possibility. Schulze's attempt at "American" (Cajun) cooking, for example, brings the three friends back together after a spat: it reunites them in misery against the spicy cuisine. Even more important, it is the first time that his friends have dined together at Schultze's place after more than twenty years of acquaintance. Lest the audience find too much possibility in such moments, the scene ends with the three complaining bitterly about the way some nebulous "they" has lied to and pushed them out. Jürgen bemoans that the time for rising up has passed, but Manfred counters, "Quatsch, für die Revolution ist man nie zu alt."[16] He takes another pull at his beer after this declaration, but otherwise remains motionless with his eyes glued to the television. While it does not restore the (ex-)working classes to their Marxist role as the carriers of history, the laughable "difference" experienced at this American meal nevertheless deepens their localized intimacy.

In some cases such an openness can have an extremely powerful effect. Precisely the difference of Cajun music touches Schultze, and being moved in this manner scares him so much that he initially fears that it signals an illness. Once he has been infected, it becomes literally impossible for him to play his old music. This is no mere rehashing of the "Amis-have-colonized-our-

---

[15] "Shitty nigger-music!" "To the nigger-music!...To Schultze."

[16] "Crap, you're never too old for the revolution!"

subconscience" motif, but neither is it a magical transformation: Schultze can only play one Zydeco tune, poorly and at an unregulated tempo, and he finally is brought up against this fact at the "Wurstfest" in Texas. Seeing all these Texans in their faux-German *Trachten*, playing fast and well, yodeling loudly, Schultze quietly puts his instrument away and leaves the arena. It remains unclear whether he goes because he feels he is not good enough or because the polka-tinged mexicali music is not what he does. The next scene, in which he stops when a band at another grandstand begins playing "Das Deutschlandlied," offers some insight. The camera pans away from Schultze across a sea of drunken passers-by and costumed Amis to rest on the brass band playing this national(ist) anthem. There is a frightening difference between the German who stops for his nation's song and the Texans who stand for it. For lack of better terms, Schultze's response is natural, while that of the others is performed: his action reflects who he is without being reflected upon; theirs seems to be both elected and performed, and thus to be far more ideologically loaded.

Schorr's film clearly recognizes the constructed nature of identity, and much of the humor in *Schultze Gets the Blues* arises from changing perspectives that expose the absurdities in such constructions, which have social conditions and received traditions as their two primary building blocks. At the same time, Schorr also seems sensitive to the fact that individuals do not always have the distance to get a perspective on the artificiality of who they (think they) are. This comes, in part, from the comfort and sloth that are embodied in a figure like the Schultze we see early on, reclining nearly motionless in his yard drinking beer and smoking cigars, surrounded by the garden gnomes he has just carefully cleaned, himself the very image of kitsch Germany. Yet this surface stillness, rather than deep contemplation and enlightenment, dissolves the identity from which it seems to arise and with which it seems so content. As Cooppan (2003) puts it in a different context, this kitsch Germany

> In its refusal to read or to know the other... frustrate[s] monolithic concepts of difference and identity and reject[s] the binarizing logic of us/them in favor of a diffuse aesthetic of the surface (270).

Thus, a potential resides in such provisional immediacy of this surface, *Schultze* seems to aver, if not for "authenticity" itself then for authentic communion, a kind of genuineness that develops out of identity's artifice. In the world from which Schultze comes, this possibility resides less in enlightened demystification than in naturalized response.

Schultze does not come to a realization about his status at the festival, just as he does not come to a deeper understanding of anything in this film. Or, to put this differently, at home he senses that his swerve from tradition is a problem, but he makes no effort to articulate this in language, and the film gives no indication that he struggles with its comprehension. Schultze's tentative, but repeated request that he be allowed to play another song for the *Musikverein* is a case in point. While fully aware of the problems this might cause, rather than trying to explain or justify the change, he simply states twice: "I think I would like to play a different song." Later, when he confronts the picture of his father the accordion player, he refrains from any pathos-laden articulation to the photo of why he feels this need to abandon the polka: he merely sets it on the shelf and then, when it slips, returns it to the nail with its face to the wall. If, as Julia Hell (1997) has argued, the GDR's *Ankunftsroman* ("novel of arrival" in socialism) was marked by a "final submission to the Law of the Father" that involved producing a *"post-facist body"* (206), then it would perhaps not be amiss to see Schultze's extreme corporeality as the embodiment of a post-socialist body turning away from the law of the (socialist) father in a parodic "Abschiedsfilm" ("film of departure") from socialism.

The problem with such a reading would be that it posits consistency in behavior where there is none. The traditional music of the father from which Schultze turns is not really to be associated with socialism; on the other hand, he turns to a tradition in his *Gartenzwerge* that has very distinct history counter to the GDR, a state that once declared the figure to be bourgeois and anticommunist and banned its production.[17] A better means of understanding these tensions would be to consider the use of memory and tradition for negotiating the everyday. Schultze may stand in for East Germans, whose memories had been rendered "irrelevant to the new life circumstances in the East after 1989" (Ten Dyke 2002, 155), but he does not choose to reenact his earlier performance of tradition as a memory in order to maintain a way of life, for that performance has always acted as an inhibitor. Hence, once in the US, he simply does not respond to the performance of a supposedly traditional culture composed of ossified markers glued together simply in order to set the tradition forward: the Lederhosen, the hats, and the Germanness in Texas are as uninteresting to him as the traditional music conserved in place of a memory of life by his *Musikverein* at home.

So why has Cajun music captivated him? The film posits links between notions of hybridity and authenticity here: it is literally "hybrid" music–creole that speaks to him, representing a cultural expression that simply *is*, arising from a true openness to others, rather than from an attempt to conserve and perform something that may never have existed in the first place. Within the parallel worlds of kitsch common to the little people of both Germany and the US in this

---

[17] Autodidactic nanologist Fritz Friedmann reports that "one look in the history books would have convinced the party hacks otherwise. The appearance and clothing of the garden gnome remind one distinctly of the miners of Thüringen" (http://www.zipfelauf.com/wienerz.htm).

film, the embrace of difference within the human community is paramount in both locations, regardless of the paucity of aesthetic sensibility or the lack actual communication that attend it.

We see this repeatedly: Schultze shares a hot tub in a parking lot next to a freeway with a woman he hardly understands; he dances with people he has just met in clapboard, backwater bars, and at a "Rock 'N' Bowl"; he acquires a nickname from a "Czech" musical group he happens upon, even though their conversation consists almost exclusively of one word. The word is "petroleum," which Schultze inadvertently substitutes for the American "gasoline." While language differences play a role, they are not primary: the band never corrects Schultze, although they do offer up a different "petroleum" (vodka) before pointing him to the gas station. Even misunderstandings are not primarily attributable to linguistic comprehension. One sad moment, when Schultze feels abandoned at a bar in the bayou, does not come because he understands neither Cajun French nor English, but because his dance partner gives no indication that she will be coming back. Finding himself embarrassingly left alone, Schultze exits without making a sign. The camera lingers, however, to show his partner return carrying two drinks, and she in turn looks crestfallen and abandoned. In each of these cases it is the social gesture that matters to communication more than the language of expression or even any sense of deep mutual or self understanding. English neither aids nor impedes his final adventures, even though, quite clearly, these are adventures that could never have taken place just within the German-language realm in which he initially moves.

Schultze Gets the Blues is by no means a perfect film: it contains continuity errors, does not provide enough overt motivation for its characters' actions for some viewers, and assumes a geography that is impossible.[18] The wrong musical form is evoked in the title (Schultze hears and plays two-steps, not blues tunes), although the English-language pun is successful, and the reference to an "American" form is compelling. Most importantly, there is clearly a kind of exoticism of difference at work here, which both fails to recognize positive moments in the German-influenced Tex-Mex sound and idealizes the hybridity of the Cajun world unrealistically. One might, indeed, be tempted to assign it to the "can't-we-all-just-get-along" category. What is most important, though, is that *Schultze* questions instrumentalized identity at each turn, without reading in a different one. For example, early in the film there is an overt instrumentalization of the miners' identity when former colleagues sing a

---

[18] The site of the "Wurstfest" shoot is New Braunfels, TX, a town off the interstate between San Antonio and Austin, which is situated far from bayou country and even further from the border with Louisiana, roughly 280 miles by road. The dreamlike quality and existential import of Schulze's journey, of course, give license to the film's creative cartography.

traditional song and award the three retirees large crystals with electric lights inside. While such an identity may well be important to these figures, this performance only poses for working-class solidarity as it sugar coats the situation of their forced retirement. The trio's lack of reaction shows this to be a performance of the legitimating shifts of cultural identification: as the coal is displaced into crystal, the ousted miners "become" the gnomes of legend. Similarly, the "Wurst" German personae in Texas are equally unmasked by Schultze's refusal to read or to know it. Hence, while focusing so much on German-isms, Schorr's is a "German" film only in the least important aspects.[19]

In the context of this volume we might ask, then, to what extent this is a "European" film. Certainly it is significant that Schultze's only outburst comes at the introduction of the Euro: "how can you do that," he screams at the travel agent who changes the sign advertising the price of the trip to Louisiana. His anger is mis-directed at this one person, but the viewer is aware that the instrumentalized notion of European identity through monetary policy and commercial alliance is at fault here. Still, it seems important to see this film in relation to the traditions of European filmmaking to which it alludes. For example, the viewer seems to recognize clear nods to the New German Cinema's "America films" such as Werner Herzog's *Stroszek* (1977) or the Wenders road movie. Unlike *Alice in den Städten* (1974) or *Paris Texas* (1984), however, this journey is not sparked by a charge that needs to be taken care of in order to return to a state of blissful cinematic sight and motion devoid of narrative. Schultze simply goes. As he moves further into the swamp country, the camera work recalls Herzog's South American films as well. The verdant surroundings shot from the boat seem to cut the screen horizontally and to cordon the world off from our sojourner, who at one point is depicted in a long take shot from the front at a slightly low angle as he steers his craft up the bayou. This echoes the shots in *Fitzcarraldo* (1982) of the Dutch pilot, another large man, as he navigates the treacherous Ucayali into uncharted regions. However, about halfway through this take, Schultze removes a tiny garden gnome from his pocket and affixes it to the console so that it, too, can look ahead. Re-introducing us to his little friend at this point shatters any false sense of profundity that may have been building in the quiet sobriety of this portion of the film. The figurine has lost none of the freight it carried in the first part of the

---

[19] While clearly neither an "anti-Heimat" nor "Heimat" film, *Schultze* contains any number of what Rick Altman (2004) calls semantic and syntactical elements from those genre. At the conclusion of Johannes von Moltke's (2005) fine exploration of Heimat in German film, the author notes two trends in post-Wall Heimat-cinema: one fostering nostalgia and consensus in the service of the "Berlin Republic," and one that is resistant to "integration into overly conciliatory frameworks" (237). See also Naughton (2002). *Schultze* perhaps indicates a third way in which the instruments of Heimat can be plated.

film—German *Spiessigkeit* now steams up the waterways of the Americas, seemingly intact and ready for what awaits it. What awaits is Schultze's quiet death beneath the stars, devoid of any meaning that needs further communication.

The aesthetic drive to difference that marked, say, *Aguirre, der Zorn Gottes* (1972), is alternately figured in *Schultze Gets the Blues*: there is no positing of depth or mystery in the swamp forest; Schultze does not go native and is not more "other" than the others he meets; he certainly is not the Wrath of God. But then, Schorr's world is not a radically relativist one in which only the charismatically powerful or the absolutely other are worthy of existence and only the impossibly grand scheme worthy of pursuit. It is a world of localities occupied by little people, some of whom have no more need for identity than their experience affords them. There has been no scheme or quest, and in the end we return, along with the remains of Schultze and those who offered him shelter as he passed, to Anhalt, where his funeral provides the setting not necessarily for a new community but an expanded one. And here, again, it is the gesture of communication that turns the potentially tragic into happy farce. The funeral sequence begins with a shot down a tree-lined path leading to the cemetery as the musicians from "Harmonie" approach blowing a slow dirge in a three-quarter beat. A cut to the grave site shows an urn being lowered as Schultze's old friends and new acquaintances (some of whom are black) look on respectfully. As the minister begins his oration, Manfred's cell phone rings inappropriately and, even more inappropriately, he answers: "Schultze?" he asks in mock surprise. The sad tension breaks, and the next shot shows the procession leaving between the trees as a happy group, the band this time playing a version of Schultze's zydeco number. An identity, which is literally no more than the name Schultze, has become the site where languages are united and contacts are opened.

Schorr's take on German and European identity in *Schultze Gets the Blues* does not stand in the traditions of filmmakers like the early Herzog nor even Fatih Akin, who averred or struggled with identity in an exclusionary framework of one cultural tradition relative to others. Nor does it follow those like Tarkovsky, who yearned for the experience of religious mystery that would relieve life's limitations. The secret knowledge of the gnome here has to do with the transnational nature of the plight and potential of the little people in this world. Building on the work of Jürgen Kocka (1991), Jarle Simensen (2004) explains the rapid change in Eastern Europe since 1989 by augmenting the notion of modernization leading inevitably to democratization through an increased middle strata with an awareness of the transnational interaction of large systems. In a way, *Schultze* shows the byproduct of that process—the interaction of small systems common to the lower strata straining upwards. In the final shot we return to the opening construction (wind turbine fore-right, slag mountain tiny in the background, vast space center and left): while Schultze does not appear this time to bike across the horizon, the funeral procession follows that same path, playing and dancing in a kind of Sachsen version of the New Orleans jazz funeral. In doing so they provide yet another riff on the fabled ending of *The Seventh Seal* (1957), and it becomes clear that this film's sense of life aligns itself with those who celebrate the human comedy, such as Ingmar Bergman or, perhaps, Woody Allen. The visions of these directors, while not without their local, national, and ethno-cultural inflections, might have once been termed humanist or universalist: it remains a question whether such sentiments now need to be spoken of, in German or in English, as transnational or postnational, or whether, like Schultze and the ubiquitous garden gnome, we can begin mutely to dismantle such labels in the new Europe.

Postscript

Two fossil fuels link Schultze to his drinking buddies on different sides of the Atlantic: the coal that he mined with Jürgen aand Manfred and the "petroleum" that he drinks with the Czech heritage band whose forebears had long since emigrated from central Europe. Doubtless Schorr uses "petroleum" in order to strengthen what he sees as a connection between the two regions that are featured in the film and to dislodge any notion that Louisiana is a paradise:

> Auf der anderen Seite wollte ich aber auch zeigen, dass es für die Leute, die dort unten leben, gar nicht das gelobte Land ist, dass es auch eine durchaus triste Realität hat und Menschen dort mit ganz ähnlichen Problemen zu kämpfen haben, wie Schultze in Sachsen-Anhalt. Louisiana, wo wir gedreht haben, hat auch eine ganz ähnliche Geschichte; statt der Bergwerke und Schwerindustrie gibt es dort eine Ölindustrie, die nach dem grossen Boom in den letzten zehn, fünfzehn Jahren langsam abgebaut wurde.[20]

In this article I have emphasized the role that local, national, and transnational identifications play in enabling the kinds of problems faced by these people across the divides that seem to separate them. Being from New Orleans, and revising this text in the wake of the Katrina disaster on the US Gulf Coast to the East of the region where Schultze meets his end, I feel compelled to stress again

---

[20] "On the other hand I wanted to show that for the people who live there this is not the promised land, that it has a very gloomy reality, and the people there struggle with very similar problems to those that Schultze has in Sachsen-Anhalt. Louisiana, where we filmed, has a similar history; instead of mines and heavy industry there is the oil industry, which since the great boom has been slowing dismantled over the past ten, fifteen years" (Schorr in Sterneborg 2004).

the manner in which class (it seems like such an anachronism to use the term!) becomes erased in both the positive and negative results of such identifications.

As stated above, "'localization and globalization are inextricably bound together in the current phase' of uneven development, not just in the economy but also in the thickets of identificatory politics" as well. For example, being "New Orleanian" has for years bonded the most diverse group of people imaginable; it also allowed for the perpetuation of the crassest division between haves and have-nots imaginable in the richest country on the planet. Nowhere has the emptiness of the "distinction" between the two dominant US political parties been more apparent over the years than in Louisiana's approach to this threat of natural disaster (recognized in the 1950s). In New Orleans the dominance of African Americans in mayoral politics since the mid-1970s shows that race alone is not the issue as many maintain (although, of course, racism and structural poverty are intimately intertwined). Vast mismanagement of resources to give preference to privilege, on the one hand, and the sense that reserving the racial makeup of representatives would be a primary move toward solving problems, on the other, led in no small measure to the disaster. They also influenced President Bush's decisions to ignore the direct, and quite accurate, warnings about the consequences of the coming storm in favor of attending a $5000 per plate fundraiser in California, and then to lie about having received the warning afterwards. The resiliency of New Orleanians in the aftermath of all this is a marvel to behold and restores faith in the human spirit; yet, it also accommodates many versions of plans to favor those in a position of significant "ownership" at the expense of those less well situated. Thus, aided by the long history of economic disenfranchisement and by identifications that push the economic from view, the hurricane removed impediments to further concentration of wealth in the hands of the few.

Without wanting to seem flippant, I would suggest that the situation in New Orleans now may be seen as paralleled in the situation at the beginning of *Schultze Gets the Blues*. Although the consequences are not so dire within the world of the film, false identifications and heartless economic policy place the characters in a desperate situation. Whether already downsized or still at work, these Sachen-Anhalters' misplaced middle-class allegiances and national representations smooth their route into the new union of Europeans that has increasingly less concern for them. But in the make-believe world of the cinema, a figure can appear who resides in these misalignments in so naturalized a manner that they implode. Schultze's superficial life, seemingly so indexically and iconically insistent on his German identity, paradoxically opens a path to difference and allows commonalities to arise, uniting people in spite of their own identities. The "jazz" funeral at the film's end is a far cry from what one might see in New Orleans, but it humorously brings together figures who have more in common than one would initially have thought. Within the new Europe, however, his burial reminds us that one can, indeed, be too old for the revolution.

Works Cited

Akin, F. 1998. *Kurz und schmerzlos* (Short, Sharp Shock). Germany: Wüste Filmproduktion; ZDF.
—. 2004. *Gegen die Wand* (Head On). Germany: Wüste Filmproduction. Universal dvd.
Allin, D. H. 2001. Uneasy triangle: Transatlantic partnership and UN governance. In *The new transatlantic agenda: Facing the challenges of global governance*. Edited by H. Gardner and R. Stefanova. 153-172. Aldershot: Ashgate.
Altman, R. 2004. A semantic/syntactic approach to film genre. In *Film Theory and Criticism*. 6th ed. 680-90. Edited by L. Braudy and M. Cohen. Oxford & New York: Oxford UP.
Becker, W. 2003. *Good-bye Lenin!* Germany: X-Filme; WDR; arte. Sony Pictures.
Bergman, I. 1957. *Det Sjunde inseglet* (The Seventh Seal). Sweden: Svensk Filmindustri. Criterion Collection dvd.
Box, S. and N. Park. 2005. *Wallace and Gromit in the Curse of the Were-Rabbit* (2005). Aardman Animation; Dreamworks.
Brown, D. 2003. *The Da Vinci code*. New York: Doubleday.
Cooppan, V. 2003. Mourning becomes kitsch: The aesthetics of loss in Severo Sarduy's *Cobra*. In *Loss: The politics of mourning*. Edited by D. L. Eng and D. Kazanjian. 251-277. Berkeley: U California Press.
Davidson, J. E. 2004. "Against Rushing Through Places Which Ought To Be Dwelt In": Kracauer, Wenders, and the Post-Turnerian impulse. *Studies in European Cinema* 1 (2): 91-104.
Dyson, K. and K. H. Goetz. 2003. Living with Europe: Power, constraint, and contestation. In *Germany, Europe, and the politics of constraint*. Edited by K. Dyson and K. H. Goetz. 3-36. Oxford & New York: Oxford UP.
Featherstone, M. 1996. Localism, globalism, and cultural identity. In *Global/Local: Cultural production and the transnational imaginery*. Edited by R. Wilson and W. Dissanayake. 46-77. Durham: Duke UP.
Frickel, T. 1997. *Deckname Dennis* (Codename Dennis). Germany: DDC Denver; HE-Films.
Gronow, J. 1997. *The sociology of taste*. New York & London: Routledge.
Hell, J. 1997. Soft-porn, kitsch, and post-fascist bodies: The East German novel of arrival. In *Socialist realism without shores*. Edited by T. Lahusen and E.

Dobrenko. 203-226. Durham & London: Duke UP.
Herzog, W. 1972. *Aguirre, der Zorn Gottes* (Aguirre, the Wrath of God). Germany: Werner Herzog Filmproduktion. New Yorker Films video.
—. 1977. *Stroszek*. Germany: Werner Herzog Filmproduktion (et al). New Yorker Films video.
—. 1982. *Fitzcarraldo*. Germany: Werner Herzog Filmproduktion (et al). New World Films video.
Jacobsen, A. 2005. *King of the Hill*. "Yard, she blows." Fox. Episode 175. 23 January.
Jeunet, J-P. 2001. *Le Fabuleux destin d'Amélie Poulain* (Amélie). France; Germany: Universal; Miramax.
Kocka, J. 1991. Überraschung und Erklärung: Was die Umbrüche von 1989/90 für die Gesellschaftsgeschichte bedeuten könnten. In *Was ist Gesellschaftsgeschichte? Positionen, Themen, Analysen*. Edited by M. Hetling and C. Huerkamp. 11-22. Munich: Beck.
Lugg, C. A. 1999. *Kitsch: From education to public policy*. New York: Falmer.
Moltke, J. V. 2005. *No place like home: Locations of heimat in German cinema*. Berkeley: University of California Press.
Mucha, S. 2004. *Die Mitte* (The Center). Germany: Hessisches Rundfunk; Strandfilm; arte. Ventura Films Distributor.
Naughton, L. 2002. *That was the Wild East: Film culture, unification, and the "new" Germany*. Ann Arbor: University of Michigan Press.
Poet, P. 2002. *Ausländer 'Raus–Schlingensiefs Container* (Foreigners Out!). Austria: Bonus Film; Real Film.
Schorr, M. 2003. *Schultze Gets the Blues*. Germany: Kombinat GmbH & Co.; ZDF. Paramount dvd.
Simensen, J. 2004. The global context of 1989. In *Transnational moments of change: Europe 1945, 1968, 1989*. Edited by G.-R. Horn and P. Kenney. 157-172. Lanham: Rowman & Littlefield.
Sterneborg, A. 2004. Amerika ist mehr als ein Klischee. *epd Film* (April): 2-4.
Ten Dyke, E. A. 2002. Memory and existence: Implications of the *Wende*. In *The work of memory: New directions in the study of German culture and society*. Edited by A. Confino and P. Fritsche. 154-72. Urbana & Chicago: U of Illionios Press.
Treut, M. 1991. *My Father is Coming*. Germany: Hyane. Tara Releasing.
Van Helsing, F. 2003. *"Ihr Gartenzwerg hat mich beleidigt!" Die verrücktesten Klagen der Welt*. Frankfurt a.M.: Eichborn.
Venske, H. 1983. Die Deutschen werden ausgewandert. *Herr Kalaschnikoff ratter den Sonntagein*. http://www.geocities.com/Athens/8307/venske/venske14.htm
Verhoeven, M. 1989. *Das schreckliche Mädchen* (The Nasty Girl). Germany:

Filmverlag der Autoren; ZDF. Mirimax video.

Voltmer, K. and Eilders, C. 2003. The media agenda: The marginalization and domestication of Europe. In *Germany, Europe, and the politics of constraint*. Edited by K. Dyson and K. H. Goetz. 173-197. Oxford & New York: Oxford UP.

Wenders, W. 1974. *Alice in den Städten* (Alice in the Cities). Germany: Filmverlag der Autoren; WDR. Pacific Arts video.

—. 1984. *Paris Texas*. Germany: Argos; Road Movies. Twentieth-Century Fox video.

CONTRIBUTORS

OLIVIER ASSELIN is Associate Professor in the Department of Art History and Film Studies at the University of Montreal. He has written articles and monographic studies on contemporary art and co-edited two special issues on *Autofictions* (2002) and *Digital Screens* (2004). He is also a filmmaker, having directed *La Liberté d'une statue* (1990) and *Le siège de l'âme* (2004).

SANDRA BARRIALES-BOUCHE is Assistant Professor of Spanish at Suffolk University where she teaches Spanish language, culture, literature and film. Her research interests include the literature of the exiles of the Spanish Civil War, the cultural interactions between Spain and Latin America, and the literature and film of Democratic Spain. She is the editor of *España: ¿laberinto de exilios?* (2005).

RUTH BARTON is O'Kane Senior Research Fellow at the School of Languages, Literatures and Film at UCD Dublin. She is the author of *Jim Sheridan: Framing the Nation* (2002), *Irish National Cinema* (2004) and co-editor of *Keeping it Real: Irish Film and Television* (2004). Her forthcoming book is titled *Acting Irish in Hollywood: From Fitzgerald to Farrell*. She is also Director of the "Screening Irish-America" project.

NEVENA DAKOVIĆ is Professor of Film Theory at the University of the Arts in Belgrade, Yugoslavia. She is the author of *Melodrama is Not a Genre* (1995) and *Dictionary of Film Theorists* (2002); editor of the multimedia publication *The Representation of the Serbian Cultural and National Identity* (2004), and co-editor of *Gender and Media* (1997) and *Mediated Identities* (2001). She has been a frequent visiting professor (Oxford, Nottingham, Warwick, Ankara, Ljubljana). Her research is focused on the issues of identity (national, multicultural) representations in cinema.

JOHN E. DAVIDSON is Associate Professor of German at the Ohio State University, where he is also Graduate Studies Committee Chair and Director of Film Studies. His areas of specializations include German film and visual culture, post-Enlightenment literature, and contemporary critical theories. He has written *Deterritorializing the New German Cinema* (1999).

CONTRIBUTORS

JEHANNE-MARIE GAVARINI is Associate Professor of Art at the University of Massachusetts-Lowell and Visiting Scholar-Artist at the Women's Studies Research Center at Brandeis University. Her artistic work has been featured nationally and internationally. She has received numerous artistic awards from the Massachusetts Cultural Council, Pennsylvania Council on the Arts, Bronx Council on the Arts, and Alliance Française of San Francisco. Her research interests include contemporary art, visual studies, film, gender studies, and cultural theory. She is co-translator of *Tomboy* which will be published in 2007 by the University of Nebraska Press.

CLAUDIO MAZZOLA teaches Italian at the University of Washington-Seattle. His areas of expertise are Contemporary Italian fiction and Italian Cinema. He has published a number of articles on contemporary Italian literature and cinema, as well as having published a reader for third year students entitled *Racconti Regionali* (1990) and a second year grammar book, *Insieme* (1995).

ALEJANDRO PARDO is Head of the Department of Culture and Audiovisual Communication at the University of Navarra and professor of Film and TV Production. Author of *David Puttnam, un productor creativo* (Rialp, Madrid, 1999) and *El oficio de producir películas: el estilo Puttnam* (Ariel, Barcelona, 2003), as well as editor of *The Audiovisual Management Handbook* (Media Business School, Madrid, 2002). He is currently working on the economic and cultural relationships between the US and the European film industries in the context of globalization.

MIREILLE ROSELLO is Professor of Comparative Analysis at the Universiteit van Amsterdam (Amsterdam School of Cultural Analysis and *Literatuurwetenschap*). Her research and teaching interests are in the fields of comparative and interdisciplinary cultural analysis of contemporary objects, visual or textual narratives (20th- and 21st-century literatures, popular culture, cinema, television, and new media). Her latest publication is *France and the Maghreb: Performing Encounters* (2005) and she is currently working on the creolization of Europe.

MARJORIE ATTIGNOL SALVODON is Assistant Professor of French at Suffolk University, where she teaches French and francophone film, French language, literature. Her research interests include literary translation and representations of exile, immigration and cultural identity in contemporary francophone cultures and literatures. She is co-translator of *Tomboy* which will be published in 2007 by the University of Nebraska Press. Her current research explores the questions of identity, difference, and belonging in contemporary French literature.

JANIS LITTLE SOLOMON is the Lucretia L. Allyn Professor of German Studies emerita at Connecticut College, where she was also Chair of the Department of German Studies and Founding Director of the Program in Film Studies until 2006. She is the author of *Die weltliche Lyrik des Martin Opitz* (1973) and *Die Kriegsdramen Reinhard Goerings* (1985), as well as articles on German literature ranging from the 16th through the 20th century. She currently has several works in progress, including "In Search of Self: Interrogation/Investigation/Narration in German Women's Films," "Gender and Genre: The Case of German Drama" and "The Blue Angel: Who Has/Is the Bird?"

INDEX

2by4 173
7° día, El (*The 7ᵗʰ Day*) 100
40m2 Deutschland 44
48 Hours 79
Abrahamson, Lenny 181-182
Adam and Paul 13, 181-182
Adelson, Leslie 48
Aguirre, der Zorn Gottes (*Aguirre, The Wrath of God*) 202
Akın, Fatih 10-11, 34-39, 41-44, 46-49, 70-71, 190, 192, 202
Air de famille, Un (*Family Resemblances*) 16
Aitkin, Ian 9
Alanyali, Iris 48
Alice in den Städten (*Alice in the Cities*) 201
Allen, Kieran 179
Allen, Woody 83, 203
Allin, Dana H. 195
Almejas y mejillones 121, 124
Almodóvar, Pedro 98, 99, 104, 107
Alquimista impaciente, El 101
Altman, Rick 201
Amelio, Gianni 12, 161, 164
Amenábar, Alejandro 98, 100, 120, 123
Americanization 174, 191-192
Andersen, Arthur 90
Anderson, Benedict 128
Angelopoulos, Théo 70
Un'anima divisa 161
Antonioni, Michelangelo 157
Aranda, Vicente 99, 120, 123-124
Aristaráin, Adolfo 99, 104, 105, 120-121, 124
Aristotle 129
Arsuaga, Diego 103
Asphalt Tango 75
Asselin, Olivier 12, 128

Augé, Marc 150
Ausländer 'Raus-Schlingensiefs Container (*Foreigners Out!*) 188
Bacri, Pierre 16
Bakhtin, Mikhail 77, 176
Balagueró, Jaume 98
Balibar, Etienne 5, 20-21
Balkanisateur (*Valkanisateur*) 11, 70-72, 75, 80
Balsa de piedra, La (*The Stone Raft*) 106
Bardem, Miguel 121, 124
Barton, Ruth 13, 170, 173, 177-178
Baser, Tevfik 44
Bauman, Zygmut 158, 168-169
Becher, Max 60
Becker, Wolfgang 191
Before the Rain 84
Belly of an Architect, The 147
Bend of the River 82
Bénédict, Sébastien 132
Benhadj, Rachid 102
Benjamin, Walter 55
Berger, Pablo 100, 121, 124
Bergfelder, Tim 6, 9
Bergman, Ingmar 203
Big Birthday, The 172
Blanco, David 101
Bloom, Harold 149
Böhm, Hark 44
Bola, El (*Pellet*) 97
Bolger, Dermot 177
Bollaín, Iciar 98
Bolter, Jay David 129
Borders 1, 129, 177, 179, 188, 195;
    Balkan 75, 80; chaotic 16, 24, 31;
    collapse of 8; deterritorialized 20;
    ethnic 11; European 1, 4-5, 9, 17, 31-32; geographic 45; geographical

5, 60, 65, 71, 156; geopolitical 58; linguistic 28; national 8, 9, 19, 47, 92, 111-112; nature of 1, 5, 10; of identity 3-4; permeable 53; political 128; porous 2, 8; tactical 25; temporal 65
Bouchy, Karine 144
Boundaries 4-5, 7-8, 29, 36, 45, 53, 55, 62, 64, 92, 100, 162, 182-183; cultural 16, 195
Bouquet, Stéphane 132
Box, Muriel 172
Brady, Eugene 173
Bread and Roses 102, 108
Brecht, Bertolt 43
Bridge 11, 22, 34, 39-41, 47-48, 55, 57-58, 62, 93, 96, 107, 110, 170; Mostar 58-59, 62
Brooks, Peter 19
Brooks, Xan 19, 21
Brown, Dan 186
Bugge, Peter 4
Butler-Cullingford, Elizabeth 172
Cabaret Balkan (*Bure baruta*) 75
Campanella, Juan José 103, 120-121, 123-124
Canícula 101
Carabiniers, Les 59
Caranfil, Nae 75
Carmen 120, 124
Carnevale, Marcos 121, 124
Carrera, Carlos 103, 121, 123
Carroll, Noel 73
Cassavetes, John 37
Çetin, Sinan 41
Chacun cherche son chat (*When the Cat's Away*) 16
Chambraud, Cécile 31
Chambre, La 16
Chaos 6, 18, 23, 25-26, 30-31, 56, 70
Chavarrías, Antonio 93, 111
Christie, Ian 110, 136
Cinema of abjection 181
Citton, Yves 27
Clayton, Sue 177
Close-up(s) 134, 136

Coixet, Isabel 107, 120, 123
Comerford, Joe 179
Cook, Fielder 172
Cook, the Thief and her Lover, The 147
Cooppan, Vilashini 189-190, 198
Co-productions 7, 11-12, 89-124, 178
Co-production treaties 90-92, 112
Corbett, Mary Jean 172
Crimen del Padre Amaro, El (*The Crime of Padre Amaro*) 101, 103, 109, 121, 123
Crimen Ferpecto (*Ferpect Crime*) 101, 109, 120, 123
Cronin, Michael 179
Crossing the Bridge: The Sound of Istanbul 38
Crowley, John 20-21
Crying Game, The 174
Curtis, Barry 172
Daković, Nevena 11, 70
Danan, Martine 7
Darkness 98
Darwish, Mahmoud 57
Das schreckliche Mädchen (*The Nasty Girl*) 191
Database(s) 130, 143-146, 149-150; logic 145
Davidson, John E. 13, 186, 191
Davis, John T. 182
Death in Venice 176
Deckname Dennis (*Codename Dennis*) 192-195
Delanty, Gerard 8
De Palma, Brian 37
Denk ich an Deutschland—Wir haben vergessen zurückzukehren (*We Forgot to Go Back*) 38
Der Untergang 48
Derrida, Jacques 3-4, 55, 66-67, 151
Desafinado (*Off Key*) 98, 106
Díaz Yanes, Agustín 120, 123
Dieckmann, Katherine 65
Die Geschichte vom weinenden Kamel 48
Die Mitte (*The Center*) 188

Digital filmmaking 179; media 129;
new digital film era 182;
technologies 134, 139, 149
Disappearance of Finbar, The 177-178
Disappearance of Rory Brophy 177
Diversity 6-7, 17, 76, 112
Donner, Richard 79
Don't Look Now 176
Dragojević, Srdjan 71
Drunken Master 38
Duck you sucker! (Giù la testa) 83
Dust 11, 70-72, 80-82, 84-85
Dyson, Kenneth 186
È già ieri 106
Eilders, Christiane 187
Eisenstein, Sergei M. 133-134
Elefant 134
Eleftheriotis, Dimitris 89, 111-112
Elliot, Bridget 140
Elsaesser, Thomas 7, 9, 11, 89, 111, 181-182
Embrujo de Shanghai, El 101, 121, 124
Émigré 71, 76
Empire 135
Engels, Josef 42
Escape 70
Espinazo del diablo, El (The Devil's Backbone) 104, 120, 123
Eurimages 7, 92-93, 113
European identity 5-8, 10, 20, 186, 192, 201-202; integration 186-187
Europeanization 186-187
European Union 1, 5-6, 46, 90-92
Europudding 105, 109
Europudding(s) 7-8, 19, 178
Evans, Dylan 63
Everett, Wendy 5, 8, 89, 95, 111
Eze, Emmanuel Chukwudi 3
Fabuleux destin d'Amélie Poulain, Le (Amelie) 189
Fall of Berlin Wall 138, 147, 157; of the Iron Curtain 191; of the Soviet Union 162
Falls, The 148
Farzanefar, Amin 37
Fassbinder, Rainer Werner 191

Featherstone, Mike 187
Fellini, Federico 157
Ferenczi, Aurélien 18, 31
Ferreira, Patri 101
Field, The 173
Figel, Ján 28
Figgis, Mike 134
Fitzcarraldo 201
Fontana, Josep 2-3
Ford, John 83, 171
Forrest Gump 83
Fortress Europe 17
Fowler, Catherine 9
Francis, Karl 107
Frickel, Thomas 192, 195
Friedman, Lawrence 159
From the Snow (Ap to Hioni) 75
Fuchs, Cynthis 79
Galt, Rosalind 8
García, Soledad 4
García-Capelo, Álvaro 101
Gardela, Isabel 97
Gates, Henry Louis Jr. 149
Gavarini, Jehanne-Marie 11, 53
Gemünden, Gerd 37, 39
Genette, Gérard 18
Gente pez 101, 120, 124
Getürkt! (Weed) 35
Giaccardi, Chiara 159
Gibbons, Luke 171-172, 179
Giordana, Marco Tullio 12, 164, 166-168
Glissant, Edouard 31
Globalization 6-7, 9, 11-12, 17, 49, 89-90, 128, 157-8, 162, 187, 204
Godard, Jean-Luc 10, 53-67
Goetz, Klaus H. 186
Goff, Patricia 1, 5
Gómez Pereira, Manuel 98, 106
Good-bye Lenin! 191-192, 195
Goritsas, Sotiris 11, 70, 75
Göttler, Fritz 42
Goulding, Daniel J. 80
Goytisolo, Juan 53, 66
Göztürk, Deniz 41

Greenaway, Peter 12, 102, 130, 137-149
Gronow, Jukka 189
Groundhog Day 106
Grusin, Richard 129
Guess Who's Come to Dinner? 105
Gutiérrez, Chus 97
Györy, Michel 90, 92
Hable con ella (Talk to Her) 98
Halévy, Daniel 150
Hall, Stuart 8
Hampton, Christopher 106
Hanauer, Florian 39
Harari, Dominic 105
Hartog, François 150-151
Hawks, 82
Hayden, Joanne 177
Head-On (Gegen die Wand) 11, 34, 38, 41-42, 44, 46-48, 70, 190, 192
Heer, Rolf de 102, 121, 124
Heinich, Nathalie 140
Hell, Julia 199
Helsing, Falk van 188
Hentz, Stefan 39
Herrero, Gerardo 105
Herzog, Werner 201-202
Heun, Sylke 45
Hijo de la novia, El 103, 120, 123
Hill, John 110
Hill, Walter 79
Hitchcock, Alfred 135
Hjort, Mete 73-74, 78
Hobsbawm, Eric 128
Home is the Hero 172
Hoskins, Colin 89-90
Hotel de Lux (Luxury Hotel) 71
Huston, John 82
Hutcheon, Linda 81
Huyssen, Andreas 48
Hybridity 199-200; hybridization 72, 170; hybrid co-productions 99, 104; hybrid identity 186; hybridized genres 81; chaotic hybrid 22
Ibarretxe Brothers 106
Ibermedia 113

Iglesia, Alex de la 101, 120, 123
Iglesias, Jorge 101, 120, 124
Illarramendi, Ángel 103
Imagining Argentina 106
Im Lauf der Zeit (Kings of the Road) 41
Immigration 1, 4-5, 12, 16, 21-22, 31, 47, 156, 159-161, 168, 171; immigrant(s) 162-167, 170-171, 179, 181, 183; anti-immigration 16
In America 173-174, 179
In July (Im Juli) 11, 34-35, 38-42, 47, 70, 74-75
Incautos 121, 124
Io non ho paura 102
Iordanova, Dina 72
Ivory, James 175
Jäckel, Anne 7-8, 89, 93-94, 110
Jaoui, Agnès 16
Jeanneney, Jean-Nöel 150
Jet Set 102
Jeunet, Jean-Pierre 189
Jordan, Neil 174
Journey to the Sun (Güneşe yolculuk) 70, 74-75
Juana la Loca 120, 123
Judt, Tony 4
Junghänel, Frank 42-43
Kael, Pauline 147
Kamchatka 103, 120, 124
Karanović, Srdjan 71, 80
Kazan, Elias 83
Kearney, Richard 170
Kennan, George F. 131
Kirby, Peader 179
Klapisch, Cédric 10, 16-17, 19-21, 27, 29-31, 105, 121, 123
Kochhar-Lindgren, Gary 140, 143-144
Koçi, Fatmir 71
Kocka, Jürgen 202
Koller, Xavier 75
Konchalovsky Andrei 79
Konstantarakos, Myrto 176
Koselleck, Reinhart 150
Krause, Tilman 44
Kristeva, Julia 24
Kujundzic, Dragan 132

Kulaoğlu, Tunçay 35
Kurz und schmerzlos (Short Sharp Shock) 11, 35-39, 46, 192
Kusturica, Emir 39, 70
Lacan, Jacques 54, 58, 63-64
Laïdi, Zaki 150
Laissez-passer (Safeconduct) 102, 108
Lamerica 12, 161, 164, 167-168
Language(s) 3, 13, 17, 19, 24-30, 47, 49, 53-54, 56-57, 61, 63-64, 66, 71, 73, 128-129, 156, 160-161, 163-164, 180, 187, 188, 190, 192-193, 198, 200, 202
L'Auberge espagnole (Pot Luck) 10, 16-20, 23-24, 26-27, 105, 109, 121, 123
Lecchi, Alberto 105
Leersen, Joep 172
Le Goff, Jacques 2, 60
León de Aranoa, Fernando 98, 100, 120, 123
Leone, Sergio 83
Lethal Weapon 79
Letter from an Unknown Woman 85
Lévinas, Emmanuel 58
Lisbon Story 20
Lista de espera 109, 123
Loach, Ken 102, 108
Local identity 188; localism 187-188; localization 187, 204
Lombard, Carl 177
Lombardi, Francisco 103, 105
Long take 130, 135-137, 196; single 134-135
López Amado, Norberto 121, 124
Lowenthal, David 150
Lucía y el sexo (Sex and Lucia) 98
Lugares comunes (Common Places) 104, 120, 124
Lugg, Catherine A. 187
Luna, Bigas 99
Luna de Avellaneda 103, 121, 124
Lunes al sol, Los (Mondays in the Sun) 98, 100, 109, 111, 120, 123
Lungulov, Darko 70
Lynch, John 175-177

Mackenna's Gold 82
MacWeeney, Alen 182-183
Magatti, Mauro 159
Magnificent Seven, The 82
Maité 99
Malraux, André 25, 56
Man Who Shot Liberty Valance, The 83
Mañas, Achero 97
Manchevski, Milcho 11, 70, 80, 82, 84-86
Manfredonia, Giulio 106
Manjar de amor (Food of Love) 107
Mann, Anthony 82
Manovich, Lev 130, 143
Mar adentro (The Sea Inside) 100, 109, 120, 123
Martin (Hache) 99
Mazierska, Ewa 20
Mazzacurati, Carlo 161
Mazzola, Claudio 12, 156
McAdam, Trish 175
McGuigan Paul 102
McIlroy, Brian 171
McLoone, Martin 171, 173-174
McNab, Geoffrey 136
Mean Streets 37
Medem, Javier 98
MEDIA Programme 7, 92-93
Medium shot(s) 134
Meet the Parents 105
Mennel, Barbara 35, 37
Merry Christmas 102
Mi vida sin mí (My Life Without Me) 107, 109, 120, 123
Miller, Toby 89-90, 92-93, 111
Mirka 102, 111
Misterio Galíndez, El (The Galindez File) 105
Moloch 133
Moltke, Johannes von 201
Monahan, Barry 172, 174
Montejo, Julia 107
Monty Python and the Holy Grail 22
Motif of the journey 170, 173; trope of the journey 181; of traveling 171; of traveler 172

Mucha, Stanislaw 188
Murphy, Pat 175, 177, 179
My Darling Clementine 82
My Father is Coming 191
Mythomoteur 71-71, 80, 84-85
Naficy, Hamid 70, 171, 178-179
Naked Spur, The 82
Narrative(s) 129, 139, 142, 170-172, 178; narrative cinema 129; narrative coherence 132; national narrative(s) 130, 151; narrative responsibility 146; narrative unity 136; micro-narratives 132; travel narrative(s) 171, 179; the return of 150;
Naughton, Leonie 201
Natale sul Nilo 102
Navarro, Antonio 120, 123
Navigators, The 102
Nebot, Jesús 107
Neorealism 157
Nephew, The 173
Nešto izmedju (*Something in Between*) 80
New German Cinema 190, 201
Nicodemus, Katja 38, 42, 44
Night Train 175
Nora 175-176
Nora, Pierre 149-151
Nos miran 121, 124
Notre musique 11, 53-58, 60, 62-67
Noys, Benjamin 143
Nueces para el amor 105
October 133
Ogden, Perry 182
O'Hara, Daniel 179-180
Olasagasti, Enoka 99
Old Man Who Read Love Stories, The 102, 109, 121, 124
Oliveros, Luis *105*
Onteniente, Fabien 102
Oosterling, Henk 146
Open City 157
Ophuls, Max 85
Oppenheim, Jean 135
O'Sullivan, Thaddeus 179

Otero, José María 91, 93
Otros, Los (*The Others*) 98
Owenson, Sidney 172
Paasi, Annsi 4
Paisá 157
Pajaczkowska, Claire 172
Palacio, Manuel 98-101, 104
Pantaleón y las visitadoras 103
Pardo, Alejandro 11-12, 89
Parenti, Nani 102
Paris Texas 201
Parsi, Vittorio Emanuele 71
Pascoe, David 140
Paskaljević, Goran 75
Pata negra 105
Pavee Lackeen (*The Traveller Girl*) 13, 182
Peckinpah, Sam 82
Pelegrí, Teresa 105
Peor imposible, ¿Qué puede fallar? 101
Perro, El (*Bombón: El Perro*) 103
Pillow Book, The 139
Piñeyro, Marcelo 103, 120, 124
Pita, Dan 71
Plata quemada 103
Plaza, Francisco 107
Poet, Paul 188
Poisson rouge 16
Pollack, Michel 140
Pollock, George 172
Pollock, Griselda 149
Poniente 97
Pons, Ventura 107
Port, Mattijs van de 79
Poschardt, Ulf 49
Poupées russes, Les (*The Russian Dolls*) 10, 16-17, 26
Pratt, Mary Louise 19
Premeditated Murder (*Ubistvo s predumišljajem*) 70
Pretty Village Pretty Flame (*Lepa sela lepo gore*) 71
Propaganda 41
Prospero's Books 139
Proust, Marcel 18

Proustian 71
Punto de mira (One of the Hollywood Ten) 107
Purdy, Anthony 140
Quando sei nato non ti piu' nascondere 12, 164
Quiet Man, The 171-173
Quinn, Bob 179
Quinn, Paul 173
Ramadanovic, Petar 65-66
Raise der Hoffnung (Journey of Hope) 75
Ray, Robert B. 71
Rebella, Juan Pablo 103
Reckoning, The 102
Remis, Harold 106
Reyes Magos, Los (The Three Wise Men) 109, 120, 123
Robbins, Andrea 60
Rocco and His Brothers 161
Rodek, Hanns-Georg 39, 42, 48
Roeg, Nicolas 176
Rohmer, Eric 102
Roma 105, 121, 124
Romasanta 107
Room With A View, A 175
Rope 15
Rosello, Mireille 10, 16, 22
Rossellini, Roberto 157
Run Lola Run (Lola rennt) 39
Russian Ark, The 12, 130, 132-137, 149
Ryan, Marie-Laure 145-146
Sabotaje (Sabotage!) 106
Sala-Molins, Louis 3
Salvatores, Gabriele 102
Santaolalla, Isabel 90, 97, 101, 103-104, 111, 122
Satantango 134
Saura, Carlos 100
Scarface 37-38
Schneider, Peter 5
Schorr, Michael 195-196, 198, 201-203
Schultze Gets the Blues 13, 195-198, 200, 202, 204
Scorsese, Martin 37, 39, 180
Seduction of Mimi, The 161

Segura, Santiago 97
Semprún, José 101
Şenocak, Zafer 48
Sensin, du bist es! 35
Seres queridos 105
Seventh Seal, The 203
Shane 82
Sheridan, Jim *173*
Shohat, Ella 76-78
Short Sharp Shock 10, 35
Simensen, Jarle 202
Sin noticias de Dios 120, 123
Sin retorno (No Turning Back) 107
Sjaj u očima (Loving Glances) 71
Slapšak, Svetlana 85
Sluizer, George 106
Smallhorne, Jimmy 173
Smith, Anthony 71
Snakes and Ladders 175
Sokurov, Aleksandr 12, 130, 133, 149
Solas 98
Soldini, Silvio 161
Solino 38
Solomon, Janis Little 10-11, 35
Someone Else's America (Tudja Amerika) 75
Sorín, Carlos 103
Stahlberg, Britta 42
Stam, Robert 73, 76-78
Steady cam 134
Sterneborg, Anke 203
Sterritt, David 65
Stevens, George 82
Stoianovich, Traian 71
Stojanović, Gorcin 70
Stoll, Pablo 103
Stroszek 201
Sturges John 82
Such' mich nicht 38
Sun 133
Sweet Sixteen 102
Taberna, Helena 105
Tabío, Juan Carlos 121, 123
Tango and Cash 79
Tarr, Bela 134
Taurus 133

Tavernier, Bertrand 102, 108
Taxi Driver 180
Te doy mis ojos (Take My Eyes) 98
Ten Dyke, Elizabeth 199
Tesson, Charles 132
Theil, Stefan 42, 47-48
This is My Father 173
This Other Eden 172
Thompson, J. Lee 82
Timecode 134
Tinta roja 105
Tirana, Year Zero 71 (*Tirana, année zéro*) 71
Todorova, Marija 77
Tomándote (*Tea for Two*) 97
Toro, Guillermo del 104, 120, 123
Torremolinos 73 100, 121, 124
Torrente 97
Touch of Evil, A 134
Tourné, Isabelle 17
Tower of Babel 55
Travel narratives 171-172, 179
Traveller 182
Traveller Girl, The 13, 182
Treasure of Sierra Madre, The 82
Treut, Monika 191
Triana-Toribio, Núria 95
Triple Agent 102
Trueba, Fernando 99, 101, 121, 124
Tulse Luper Suitcases: A Personal History of Uranium, The 12, 102, 130, 137-138, 140-149, 151
Último tren, El 103
Ulysses' Gaze (*To Vlemma tou Odyssea*) 70, 74, 82
Underground (*Podzemlje*) 70-71, 74, 83-84
Uribe, Imanol 121, 124
Ustaoğlu, Yesim 70
Van Sant, Gus 134
Vázquez Montalbán, Manuel 105
Venske, Henning 188
Verhoeven, Michael 191

Vertical Features Remake 148
Vesna va veloce 161
Viaje de Carol, El 121, 123
Visconti, Luchino 161, 176
Visit of the Sultan Rašid V to Kumanovo and Skopje, The 82
Viva Zapata! 83
Voltmer, Katrin 187
Walk Through H, A 148
Wallace and Gromit in the Curse of the Were-Rabbit 188
War(s) 1, 3-5, 12, 48, 54-57; Cold War 128, 138, 195; post-war 42; Spanish Civil War 104-105; World War I 1, 131; World War II 1, 12, 147, 156-157
Warhol, Andy 135
Wayne, Mike 7, 89, 93, 97-99, 100-101, 104, 111
Wenders, Wim 20, 39, 41, 191, 201
Wertmuller, Lina 161
West, Rebecca 70, 84
Westphal, Anke 42-43
Wewer, Antje 44
Whisky 103
White, Rob 178
Wide-angle lens 134
Wild Bunch 82
Wild Irish Girl, The 172
Wilson, George Macklin 85
Winchester 73 82
Winterbottom, Michael 175
With or Without You 175
Yasemin 44
Yoyes 105
Yu Ming is my Name 13, 179-182
Zabala, Carlos 88
Zaimoğlu, Feridun 44, 47
Zambrano, Benito 98
Zander, Peter 45-46
Zelig 83
Zemeckis, Robert 83